THE
HARLEM RENAISSANCE
An Anthology

Edited by

Cary D. Wintz

Brandywine Press • Maplecrest, NY

W ¥ 39-51, 58-72
72-74, 94-119, 130-44
F 147-199

TABLE OF CONTENTS

I. Introduction: A Historical Overview of the
Harlem Renaissance **1**

II. African American Literature Before the
Renaissance **20**
Paul Laurence Dunbar: Poems **21**
Charles W. Chesnutt:
"The Wife of His Youth" **25**
Criticism and Assessment:
William Dean Howells **33**

III. African American Literature in
Transition **39**
W.E.B. Du Bois: Poems **41**
W.E.B. Du Bois:
The Quest of the Silver Fleece **45**
James Weldon Johnson: Poems **50**
James Weldon Johnson: *The Autobiography of
an Ex-Colored Man* **54**
Claude McKay: Poems **58**
Jean Toomer: *Cane* **61**
Criticism and Assessment **65**

IV. The Origins of the Harlem Renaissance:
1924–1926 . . . . **72**
Jessie Fauset: *There Is Confusion* **74**
Walter White: *The Fire in the Flint* **81**
The Civic Club Dinner **90**

Alain Locke: *Survey Graphic—Harlem:*
Mecca of the New Negro **94**

Alain Locke: *The New Negro* **100**

The *Opportunity* Literary Contest **111**

Carl Van Vechten: *Nigger Heaven* **119**

Reviews of *Nigger Heaven* **125**

Fire!! **130**

V. The Harlem Renaissance, 1926–1930 . . . . **147**

Langston Hughes: "The Negro Artist and
the Racial Mountain" **148**

W.E.B. Du Bois on Artistic Freedom and
Responsibility **151**

Langston Hughes: Poems, 1922–1930 . . . . **159**

Countee Cullen: Poems from *Color* **163**

James Weldon Johnson:
God's Trombones **169**

Claude McKay: *Home to Harlem* and
Two Reviews **171**

Nella Larsen: *Passing* **179**

Wallace Thurman: *The Blacker the Berry* **186**

Langston Hughes: *Not Without Laughter* **194**

VI. Slow Fade to Black: The 1930s **200**

Alain Locke: "This Year of Grace" **201**

Arna Bontemps: *God Sends Sunday* **203**

Sterling Brown:
Poems from Southern Road **208**

Langston Hughes: A "Social Poet" **213**

Zora Neale Hurston: *Mules and Men* **217**

Criticism from *The New Challenge*:
Alain Locke and Richard Wright **224**

Selected Bibliography **233**

I

INTRODUCTION:
A HISTORICAL OVERVIEW OF THE
HARLEM RENAISSANCE

The Harlem Renaissance was the most important event in twentieth-century African American intellectual and cultural life. Its most obvious manifestation was in a self-conscious literary movement, but literature and the Renaissance touched every aspect of African American literary and artistic creativity from the end of World War I through the Great Depression of the 1930s. Literature, critical writing, music, theater, musical theater, and the visual arts were encompassed by this movement; it also affected politics, social development, and almost every phase of the African American experience from the mid-1920s through the mid-1930s. The Renaissance emerged from the great demographic transformation that brought hundreds of thousands of African Americans from the rural South to the urban North; it gave voice to the reinvigorated demand for equality, justice, and pride that grew out of such diverse movements and individuals as Booker T. Washington, the National Association for the Advancement of Colored People and W.E.B. Du Bois, and Marcus Garvey and his Universal Negro Improvement Association.

The Harlem Renaissance, then, was an African American literary and artistic movement centered in Harlem, but influencing African American communities across the country; it flourished in the late 1920s and early 1930s, but its antecedents and legacy spread many years before 1920 and after 1930. It had no universally recognized name, but was known variously as the New Negro movement, the New Negro Renaissance, and the Negro Renaissance, as well as the Harlem Renaissance. It had no clearly defined beginning or end, but emerged out of the social and intellectual upheaval in the African American community that followed World War I, blossomed in the mid to late 1920s, and then faded away in the mid 1930s. While at its core it was primarily a literary movement, it touched all of the African American creative arts. While its participants shared a commitment to representing honestly and completely the African American experience, and believed in racial pride and equality, no common political philosophy, social belief, artistic style, or aesthetic principle bound them together. This was a movement of individuals free of any overriding manifesto. While central to African American artistic and intellectual life, by no means did it enjoy the full support of the black or white intelligentsia; it generated as much hostility and criticism as it did support and praise. From the moment of its birth its legitimacy was debated. Nevertheless, by at least one measure its success was clear: the Harlem Renaissance was the first time that a considerable number of mainstream publishers and critics took African American literature seriously, and it was the first time that African American literature and the arts attracted significant attention from the nation at large.

Nineteenth-Century African American Literature

The roots of the Harlem Renaissance are found in the emergence of African American literature during the nineteenth century. Writers during this period attempted to give expression to black life at a time when slavery, the Civil War, emancipation, segregation, oppression, and the struggle for freedom and equality defined the black experience. Through their literary efforts they grappled with the fundamental question of African American art: were African American writers simply darker skinned versions of American writers, or did they produce a distinctive literature based on African and African American themes and folk traditions?

During the first two-thirds of the nineteenth century slavery dominated African American literature. The most pervasive literary product was the slave narrative, of which the best known were Frederick Douglass's *The Narrative of the Life of Frederick Douglass, an American Slave, Written by Himself,* published in 1845, and two years later William Well Brown's *Narrative of William W. Brown, a Fugitive Slave.* Some two dozen slave narratives were published during the 1840s and 1850s, along with pioneering works of African American fiction including William Well Brown's *Clotel; or, The President's Daughter,* the first novel by an African American, and Harriet E. Wilson's publication in 1859 of *Our Nig; or Sketches from the Life of a Free Black,* the first novel by an African American woman. The slave narratives enjoyed the greatest commercial success. They provided literary material for the emerging African American religious and anti-slavery publications, as well as for white-owned abolitionist journals, and found an audience among both whites and free blacks.

Following emancipation African American literature shifted its focus significantly. Memoirs of African American life remained popular, but instead of concentrating on the horrors of slavery, they emphasized individualism, self-reliance, moral rectitude, and personal achievement—traits that brought success in the post-emancipation era. Booker T. Washington's *Up From Slavery,* published in 1901, is the best known but not the only example of this genre. The audience also shifted during this period. The end of slavery, the decline of the abolitionist movement, and the hardening of racial lines greatly diminished the interest of whites in African American literature. Instead, growing literacy among blacks, the proliferation of black periodicals, and the emergence of small, usually church-affiliated black publishing operations created a new but limited market for black writing within the black community. Consequently, a small African American literary subculture developed that produced writing of uneven quality that was published and distributed within the black community by black institutions, and was largely invisible to the white literary world.

As this segregated literary tradition developed, black writers frequently turned their attention to African American folk culture and history. Much of the work in uncovering the rich African American folk tradition was done in the black community, especially at the emerging black colleges and universities. The Jubilee Singers of Fisk University, organized in 1871, popularized the spirituals as an art form, while at Hampton Institute writers for the *Southern Workman* collected and published African American folk materials. The Fisk Jubilee Singers, along with white author Joel Chandler Harris, whose Uncle Remus stories popularized traditional black trickster tales, and black writer-performers such as Bob Cole and Rosamond Johnson, who used spirituals and traditional black musical forms to create the basis for black musical theater, brought black culture and folk traditions to an audience outside the black community in the late nineteenth century.

At the century's end, literature lagged behind black music and musical theater, limited primarily by the difficulty black authors faced in getting published and having their books distributed. The black press simply did not have the resources to produce and market on a mass scale. Works that challenged popular stereotypes of blacks were particularly affected. As the twentieth century began only two African American literary figures had managed to break through these barriers and attain, at least on a limited scale, a national reputation. Poet Paul Laurence Dunbar and novelist Charles Waddell Chesnutt were discovered and promoted by critic William Dean Howells, published by commercial presses, and marketed nationally. But even these two achieved their greatest success when they embraced black folk traditions and conformed to white stereotypes of black literature. They were far less successful when they challenged these conventions, and especially when they addressed issues of race and racial oppression.

Social, Political, and intellectual Background

The emergence of the Harlem Renaissance was connected to the rapidly changing social and political environment of the early twentieth-century United States. Underlying the Renaissance was the Great Migration that brought hundreds of thousands of African Americans from the rural South to the industrial cities of the North. Central to this process was the development of Harlem as the political and cultural center of African America. Equally important was the political militancy that arose in the African American community in the second decade of the twentieth century. This militancy was reflected in the emergence of W.E.B. Du Bois and the NAACP as champions of racial equality, and the rise and fall of Marcus Garvey and his message of racial pride.

The migration of African Americans northward was part of a general movement from rural to urban America that began in the second half of the nineteenth century and continued through most of the twentieth. This movement involved both black and white Americans, and connected directly to the transformation of the country from an agricultural to an urban and industrial economy. Along with economic forces the movement of African Americans was influenced by the deteriorating racial situation, especially in the southern states, during the late nineteenth and early twentieth centuries. The growth of segregation, the systematic disfranchisement of African Americans, and most importantly, the intensification of racial violence, especially lynching and race riots, combined with economic factors to precipitate the migration. African American migration patterns were extremely complex, and involved movement from one area of the South to another, and from rural to urban areas within the South, as well as from the South to the North. Nevertheless, the movement of African Americans out of the rural South to the urban North was significant enough to warrant comment and concern in the South and to transform radically the racial composition of northern cities.

While African Americans migrated to industrial cities across the Northeast and

Great Lakes region, the impact on New York City was especially notable. In 1890 approximately 20,000 African Americans resided in Manhattan. The largest number were concentrated in the Tenderloin district on the west side of Manhattan between 27th Street and 53rd Street, and in the San Juan Hill district, on the west side above 57th Street. These areas were slums with a high population density, dilapidated housing, and high crime rates; black residents were victims of various expressions of racial hostility including a race riot that swept through the Tenderloin in 1900. By 1930 the black population of Manhattan had increased tenfold to over 224,000. Harlem, north of Central Park, from 126th Street to 159th Street, was home to almost three-quarters of this population.

More important than its physical growth was the role that Harlem assumed in the imagination of black Americans in the early twentieth century. By the 1920s Harlem had supplanted Washington, Philadelphia, and Atlanta as the focal point of black America. It was the home to most of its important institutions and people—the NAACP and the Urban League, Marcus Garvey and his UNIA; it also had become the center of African American art and culture and a magnet that attracted the creative and ambitious of the race from across the country and the world. James Weldon Johnson gave voice to this image of Harlem in his 1930 book, *Black Manhattan*, "So here we have Harlem—not merely a colony, or a community, or a settlement—not at all a 'quarter' or a slum or a fringe—but a black city located in the heart of white Manhattan, and containing more Negroes to the square mile than any other spot on earth. It strikes the uninformed observer as a phenomenon, a miracle straight out of the skies." Johnson continued in increasingly glowing terms, describing Harlem as "one of the most beautiful and healthy" neighborhoods in the city, characterized not by overcrowded tenements but by "new-law apartment houses and handsome dwellings, with streets as well paved, as well lighted, and as well kept as in any other part of the city." Johnson's optimism captured that magic that was reflected in the Harlem Renaissance, but it ignored the reality that by 1930 Harlem was well on its way to becoming a blighted, inner-city slum.

At the same time that the black migration was altering African American demographic patterns, an intense struggle was underway for leadership in the black community. Initially this struggle focused on efforts to achieve equal rights, and was embodied in the conflict between the two most prominent African American leaders, Booker T. Washington and W.E.B. Du Bois. Actually in their goals these two men were never far apart. They both wanted full civil and political rights for African Americans; they both opposed segregation in public accommodations and the disfranchisement of African Americans based on race; they both believed that education was a key to racial progress; and they both bitterly condemned lynching and other forms of racial violence. Many of their differences were in style and strategy. Washington, based in the rural South, avoided direct confrontation with southern racism, preferring to work behind the scenes, while Du Bois, based first in Atlanta, then in Harlem, advocated a more confrontational strategy. More significant was the personal clash that developed between the two and their followers as they struggled for dominance during the period after 1903. Ultimately the deteriorating racial situation in the early 1900s undermined confidence in Washington's leadership, while Du Bois's power base in the new NAACP provided him a forum from which to effectively challenge the Tuskeegean; Washington's death in 1915 ended the contest.

After 1915 Du Bois and the NAACP also faced challenges to their leadership. The most vocal, and for a time the best-organized came from Marcus Garvey and his United Negro Improvement Association. Garvey, a Jamaican, arrived in the United States in 1916; a year later he made Harlem the center of his political movement. Initially Garvey advocated a fairly moderate program, combining a self-help, black capitalist message, similar to that of Booker T. Washington, with Pan-Africanism, a vision of unity among all of the peoples of the African diaspora. By 1919 he had become more radical, advocating a separatist-nationalist program that called for the creation of black institutions and businesses, the liberation of colonized Africa, and ultimately the migration of African Americans back to an African homeland. By the end of 1920 Garvey's UNIA claimed over 1,000,000 members, mostly among the black working classes; two years later his movement was in shambles and he had been indicted for mail fraud.

Against this background blacks responded to the worsening racial situation by intensifying their demands for equal rights and debating new strategies to attain these rights. This heightened racial consciousness was embodied in the concept of the "New Negro" initially defined at the beginning of the new century, then revived to capture the renewed sense of racial pride and militancy that followed World War I. Actually the term was associated with a variety of political and racial views: from a belief in racial pride, self-reliance, and assimilation; a more radical and confrontational demand for equal rights; or a Pan-African and nationalist perspective. The term "New Negro" can best be understood as the culmination of extensive social and intellectual developments within the African American community in the last quarter of the nineteenth century, and as a synthesis of the divergent black political and racial strategies that had dominated African American political thought prior to and immediately following World War I. These included the more moderate approach of Booker T. Washington, the more confrontational and militant strategy of W.E.B. Du Bois and the NAACP, and the nationalistic, Pan-African ideology of Marcus Garvey. It also included the racial pride and awareness expressed in organizations such as historian Carter G. Woodson's Association for the Study of Negro Life and History, and political efforts that led to the election of the first northern blacks to congress.

In an essay he wrote for the Harlem issue of *Survey Graphic* in 1925, which celebrated the new literary creativity, Alain Locke connected the New Negro with the emerging Harlem Renaissance. The "younger generation is vibrant with a new psychology," he declared, that reflected its shift "from social disillusionment to race pride." These New Negro writers, Locke continued, rejected the old stereotypes of black "aunties, uncles, and mammies" and the sentimental appeal against racial injustice that had characterized the work of the previous generation of black writers. Instead they embraced the more positive attitudes of self-respect and self-reliance; they repudiated social dependence and strongly asserted their racial pride.

African American Literature on the Eve of the Harlem Renaissance

In spite of its shortcomings and limitations, the nineteenth century left a rich tradition in African American literature. In the twentieth century Chesnutt and Dunbar would be joined by a host of other black poets and writers, several of whom began writing prior to the First World War, and continued into the period of the Harlem Renaissance. Of these the most notable were James Weldon Johnson and W.E.B. Du Bois.

Du Bois, best known as a historian, sociologist, and civil rights leader, wrote a novel and several poems during the pre-war period. His collection of essays, *The Souls of Black Folk*, and his early historical and sociological works had already established his credentials as a writer before he turned to fiction. In 1911 he published his first novel, a long, complex work that examined race, class, sectional, and economic conflict against the background of cotton production, marketing, and financing. Its exposé of political and economic corruption in American industry bore some resemblance to that depicted in Frank Norris's naturalistic novels, *The Octopus*, which came out in 1901, and *The Pit* published two years later. But Du Bois combined this naturalism with a complex plot that ranged from black characters to whites, and from the rural South to the centers of political and financial power in Washington and New York. Although the novel suffered from the intricacies of its plot, and the tension between its efforts at social realism and its romantic tendencies, it had two redeeming characteristics. First, Du Bois developed a set of extremely forceful women characters; secondly, the novel was significant because Du Bois, who by 1911 had become the most important African American intellectual in the country, wrote it. The novel received fairly good reviews, perhaps aided by the stature of its author, but it did not sell well. Du Bois would not attempt another novel for seventeen years.

James Weldon Johnson's only novel, *The Autobiography of an Ex-Colored Man*, appeared in 1912, the year after Du Bois's effort. Johnson had a varied background as a teacher, lawyer, political activist, poet, and songwriter. He had gained significant success in black musical theater as a non-performing member of the very popular songwriting and performing team, Rosamond Johnson and Bob Cole. Not satisfied with songwriting, Johnson turned to writing serious poetry and began work on his novel. *The Autobiography of an Ex-Colored Man* was the most significant novel published by an African American prior to the Harlem Renaissance. In many ways it was a transition piece that moved beyond the work of Dunbar and Chesnutt, and anticipated many of the themes that would appear in the Harlem movement. It tells of the effort of a light-skinned African American to find racial justice in the United States. Initially he lives as a black man, but ultimately, he achieves his goals by crossing the color line and passing for white. Like Chesnutt, Johnson exposed the racial problems confronting African Americans, but he also went much further, exploring the meaning of the black experience in America, especially the psychological impact of racism. Racial prejudice was important, but to Johnson the black response to race was far more so. Johnson also expanded on another theme, first introduced by Dunbar in his novel, *The Sport of the Gods*. Like Dunbar, Johnson explored the local color of the emerging black ghetto, depicting vividly and realistically the lives of the black actors and musicians who lived and worked along 53rd Street in Manhattan. In spite of its quality, *The Autobiography of an Ex-Colored Man* suffered from poor marketing and distribution, and did not do well until it was re-released during the Harlem Renaissance.

Johnson had somewhat more success with his poetry. Two pieces in particular secured his early literary reputation. The first he wrote to celebrate Abraham

Lincoln's birthday; his brother, Rosamond, set it to music and it was performed by a school choir in February 1900. The poem and song, "Lift Every Voice and Sing," is now celebrated as the Negro National Anthem. Johnson wrote the second poem, "Fifty Years," to mark the occasion of the fiftieth anniversary of the Emancipation Proclamation. The *New York Times* published it, to great acclaim, on its editorial page on January 1, 1913. Four years later Johnson published his first book of poetry, *Fifty Years and Other Poems*. This venture was less successful. The title poem and ten others were strong, but the rest, a combination of dialect pieces, some patterned after Dunbar's work, others drawn from his writing for the theater and nonracial verses, were second rate.

By the end of World War I literary foundations laid by Chesnutt, Dunbar, Johnson, and Du Bois, together with the racial, social, cultural, and political ferment that was brewing in Harlem, led to the movement known as the Harlem Renaissance. Several young black writers contributed to this ferment, but it involved much more than literature. World War I brought in its wake a series of devastating race riots culminating in the 1919 outbreaks in Washington and Chicago. Black politics shifted as Marcus Garvey mobilized tens of thousands of supporters and confronted the NAACP and the African American establishment with a mass movement, while A. Philip Randolph and the *Messenger* challenged the conventional leadership from the socialist left. Along with the thousands coming North into Harlem with the black migration, jazz and the blues followed from the South and Midwest into the city's bars and cabarets. These creative energies spread to the stage. *Shuffle Along* played in 1921 to standing-room-only crowds, and launched a series of black-oriented musicals and musical reviews. Claude McKay's volume of poetry, *Harlem Shadows*, appeared in 1922, Jean Toomer's experimental novel *Cane* followed the next year, and these as well as the initial published works of other young black writers contributed to Harlem's burgeoning cultural life.

Claude McKay, born and raised in Jamaica, had already published two volumes of dialect island poetry before he came to the United States in 1912 to study agriculture. By 1915 he was living in Harlem pursuing a writing career. McKay's literary connections during this period were not in Harlem, but in Greenwich Village. His first American poem appeared in *Seven Arts*; others followed in *Pearson's* and *The Liberator*. However, Harlem and the African American experience were the source and content of his best writing during this period, as evidenced in *Harlem Shadows*, his first and his finest American book of poetry. Like McKay, Jean Toomer's primary literary connections were among whites—Waldo Frank, who helped guide the publication of his book, poet Hart Crane, editor Gorham Munson, artist Georgia O'Keeffe, and photographer Alfred Stieglitz. His writing, though, was purely black in content and theme. His experimental book *Cane* excited African American critics who praised the book for its poetic style and for its probing of the black experience.

Other young writers also surfaced in the early 1920s. Langston Hughes published his first poem, "A Negro Speaks of Rivers" in *The Crisis* in 1921, when he was a nineteen-year-old freshman at Columbia; by the spring of 1924 when he returned to New York after spending the better part of two years abroad, he was already something of a literary celebrity. Walter White, an officer of the NAACP, published his first novel, *The Fire in the Flint*, in 1924, as did Jessie Fauset, Du editorial assistant at *The Crisis*. Yet up to this point there was no literary movement—only a growing amount of literary activity.

Origins of the Harlem Renaissance

Against this background of increasing literary activity, three events occurred between 1924 and 1926 that launched the Harlem Renaissance. The first of these established a link between three major players in the literary Renaissance—the black literary and political intelligentsia, the white publishers and critics, and the young black writers. The occasion was the dinner that Charles S. Johnson of the Urban League hosted on March 21, 1924 to recognize the new literary talent in the black community and to present this to New York's white literary establishment. Out of this dinner came the March 1925 "Harlem issue" of the avant-garde magazine *The Survey Graphic*, edited by Alain Locke and devoted to defining the aesthetic of black literature and art. The next event signaled the unprecedented white fascination with Harlem, African Americans, and their art and culture. This was the publication in early 1926 of white novelist Carl Van Vechten's *Nigger Heaven*, a spectacularly popular exposé of Harlem life that helped create the "Negro vogue" that drew thousands of sophisticated New Yorkers to Harlem's exotic night life and stimulated the national market for African American literature and music. The final event symbolized the coalescence of a core group of young writers and artists into a movement. In the fall of 1926 a group of young black writers produced their own literary magazine, *Fire!!* With *Fire!!* poet Langston Hughes, writers Wallace Thurman and Zora Neale Hurston, artist Aaron Douglas, along with other young writers and artists declared their intent to assume ownership of the literary Renaissance.

The Harlem Renaissance

Despite the efforts of Thurman and his young colleagues to launch a magazine that would define the new literary movement, *Fire!!* fizzled out after only one issue, and the literary movement remained ill defined. No common literary style or political ideology was associated with the Harlem Renaissance. It was far more an identity than an ideology or a literary or artistic school. What united participants was their sense of taking part in a common endeavor and their commitment to giving artist expression to the African American experience. If any statement defined the philosophy of the new literary movement, it was Langston Hughes's essay, "The Negro Artist and the Racial Mountain," published in *The Nation* on June 16, 1926. This essay was an artistic declaration of independence—independence from the stereotypes that whites held about African Americans and the expectations that they had for black literary works. Independence also from the expectations that black leaders and critics had for black writers, and the hopes that they placed in their work. As Hughes concluded:

> We younger Negro artists who create now intend to express our individual dark-skinned selves without fear or shame. If white people are pleased we are glad. If they are not, it doesn't matter. We know we are

beautiful. And ugly, too. The tom-tom cries and the tom-tom laughs. If colored people are pleased we are glad. If they are not their displeasure doesn't matter either. We will build our temples for tomorrow, strong as we know how, and we will stand on top of the mountain, free within ourselves.

The determination of black writers to follow their own artistic vision and the diversity that this created were the principal characteristics of the Harlem Renaissance. This diversity ranged from Langston Hughes weaving the stylistic forms of African American music into his experimental poems of ghetto life ("The Weary Blues"); Claude McKay adopting the sonnet as the vehicle for his militant poems attacking the racial violence of 1919 ("If We Must Die"), or for presenting glimpses of Harlem life ("The Harlem Dancer"); Countee Cullen employing classical literary allusions as he explored the African roots of black life ("Heritage"); Nella Larsen presenting a powerful psychological study of an African American women's loss of identity (*Quicksand*, in 1928); or Zora Neale Hurston using the folk life of the black rural south in her brilliant exploration of race and gender (*Their Eyes Were Watching God*, in 1937). Diversity and experimentation were also reflected in the blues of Bessie Smith, the range of jazz from the early rhythms of Jelly Roll Norton to the instrumentation of Louis Armstrong or the sophisticated orchestration of Duke Ellington, and in the primitivism and African images in the paintings and illustrations of Aaron Douglas. During the course of the Harlem Renaissance from the mid-1920s through the mid-1930s, sixteen black writers published over fifty volumes of poetry and fiction, while dozens of other African American artists made their mark in painting, music, and theater.

And yet, within this diversity, several themes emerge which set the character of the Harlem Renaissance. No black writer expressed all of these, but each did address one or more. The first of these themes was the effort to recapture the African American past, both its rural southern roots and its African heritage. Interest in the African past corresponded with the rise of Pan-Africanism in African American politics, which was at the center of Marcus Garvey's ideology, and also a major concern of W.E.B. Du Bois in the 1920s. Countee Cullen and Langston Hughes addressed their African heritage in their poems, while Aaron Douglas used African motifs in his paintings and drawings. A number of musicians, from the classical composer William Grant Still to jazz great Louis Armstrong, introduced African inspired rhythms and themes in their compositions. For most writers and artists the exploration of their Africanism was a positive experience, even though some white patrons attempted to channel black artistic creativity into their vision of African primitivism.

A number of black writers explored their southern heritage. Jean Toomer's *Cane* won wide acclaim for its use of southern black culture to understand the African American experience. Ironically, Toomer himself had little direct knowledge of the South. Zora Neale Hurston, on the other hand, was an experienced folklorist who not only published two collections of black southern folklore, *Mules and Men* in 1935 and *Tell My Horse* in 1938, but also provided an extensive study of rural southern black life in her 1937 novel, *Their Eyes Were Watching God*.

Another theme Harlem Renaissance writers used was the exploration of life in Harlem and other urban centers. Both Hughes and McKay drew on Harlem images for their poetry, and McKay used the ghetto as the setting for his first novel, *Home to Harlem*, published in 1928. Some black writers, including McKay and Hughes as well as Rudolph Fisher and Wallace Thurman, were accused of overemphasizing crime, sexuality, and other less savory aspects of ghetto life in order to feed the voyeuristic desires of white readers and publishers; white novelist Carl Van Vechten was blamed for pioneering this exploitive literature in his controversial 1926 novel *Nigger Heaven*. Other black writers like Jessie Fauset wrote about the black middle-class urban experience.

A third major theme addressed by the literature of the Harlem Renaissance was race. Virtually every novel and play and most of the poetry explored race in America, especially the impact of race and racism on African Americans. In their simplest form these works protested racial injustice. Claude McKay's "If We Must Die" was among the best of this genre. Langston Hughes also wrote protest pieces, as did almost every black writer at one time or another. The struggle against lynching in the mid-1920s stimulated anti-lynching poetry as well as Walter White's carefully researched study of the subject, *Rope and Faggot*, which came out in 1929; in the early 1930s the Scottsboro incident motivated considerable protest writing, as well as *Negro*, a 1934 anthology that addressed race in an international context. Most of the literary efforts of the Harlem Renaissance eschewed overt protest or propaganda, focusing instead on the psychological and social impact of race. Among the best of these studies were Nella Larsen's two novels, *Quicksand* published in 1928 and, a year later, *Passing*; both explore characters of mixed racial heritage who struggle to define their racial identity in a world of prejudice and racism. Langston Hughes used similar themes in his poem "Cross" and his 1931 play, *Mulatto*, as did Jessie Fauset in 1929 in her novel *Plum Bun*. That same year Wallace Thurman made color discrimination within the urban black community the central theme of his novel *The Blacker the Berry*.

Along with its other themes and materials, the Harlem Renaissance incorporated all aspects of African American culture in its literature, from the use of black music as an inspiration for poetry to black folklore as an inspiration for novels and short stories. Best known for this was Langston Hughes, who used the rhythms and styles of jazz and the blues in much of his early poetry. James Weldon Johnson, who published two collections of black spirituals in 1927 and 1928, and Sterling Brown, who used the blues and southern work songs in many of the poems in his 1932 book of poetry *Southern Road*, continued the practice that Hughes had initiated. Other writers drew from black religion as a literary source. Johnson made the black preacher and his sermons the basis of the poems in *God's Trombones*, while Hurston and Larsen used black religion and black preachers in their novels. Hurston's first novel, *Jonah's Gourd Vine* (1934) described the exploits of a southern black preacher, while in the last portion of *Quicksand* Larsen's heroine is ensnared by religion and a southern black preacher.

Through all of these themes Harlem Renaissance writers were determined to express the African American experience in all of its variety and complexity as realistically as possible. This commitment to realism ranged from the ghetto realism that created such controversy when writers exposed negative aspects of African American life, beautifully crafted and detailed portraits of black life in small towns such as in Hughes's 1930 novel, *Not Without Laughter*, or the witty and biting depiction of Harlem's black literati in Wallace Thurman's *Infants of the Spring*.

The Harlem Renaissance appealed to a mixed audience—the African American middle class and the white book-buying public. African American magazines such as the NAACP monthly journal, *The Crisis*, and *Opportunity*, the Urban League's monthly publication, employed Harlem Renaissance writers on their editorial staff, published their poetry and short stories, and promoted African American literature through articles, reviews, and annual literary prizes. Black writers attempted to produce their own literary venues as well. In addition to the short-lived *Fire!!*, Wallace Thurman spearheaded another single-issue literary magazine, *Harlem*, in 1927, while poet Countee Cullen edited a "Negro Poets" issue of the avant-garde poetry magazine *Palms* in 1926, and in 1927 brought out an anthology of African American poetry, *Caroling Dusk*.

As important as these literary outlets were, Harlem Renaissance literature relied heavily on white-owned publishing houses and magazines. Indeed, one of the major accomplishments of the Renaissance was to push open the door to mainstream periodicals and publishers. African American music also played to mixed audiences. Harlem's cabarets attracted both Harlem residents and white New Yorkers seeking out Harlem nightlife. The famous Cotton Club carried this to a bizarre extreme by providing black entertainment for exclusively white audiences. Ultimately, the more successful black musicians and entertainers moved their performances downtown. The relationship of the Harlem Renaissance to white publishers and white audiences created controversy. While most African American critics strongly supported the movement, others like Benjamin Brawley and even W.E.B. Du Bois were sharply critical and accused Renaissance writers of reinforcing negative African American stereotypes. Langston Hughes's assertion that black artists intended to express themselves freely, no matter what the black or white public thought, accurately reflected the attitude of most, but not all writers of the movement.

The Harlem Renaissance declined in the mid-1930s. A number of factors contributed to this. The Great Depression increased the economic pressure on both writers and publishers. As a result organizations like the NAACP and the Urban League, which had actively promoted the Renaissance in the 1920s, shifted their interests to economic and social issues. Reflecting this change, both *The Crisis* and *Opportunity* suspended their literary prizes in the early 1930s. Actually, the role of *The Crisis* in promoting the Harlem Renaissance had diminished in the latter years of the pervious decade following the departure of Jessie Fauset as literary editor in 1926 and Du Bois's growing disillusionment with the direction of black literature had taken and his inability to influence that direction. Charles S. Johnson's 1927 resignation from the Urban League redirected *Opportunity* back toward social and economic issues in subsequent years.

A second factor contributing to the decline of the Renaissance was the departure of many key figures in the late 1920s and the early 1930s. In addition to Charles S. Johnson, James Weldon Johnson moved from Harlem back to the South in 1931, and W.E.B. Du Bois followed in 1934; Langston Hughes left Harlem in 1931 and did not return permanently until World War II. Rudolph Fisher and Wallace Thurman died in 1934, as did James Weldon Johnson four years later. Many who did not die or leave, stopped writing. Countee Cullen, faced with a significant decline in his literary income, took a full-time job teaching school in 1934; most of his writing after that time was children's stories. Nella Larsen suffered an emotional breakdown, and never completed her projected third novel. Claude McKay, returning to Harlem in 1934 after an absence of about twelve years, wrote that the few writers from the old days who were still around seemed to be at loose ends. His writing after his return consisted of his autobiography and a history of Harlem. In contrast Zora Neale Hurston actually enjoyed her greatest period of literary output in the 1930s, but fell silent and largely dropped out of sight after the 1940s. Sterling Brown and Arna Bontemps shifted their base of operations to black universities and their writing to literary criticism and literary history. Only Langston Hughes continued to support himself through writing after the 1930s, but he no longer considered himself part of a literary movement.

Any doubt that the era of the Harlem Renaissance had ended was put to rest by the Harlem Riot of 1935. This event shattered the illusion of Harlem as the "Mecca" of the New Negro that had figured so prominently in the folklore of the Renaissance. Harlem was a ghetto, with all of the problems associated with American urban ghettos—high rates of poverty and crime, poor and overcrowded housing, inadequate city services, job discrimination, and control of government, the police force, and employment by the dominant white power structure.

Yet the Renaissance did not disappear overnight. Almost one-third of the books published during the Renaissance appeared after 1929, and Zora Neale Hurston's *Their Eyes Were Watching God*, arguably the best novel of the Renaissance, came out in 1937. In the final analysis, the Harlem Renaissance ended when most of those associated with it left Harlem or stopped writing, and the new young artists who emerged in the 1930s and 1940s chose not to associate with the movement.

Promoters and Critics of the Harlem Renaissance

The Harlem Renaissance has endured a troubled history at the hands of critics and chroniclers. Even during its heyday its reputation and very existence were challenged, most frequently from within the African American intelligentsia.

Supporters and promoters of the movement included James Weldon Johnson, Alain Locke, and Charles S. Johnson. A poet, novelist, and literary anthologist in his own right, James Weldon Johnson both praised and promoted the literary endeavors of black artists. Tolerant of the diverse themes and topics addressed by the movement, he argued that the flowering of black literary and artistic creativity constituted the wedge that would crack open the wall of prejudice and discrimination that defined race relations in the U.S. Sociologist Charles S. Johnson concurred, adding that literature, by finding meaning in the African American experience, could assist in easing the social and psychological stress that accompanied the black migration and rapid urbanization. Alain Locke was concerned more with defining the aesthetic of the Renaissance than with its social or political consequences. In his essay "Negro Youth Speaks" he praised the "lusty vigorous realism" that Hughes, Rudolph Fisher, and others brought to their literature, not because they typified a racial stereotype, but because they were unique creations. In his mind the purpose of art (including black art) was not to produce stereotypes, but to explore the variety and uniqueness of life. The literature of the Harlem Renaissance should be racial, not for the sake of propaganda, but "purely for the sake of art," and the artist should use race as an "added enriching adventure and discipline, giving subtler overtones to life, making it more beautiful and interesting, even if more poignantly so."

Countering these promoters and supporters of the Renaissance was a group of African intellectuals whose assessment of the literary movement ranged from ambivalent to negative. William Stanley Braithwaite, literary critic for the Boston *Evening Transcript* and the most successful black literary critic during first decades of the twentieth century, was out of step with the racial consciousness of the young writers. He opposed the realistic descriptions of ghetto life that characterized the writings of Hughes, McKay, and other writers and accused these young writers of praising degradation, which, he feared, would stigmatize African Americans. In spite of these concerns Braithwaite continued to assist black writers in getting published, but encouraged them to produce more traditional works that would reflect middle class values, or at least focus on the lives of educated middle class black characters. Literary historian Benjamin Brawley agreed with much of Braithwaite's assessment of the Harlem Renaissance, especially the tendency of many of its artists to focus on "primitivism" and what he termed "the popular demand for the exotic and exciting" which led to the celebration of a mood of "hedonism and paganism" in which "introspection and self-pity ran riot." Bad literature rather than the promotion of negative racial stereotypes was Brawley's principal concern.

Most complex and enigmatic of the contemporary black critics was W.E.B. Du Bois, the preeminent black intellectual of the period as well as a poet and novelist himself. From his position in the NAACP and as editor of *The Crisis*, Du Bois was strategically placed to promote the movement. And for a time he did so. In the early to mid 1920s he (or his literary editor, novelist Jessie Fauset) competed with the Urban League's Charles S. Johnson and their journal, *Opportunity* in promoting and publishing the African American arts. He even established a theater group to preserve authentic African American theater from the onslaught of the popular "black musical reviews" on Broadway. Later in the decade, as his personal political and economic views shifted leftward, Du Bois became increasingly intolerant of much of the Harlem Renaissance—particularly the realistic renderings of Harlem street life and the life of its lower classes and criminal element. This was most clearly reflected in his comments in *The Crisis* in 1926 on Carl Van Vechten's *Nigger Heaven*—he called that novelist's bestseller "a blow in the face" and "an affront to the hospitality of black folk,"—and in his review two years later of Claude McKay's *Home to Harlem*, which he wrote, "for the most part, nauseates me, and after the dirtier parts of its filth, I feel distinctly like taking a bath." The root of Du Bois's concern was his belief that the practitioners of the Harlem Renaissance subordinated the political needs of African Americans to their sense of art and the freedom of artistic expression, and, not coincidentally, to the tastes of white publishers and white readers. He most clearly expressed his disdain with these views in an address to the annual NAACP convention in June 1926 in Chicago, which he reprinted in the October 1926 issue of *The Crisis*:

> Thus all art is propaganda and ever must be, despite the wailing of the purists. I stand in utter shamelessness and say that whatever art I have for writing has been used always for propaganda for gaining the right of black folk to love and enjoy. I do not care a damn for any art that is not used for propaganda.

And in 1928 he wrote his second novel, *Dark Princess*, in an effort to offer a literary model to wean young writers away from the Van Vechten school.

Harlem Renaissance RIP

During the 1930s, as the Harlem Renaissance began to wane, criticism of the movement continued and took on a new form. Alain Locke, one of the movement's staunchest supporters in the 1920s, backed away in the early 1930s. In a 1931 essay in *Opportunity* he even celebrated (prematurely) its demise:

> Has the afflatus of Negro self-expression died down? Are we out-living the Negro fad? Has the Negro creative artist wandered into the ambush of the professional exploiters? By some signs and symptoms. Yes. But to anticipate my conclusion, —'Let us rejoice and be exceedingly glad.' The second and truly sound phase of the cultural development of the Negro in American literature and art cannot begin without a collapse of the boom, a change to a more responsible and devoted leadership, a revision of basic values, and along with a penitential purgation of spirit, a wholesale expulsion of the moneychangers from the temple of art.

This analysis reflected much of the 1920s criticism of Du Bois and others. Locke, though, added the charge that the works created in the Harlem Renaissance failed to depict accurately the nature of African Americans and the African American experience. "I think the main fault of the movement this far," he wrote, "has been a lack of any deep realization of what was truly Negro, and what was merely superficially characteristic."

A more systematic attack on the Harlem Renaissance in the 1930s came from the radical left, centered in the journal *The New Masses* and including two writers, Langston Hughes and Richard Wright. *The New Masses* had initially embraced African American literature, especially that which gave voice to the experiences of the black masses, and avoided false exoticism and primitivism. In the 1930s, under the leadership of Michael Gold, the magazine became increasingly critical of the Harlem Renaissance, especially the influence of Carl Van Vechten, who, Gold charged, "created a brood of Negro literary bums" who wasted "their splendid talents on the gutter-life side of Harlem." From their increasingly Soviet Communist perspective, Gold and *The New Masses* group attacked the Van Vechten influence as bourgeois decadence, rejected jazz as another inferior musical expression linked to the capitalist exploitation of blacks, and backed away from any concept of an African American culture that was distinct from proletarian culture.

In the early 1930s Langston Hughes became the poster child for *The New Masses'* vision of black proletarian literature. Hughes became a frequent contributor to *The New Masses* as his politics moved leftward. The clearest expression of this leftward trend in his writing was a series of proletariat poems, many inspired by his travels in the Soviet Union during 1932 and 1933, that he sought to publish under the title *A New Song*. After a lengthy discussion with his publisher, Blanche Knopf, that centered on the effect of such a volume on his literary career, Hughes withdrew them, and in 1938 had them published and distributed by The International Workers Order, a radical labor press. *The New Masses*, aware of Hughes's shifting politics, celebrated him, proclaiming his 1930 novel, *Not Without Laughter*, the beginning of a break with the "vicious Harlem tradition of Negro literature sponsored by Van Vechten and illustrated by Covarrubias." In his October 1930 review of the novel Walt Cameron found Hughes's novel, while not entirely free from the Van Vechten influence, a major step forward. "[It] is a race novel. It concludes in a misty pointless fashion. There is no clear class-consciousness or revolutionary spirit, which distinguished some of Hughes's early poems. But under its black skin, there is red proletarian blood running through it. With all its faults, *Not Without Laughter* goes far beyond Harlem. It is *our* novel."

The young Richard Wright was another African American author who joined *The New Masses* circle, at least early in his career. In a 1937 essay, "Blueprint for Negro Writing," Wright echoed the charges of his mentors, that the literature of the Harlem Renaissance catered to white audiences, and that to reach this audience it either "crept in through the kitchen in the form of jokes," or became the "fruits of that foul soil which was the result of a liason [sic] between inferiority-complexed Negro 'geniuses' and burnt-out white Bohemians with money." Though this process, he continued, it almost always ignored "the Negro himself, his needs, his sufferings, his aspirations."

African American Literature After the Harlem Renaissance

The decline of the Harlem Renaissance was not a failure of African American literature. If anything black literature emerged from the Harlem Renaissance healthier than it had ever been. Certainly the quality of post-Renaissance black writing did not decline, nor did the market for black literature or the attention paid to it by white critics. From 1940 to 1960 African American literature achieved a series of breakthroughs in several areas. First the selection of Richard Wright's novel, *Native Son*, as a Book-of-the-Month Club selection represented a major market breakthrough for a black writer, guaranteeing the critically acclaimed novel best-seller status, and its author a literary income never achieved by his predecessors. The next breakthrough came in the area of critical recognition. Gwendolyn Brooks won the Pulitzer Prize in 1950 for her book of poetry, *Annie Allen*; in 1952 Ralph Ellison won the National Book Award for *Invisible Man*; and Lorraine Hansberry received the New York Drama Critics Circle Award for her 1959 play, *A Raisin in the Sun*. The final breakthrough came in the area of popular fiction where Chester Himes and Frank Yearby achieved considerable success. Himes became a very successful mystery writer, especially in France, while Yearby published thirty popular novels, including the 1946 best seller *The Foxes of Harrow*. Margaret Walker, Melvin Tolson, and Robert Hayden, in poetry, together with Ann Petry and James Baldwin in fiction added luster to African American literature in the decades following the Harlem Renaissance.

The political and social upheavals of the civil rights movement and the rise of the black power movement dominated the 1960s and early 1970s. Much of the best-known black writing of these years was political—*The Autobiography of Malcolm X*, Martin Luther King's "Letter from Birmingham Jail" and "I Have a Dream" speech, and Eldridge Cleaver's *Soul on Ice*. Poet and playwright Amiri Baraka (LeRoi Jones) was the preeminent literary figure of the period. Black literature reflected this political bent. The Black Arts movement consciously connected itself to the black community, especially the struggles for civil rights and black power. Larry Neal, co-editor with Baraka of *Black Fire: An Anthology of African Ameri-*

can Writing, a collection as influential to the Black Arts movement as Locke's *New Negro* was to the Harlem Renaissance, explained:

> The Black Arts Movement is radically opposed to any concept of the artist that alienates him from the community. Black Art is the aesthetic and spiritual sister of the Black Power concept. . . . The Black Arts and the Black Power concept both relate broadly to the Afro-American desire for self-determination and nationhood. Both concepts are nationalistic.

The Black Arts movement attempted to implement a literary nationalism by developing its own journals and publishing houses; however, as the marketability of works by black writers was established, mainstream presses signed up many of them. The Black Arts movement also renewed popular interest in black literature, which resulted in the reprinting of many of the Harlem Renaissance works in the 1960s and 1970s.

In the last quarter of the twentieth century African American literature flowered. The dominant trend during this period was the predominance of women writers. One characteristic of the literature of this period was the application of the findings of African American history to literature. The best-known example of this is Alex Haley's immensely popular *Roots*, which appeared in 1976. Other examples include Ernest Gain's *The Autobiography of Miss Jane Pittman* published in 1971, in 1977 Toni Morrison's *Song of Solomon* and ten years later her *Beloved*, August Wilson's plays, which follow black history decade by decade through the twentieth century, as well as popular mystery writer Walter Mosely's examination of the history of post-war black Los Angeles in his Easy Rollins novels. The impact of women writers during this period is illustrated by Alice Walker, whose 1974 book *In Search of Our Mothers' Gardens* was an effort to elevate the cultural contributions of southern black women, and who was largely responsible for refocusing critical attention on Zora Neale Hurston. It is also seen in the autobiographical writings of poet Maya Angelou, beginning with her first, *I Know Why the Caged Bird Sings* in 1970. Unprecedented critical acclaim and popular response came with the award of the Nobel Prize for literature to Toni Morrison in 1993, and the incredible popularity of the television production of Alex Haley's *Roots*. Alice Walker won the 1982 Pulitzer Prize for *The Color Purple*, playwright August Wilson received two Pulitzers, one for *Fences* and one for *The Piano Lesson*, and novelist Gloria Naylor achieved the American Book Award in 1982 for *The Women of Brewster Place*. African American writers during the last twenty-five years have achieved the popularity, critical success, and financial rewards so eagerly sought by the writers of the Harlem Renaissance.

The Critics and the Harlem Renaissance: The 1950s and 1960s

Richard Wright soon freed himself from the dogma-dominated literary approach of the *New Masses* crowd, and along with Ralph Ellison, James Baldwin, and other mid-twentieth century African American writers contributed to another outburst of literary creativity in the decade before and after the second world war. Although they distanced themselves from the Harlem Renaissance, they were not overtly hostile to it. The post-World War II period also witnessed the first significant efforts to reappraise the Harlem Renaissance; these efforts led to several retrospectives of the movement, including one in 1950 by *Phylon*, and one from Howard University Press in 1955 entitled *The New Negro Thirty Years Afterwards*. A number of the works of the Harlem Renaissance were reprinted during the 1950s and 1960s, along with the publication of several anthologies of African American literature and critical writing. Much of this occurred as the civil rights movement stimulated interest in black history and black literature, and as the first courses in these subjects began to appear in the white universities. However, the study of the Harlem Renaissance remained segregated—it might appear in "black" courses and "black" books, but it was generally ignored in literary histories, literary anthologies, and survey courses on twentieth century literature or history.

Critical interpretation of the Harlem Renaissance became increasingly negative in the late 1960s as the civil rights movement gave way to the black power movement, and as the politically-oriented Black Arts movement emerged. The scholarly studies of the Harlem Renaissance that appeared at this time reinforced the criticisms of the 1920s and 1930s and added a more nationalistic perspective that grew out of the political perspectives of the black power and Black Arts movements. Harold Cruse in his book, *The Crisis of the Negro Intellectual*, and Nathan Huggins, who wrote the first scholarly study of the movement, pioneered this reassessment of the Renaissance.

Harold Cruse in 1967 placed his examination of the Harlem Renaissance within his larger analysis of the African American intellectual. Like a number of earlier critics, he lambasted the movement for its dependence on white patronage, which, he argued, caused the movement to become "partially smothered in the guilty, idealistic, or egotistical interventions of cultural paternalism" that was typical of NAACP "interracialism" and the efforts of James Weldon Johnson to extend its "politics of civil rights to the politics of culture." Cruse added two elements to this criticism. First, he emphasized the failure of the African American middle class to "support the Harlem Renaissance movement morally, aesthetically, or financially," and second, he stressed the failure of African American intellectuals to provide direction for the movement, and to provide it with critical and aesthetic standards.

Four years later in his book, *Harlem Renaissance*, Nathan Huggins echoed many of Cruse's arguments, especially the tendency of black writers to surrender their artistic vision to white promoters and patrons. As a result of this surrender, Huggins contended that black writers strayed from more authentic expressions of the black experience and either were led into exoticism and primitivism, or allowed themselves to become enslaved to white forms and values. Even though both Cruse and Huggins had underestimated the critical and aesthetic direction that the African American intelligentsia provided, or attempted to provide to the movement, other critics of the period concurred with their arguments. They found similar weaknesses in the movement and the consensus among them was that the Harlem Renaissance had been in large part a failure, or perhaps a missed opportunity.

The Harlem Renaissance at the End of the Century

A more positive and more sophisticated analysis of the Harlem Renaissance appeared in the 1980s and 1990s when the Harlem Renaissance itself enjoyed a renaissance. A new generation largely of African American scholars produced a series of excellent biographies of participants and critical studies of their works. These efforts added greatly to the knowledge of the period and provided a deeper and more critically based assessment of the Harlem Renaissance. This development coincided with the resurgence of African American literature, especially writing by African American women, which stimulated greater interest in the literary antecedents of these modern works. Related to this was the rediscovery of Zora Neale Hurston and her rise to a dominant position both African American and women's literary studies. Accompanying this was the expansion of African American studies programs and the scholarship that these programs generated. As African American studies programs matured, they stimulated the production of new anthologies and editions of Harlem Renaissance literature and African American literature. The most obvious example of this was the *Norton Anthology of African American Literature*, but it also included complete collections of the poetry of Countee Cullen and Langston Hughes, and new releases of novels of Wallace Thurman, Rudolph Fisher, and Claude McKay, among others. Equally important are developments such as the University of Missouri Press' publication of the complete works of Langston Hughes, and, perhaps most important, the publication of the works of several black writers, including Zora Neale Hurston, by the prestigious Library of America. If there is an American literary cannon, it is defined by inclusion in the Library of America. The appearance of African American writers in this series, especially writers from the Harlem Renaissance, is the strongest sign yet that African American literature has finally moved into the mainstream, and that the significance of the Harlem Renaissance to American literature is no longer in dispute.

This Anthology

This anthology concentrates on the literary aspects of the Harlem Renaissance; it does include several examples of the visual arts associated with the movement. The literary texts are arranged more or less chronologically, from materials that preceded the Renaissance through the mid 1930s. For the most part shorter pieces have been selected that could be presented in their entirety; there are some excerpts from longer works, especially if these passages are central to an understanding of an author's contribution to the Harlem Renaissance. All of the major authors are represented as well as some who are less well known, but nevertheless important to the Renaissance. Selections range from the most familiar writings to pieces that are not commonly anthologized. This anthology also includes selections that help frame the history of the movement, several essays on the Harlem Renaissance, as well as some criticism contemporary to the writing. The purpose of these pieces is to provide some insight into how the artists of this period perceived themselves, and how their contemporaries perceived them, and give some sense of the development of the movement. The critical pieces were selected, not in order to assess the literary or cultural value in the work under review, but to illustrate the range of critical reaction. This brief volume contains only a small sample of the literary work produced during the Harlem Renaissance, and an even smaller sample of the critical response to this work; its purpose is to serve as an introduction to the Renaissance, its writers, and the rich body of literature that they produced.

Finally, a word on the texts. Wherever possible the version of a work presented is the standard version as initially published and as most commonly reprinted. Errors in the original text are included, but some standards have been imposed. The anthology, for example, always capitalizes the term "Negro," which in the early part of the twentieth century was usually in lower case; and current style is employed regarding the italicization of book and journal titles. Otherwise the texts appear as they were written and published.

II
AFRICAN AMERICAN LITERATURE BEFORE THE RENAISSANCE

The two most significant African American writers at the turn of the century were poet and novelist Paul Laurence Dunbar and novelist and short story writer Charles Waddell Chesnutt. Dunbar and Chesnutt shared a number of traits. Both were born in Ohio, although Chesnutt spent much of his childhood in North Carolina; both achieved most of the white critical acclaim with their dialect pieces, while their more serious work in standard English was less favorably received; and, both broke into the literary mainstream through the attention and intervention of novelist and literary critic William Dean Howells. The two also wrote about race and its impact on blacks and whites in a manner that anticipated the work of later African American writers, and both faced many of the same problems and frustrations that their counterparts in the 1920s were to encounter.

Of the two Dunbar achieved the greater public recognition. Booker T. Washington acclaimed him as "the Poet Laureate of the Negro Race" and after his untimely death in 1906, schools, literary societies, and literary prizes took his name. Dunbar's brief literary career began in 1893 when he self-published a collection of poems, *Oak and Ivy*. Like all of his work it contained dialect pieces, which some interpreted as sentimental and nostalgic for the carefree ante-bellum plantation life, along with other poems that addressed more serious racial themes in standard English. The dialect poems attracted the attention of Howells, who arranged for Dodd, Mead, and Company to published his next two books, *Majors and Minors* in 1895 and a year later *Lyrics of a Lowly Life*. Many critics underestimated Dunbar's dialect poetry, the most powerful of which projected a strong sense of African American humanity and dignity. Dunbar was even more effective, though far less popular, when he moved away from dialect poetry and celebrated black history, or addressed the psychological cost of racism such as he did in "We Wear the Mask."

Around the turn of the century Dunbar's literary career seemed to be blossoming. In 1898 he married Alice Ruth Moore, a poet who would accomplish much in her own right, and during the next six years he published four books of short stories and four novels. Yet throughout this period Dunbar's literary frustrations continued. His dialect stories were popular; his attempts to write seriously about race were not. His last novel, *The Sport of the Gods*, examined for the first time the problems and conflicts that accompanied migration from the rural South to the urban North.

Chesnutt faced many of the same frustrations as Dunbar. His first successful writing utilized dialect and an elderly black man, Uncle Julius, who recited folk tales about slavery in Uncle Remus fashion. In spite of surface similarities, Uncle Julius is no Uncle Remus, and Chesnutt's plantation is darker, more violent, and thoroughly deromanticized. With the help of Howells, Chesnutt found a commercial press for his first volume of Uncle Julius stories, *The Conjure Woman*, published in 1899. That same year Chesnutt published a second volume of short stories, *The Wife of his Youth and Other Stories*, that dropped dialect and concentrated on race and the African American urban elite.

Chesnutt followed his short stories with three novels written in quick succession. Each addressed different racial issue, and explored the social and psychological trauma that arose from race prejudice in America. The first, *The House Behind the Cedars*, which came out in 1900, examined the stresses involved in passing and the impact that this act had on the personal relations among both whites and blacks. The third novel, *The Colonel's Dream* (1905), was his most pessimistic. It chronicled the well-intentioned efforts of a northern liberal to upgrade economic and social conditions in the South. These efforts fail disastrously when they run head on into southern racism; the Colonel retreats back to the North, his plans in ruin and his hopes dashed. Chesnutt most ambitious novel was his second, *The Marrow of Tradition*, which he published in 1901. Here he hoped to write a modern version of *Uncle Tom's Cabin* that would arouse the conscience of the nation, and mobilize it against the segregation, disfranchisement, and violence that was sweeping the South and subjecting blacks to a new condition of bondage and servitude. The novel also exposed the impotence of moderate blacks and paternalistic whites when confronted by the fury of the white mob, as well as the use of racial fear by white politicians to achieve power.

Although Chesnutt's novels clearly took the perspective of the black bourgeoisie, and his writing and plotting reflected much of the romanticism common to popular fiction at the turn of the century, their direct examination of race in a contemporary setting imbued them with a radicalism that made many whites uncomfortable; they received a mixed critical response and their sales steadily declined. The frustration over the lack of literary success prompted Chesnutt to give up full-time writing after his second novel; following the commercial failure of his last novel, Chesnutt largely abandoned writing. Except for a handful of short stories and an occasional essay, his literary career was over. Yet Chesnutt remained popular among black readers, and in recognition the NAACP awarded him the Spingarn Medal in 1928 for his pioneering work in African American literature.

PAUL LAURENCE DUNBAR:
Poems

The poems here reflect two sides of Dunbar's work—the dialect poems and the more serious pieces that address racial issues. The works in dialect are characterized by richness in content and style that do more than most verse of this kind to reflect African American life and experience. Dunbar also used dialect occasionally as a mask to conceal deeper meaning in his poems. The "boogah man" was an imaginary character derived from folklore, but it also reflected the danger of family separation under slavery. In the traditional poems Dunbar voices the frustrations that he faced as a black poet: prized for his dialect work but ignored when he attempted anything more serious. The images that he developed of the "caged bird" ("Symphony") and the "mask" (We Wear the Mask") recur through African American writing, both during and after the Harlem Renaissance. Dunbar also used his poetry to express his political concerns. "Douglass" laments the loss of the great nineteenth century civil rights leader.

"We Wear the Mask"
1895

We wear the mask that grins and lies,
It hides our cheeks and shades our eyes,
This debt we pay to human guile;
With torn and bleeding hearts we smile,
And mouth with myriad subtleties.

Why should the world be overwise,
In counting all our tears and sighs?
Nay, let them only see us, while
    We wear the mask.

We smile, but, O great Christ, our cries
To thee from tortured souls arise.
We sing, but oh the clay is vile
Beneath our feet, and long the mile;
But let the world dream otherwise,
    We wear the mask!

"A Negro Love Song"
1895

Seen my lady home las' night,
    Jump back, honey, jump back.
Hel' huh han' an' sque'z it tight,
    Jump back, honey, jump back.
Hyeahd huh sigh a little sigh
Seen a light gleam f'om huh eye,
An' a smile go flittin' by—
    Jump back, honey, jump back.

Hyeahd de win' blow thoo de pine,
    Jump back, honey, jump back.
Mockin'-bird was singin' fine,
    Jump back, honey, jump back.
An' my hea't was beatin' so,
When I reached my lady's do',
Dat I could n't ba' to go—
    Jump back, honey, jump back.

Put my ahm aroun' huh wais',
    Jump back, honey, jump back.

Raised huh lips an' took a tase,
Jump back, honey, jump back.
Love me, honey, love me true?
Love me well ez I love you?
An' she answe'd, "'Cose I do"—
Jump back, honey, jump back.

"The Boogah Man"

W'en de evenin' shadders
Come a-glidin' down,
Fallin' black an' heavy
Ovah hill an' town,
Ef you listen keerful,
Keerful ez you kin,
So's you boun' to notice
Des a drappin' pin;
Den you'll hyeah a funny
Soun' ercross de lan';
Lay low; dat's de callin'
Of de Boogah Man!

Woo-oo, *woo-oo!*
Hyeah him ez he go erlong de way;
Woo-oo, woo-oo!
Don' you wish de night 'ud tu'n to day?
Woe-oo, woo-oo!
Hide yo' little peepers 'hind yo' han';
Woo-oo, woo-oo!
Callin' of de Boogah Man.

W'en de win's a-shiverin'
Thoo de gloomy lane,
An' dey comes de patterin'
Of de evenin' rain,
Wen de owl's a-hootin',
Out daih in de wood,
Don' you wish, my honey,
Dat you had been good?
'T ain't no use to try to
Snuggle up to Dan;
Bless you, dat's de callin'
Of de Boogah Man!

Ef you loves yo' mammy,
An' you min's yo' pap,
Ef you nevah wriggles
Outen Sukey's lap;

Ef you says yo' "Lay me"
        Evah single night
'Fo' dey tucks de kivers
        An' puts out de light,
Den de rain kin pattah
        Win' blow lak a fan,
But you need n' bothah
        'Bout de Boogah Man!

"Sympathy"
1899

I know what the caged bird feels, alas!
        When the sun is bright on the upland slopes;
When the wind stirs soft through the springing grass,
And the river flows like a stream of glass;
        When the first bird sings and the first bud opes,
And the faint perfume from its chalice steals—
I know what the caged bird feels!

I know why the caged bird beats his wing
        Till its blood is red on the cruel bars;
For he must fly back to his perch and cling
When he fain would be on the bough a-swing;
        And a pain still throbs in the old, old scars
And they pulse again with a keener sting—
I know why he beats his wing!

I know why the caged bird sings, ah me,
        When his wing is bruised and his bosom sore,—
When he beats his bars and he would be free;
It is not a carol of joy or glee,
        But a prayer that he sends from his heart's deep core,
But a plea, that upward to Heaven he flings—
I know why the caged bird sings!

"Douglass"
1903

Ah, Douglass, we have fall'n on evil days,
        Such days as thou, not even thou didst know,
        When thee, the eyes of that harsh long ago
Saw, salient; at the cross of devious ways,
And all the country heard thee with amaze.
        Not ended then, the passionate ebb and flow,
        The awful tide that battled to and fro;
We ride amid a tempest of dispraise.

Now, when the waves of swift dissension swarm,
   And Honor, the strong pilot, lieth stark,
Oh, for thy voice high-sounding o'er the storm,
   For thy strong arm to guide the shivering bark,
The blast-defying power of thy form,
   To give us comfort through the lonely dark.

"The Poet"
1903

He sang of life, serenely sweet,
   With, now and then, a deeper note.
   From some high peak, nigh yet remote,
He voiced the world's absorbing beat.

He sang of love when earth was young,
   And Love, itself, was in his lays.
   But ah, the world, it turned to praise
A jingle in a broken tongue.

CHARLES W. CHESNUTT:
"The Wife of His Youth"
1899

The title piece from his second book of short stories represented a dramatic shift from the dialect slave tales of his first book. But although the characters, setting, and language are thoroughly upper middle class, Chesnutt uses this story to remind his readers both of how far blacks have come since slavery and of how close they still are to it.

"The Wife of His Youth"

I

Mr. Rider was going to give a ball. There were several reasons why this was an opportune time for such an event.

Mr. Ryder might aptly be called the dean of the Blue Veins. The original Blue Veins were a little society of colored persons organized in a certain Northern city shortly after the war. Its purpose was to establish and maintain correct social standards among a people whose social condition presented almost unlimited room for improvement. By accident, combined perhaps with some natural affinity, the society consisted of individuals who were, generally speaking, more white than black. — *How?* Some envious outsider made the suggestion that no one was eligible for membership who was not white enough to show blue veins. The suggestion was readily adopted by those who were not of the favored few, and since that time the society, though possessing a longer and more pretentious name, had been known far and wide as the "Blue Vein Society," and its members as the "Blue Veins."

The Blue Veins did not allow that any such requirement existed for admission to their circle, but, on the contrary, declared that character and culture were the only things considered; and that if most of their members were light-colored, it was because such persons, as a rule, had had better opportunities to qualify themselves for membership. Opinions differed, too, as to the usefulness of the society. There were those who had been known to assail it violently as a glaring example of the very prejudice from which the colored race had suffered most; and later, when such critics had succeeded in getting on the inside, they had been heard to maintain with zeal and earnestness that the society was a lifeboat, an anchor, a bulwark and a shield,—a pillar of cloud by day and of fire by night, to guide their people through the social wilderness. Another alleged prerequisite for Blue Vein membership was that of free birth; and while there was really no such requirement, it is doubtless true that very few of the members would have been unable to meet it if there had been. If there were one or two of the older members who had come up from the South and from slavery, their history presented enough romantic circumstances to rob their servile origin of its grosser aspects.

While there were no such tests of eligibility, it is true that the Blue Veins had their notions on these subjects, and that not all of them were equally liberal in regard to the things they collectively disclaimed. Mr. Ryder was one of the most conservative. Though he had not been among the founders of the society, but had come in some years later, his genius for social leadership was such that he had speedily become its recognized adviser and head, the custodian of its standards, and the preserver of its traditions. He shaped its social policy, was active in providing for its entertainment, and when the interest fell off, as it sometimes did, he fanned the embers until they burst again into a cheerful flame.

There were still other reasons for his popularity. While he was not as white as some of the Blue Veins, his appearance was such as to confer distinction upon them. His features were of a refined type, his hair was almost straight; he was always neatly dressed; his manners were irreproachable, and his morals above suspicion. He had come to Groveland a young man, and obtaining employment in the office of a railroad company as messenger had in time worked himself up to the position of stationery clerk, having charge of the distribution of the office supplies for the whole company. Although the lack of early training had hindered the orderly development of a naturally fine mind, it had not prevented him from doing a great deal of reading or from forming decidedly literary tastes. Poetry was his passion. He could repeat whole pages of the great English poets; and if his pronunciation was sometimes faulty, his eye, his voice, his gestures, would respond to the changing sentiment with a precision that revealed a poetic soul and disarmed criticism. He was economical, and had saved money; he owned and occupied a very comfortable house on a respectable street. His residence was handsomely furnished, containing among other things a good library, especially rich in poetry, a piano, and some choice engravings. He generally shared his house with some young couple, who looked after his wants and were company for him; for Mr. Ryder was a single man. In the early days of his connection with the Blue Veins he had been regarded as quite a catch, and young ladies and their mothers had manoeuvred with much ingenuity to capture him. Not, however, until Mrs. Molly Dixon visited Groveland had any woman ever made him wish to change his condition to that of a married man.

Mrs. Dixon had come to Groveland from Washington in the spring, and before the summer was over she had won Mr. Ryder's heart. She possessed many attractive qualities. She was much younger than he; in fact, he was old enough to have been her father, though no one knew exactly how old he was. She was whiter than he, and better educated. She had moved in the best colored society of the country, at Washington, and had taught in the schools of that city. Such a superior person had been eagerly welcomed to the Blue Vein Society, and had taken a leading part in its activities. Mr. Ryder had at first been attracted by her charms of person, for she was very good looking and not over twenty-five; then by her refined manners and the vivacity of her wit. Her husband had been a government clerk, and at his death had left a considerable life insurance. She was visiting friends in Groveland, and, finding the town and the people to her liking, had prolonged her stay indefinitely. She had not seemed displeased at Mr. Ryder's attentions, but on the contrary had given him every proper encouragement; indeed, a younger and less cautious man would long since have spoken. But he had made up his mind, and had only to determine the time when he would ask her to be his wife. He decided to give a ball in her honor, and at some time during the evening of the ball to offer her his heart and hand. He had no special fears about the outcome, but, with a little touch of romance, he wanted the surroundings to be in harmony with his own feelings when he should have received the answer he expected.

Mr. Ryder resolved that this ball should mark an epoch in the social history of Groveland. He knew, of course,—no one could know better,—the entertainments that had taken place in past years, and what must be done to surpass them. His ball must be worthy of the lady in whose honor it was to be given, and must, by the quality of its guests, set an example for the future. He had observed of late a growing liberality, almost a laxity, in social matters, even among members of his own set, and had several times been forced to meet in a social way persons whose complexions and callings in life were hardly up to the standard which he considered proper for the society to maintain. He had a theory of his own.

"I have no race prejudice," he would say, "but we people of mixed blood are ground between the upper and the nether millstone. Our fate lies between absorption by the white race and extinction in the black. The one doesn't want us yet, but may take us in time. The other would welcome us, but it would be for us a backward step. 'With malice towards none, with charity for all,' we must do the best we can for ourselves and those who are to follow us. Self-preservation is the first law of nature."

His ball would serve by its exclusiveness to counteract leveling tendencies, and his marriage with Mrs. Dixon would help to further the upward process of absorption he had been wishing and waiting for.

II

The ball was to take place on Friday night. The house had been put in order, the carpets covered with canvas, the halls and stairs decorated with palms and potted plants; and in the afternoon Mr. Ryder sat on his front porch, which the shade of a vine running up over a wire netting made a cool and pleasant lounging place.

He expected to respond to the toast "The Ladies" at the supper, and from a volume of Tennyson—his favorite poet—was fortifying himself with apt quotations. The volume was open at "A Dream of Fair Women." His eyes fell on these lines, and he read them aloud to judge better of their effect:—

> "At length I saw a lady within call,
>   Stiller than chisell'd marble, standing there;
> A daughter of the gods, divinely tall,
>   And most divinely fair."

He marked the verse, and turning the page read the stanza beginning,—

> "O sweet pale Margaret,
>   O rare pale Margaret."

He weighed the passage a moment, and decided that it would not do. Mrs. Dixon was the palest lady he expected at the ball, and she was of a rather ruddy complexion, and of lively disposition and buxom build. So he ran over the leaves until his eye rested on the description of Queen Guinevere:—

> "She seem'd a part of joyous Spring:
> A gown of grass-green silk she wore,
> Buckled with golden clasps before;
> A light-green tuft of plumes she bore
> Closed in a golden ring.
>
> . . . .
>
> "She look'd so lovely, as she sway'd
> The rein with dainty finger-tips,
> A man had given all other bliss,
> And all his worldly worth for this,
> To waste his whole heart in one kiss
> Upon her perfect lips."

As Mr. Ryder murmured these words audibly, with an appreciative thrill, he heard the latch of his gate click, and a light footfall sounding on the steps. He turned his head, and saw a woman standing before his door.

She was a little woman, not five feet tall, and proportioned to her height. Although she stood erect, and looked around her with very bright and restless eyes, she seemed quite old; for her face was crossed and recrossed with a hundred wrinkles, and around the edges of her bonnet could be seen protruding here and there a tuft of short gray wool. She wore a blue calico gown of ancient cut, a little red shawl fastened around her shoulders with an old-fashioned brass brooch, and a large bonnet profusely ornamented with faded red and yellow artificial flowers. And she was very black,—so black that her toothless gums, revealed when she opened her mouth to speak, were not red, but blue. She looked like a bit of the old plantation life, summoned up from the past by the wave of a magician's wand, as the poet's fancy had called into being the gracious shapes of which Mr. Ryder had just been reading.

He rose from his chair and came over to where she stood.

"Good-afternoon, madam," he said.

"Good-evenin', suh," she answered, ducking suddenly with a quaint curtsy. Her voice was shrill and piping, but softened somewhat by age. "Is dis yere whar Mistuh Ryduh lib, suh?" she asked, looking around her doubtfully, and glancing into the open windows, through which some of the preparations for the evening were visible.

"Yes," he replied, with an air of kindly patronage, unconsciously flattered by her manner, "I am Mr. Ryder. Did you want to see me?"

"Yas, suh, ef I ain't 'sturbin' of you too much."

"Not at all. Have a seat over here behind the vine, where it is cool. What can I do for you?"

"'Scuse me, suh," she continued, when she had sat down on the edge of a chair, "'scuse me, suh, I's lookin' for my husban'. I heerd you wuz a big man an' had libbed heah a long time, an' I 'lowed you wouldn't min' of I'd come roun' an' ax you ef you'd ever heerd of a merlatter man by de name er Sam Taylor 'quirin' roun' in de chu'ches ermongs' de people fer his wife 'Liza Jane?"

Mr. Ryder seemed to think for a moment. "There used to be many such cases right after the war," he said, "but it has been so long that I have forgotten them. There are very few now. But tell me your story, and it may refresh my memory."

She sat back farther in her chair so as to be more comfortable, and folded her withered hands in her lap.

"My name's 'Liza," she began, "'Liza Jane. Wen I wuz young I us'ter b'long ter

Marse Bob Smif, down in ole Missoura. I wuz bawn down dere.   Wen   I wuz a gal I wuz married ter a man named Jim. But Jim died, an' after dat I married a merlatter man named Sam Taylor. Sam wuz freebawn, but his mammy and daddy died, an' de w'ite folks 'prenticed him ter my marster fer ter work fer 'im 'tel he wuz growed up. Sam worked in de fiel', an' I wuz de cook.   One day Ma'y Ann, ole miss's maid, came rushin' out ter de kitchen, an' says she, ''Liza Jane, ole marse gwine sell yo' Sam down de ribber.'

" 'Go way f'm yere,' says I; 'my husban''s free!'

" 'Don' make no diff'ence. I heerd ole marse tell ole miss he wuz gwine take yo' Sam 'way wid 'im ter-morrow, fer he needed money, an' he knowed whar he could git a t'ousan' dollars fer Sam an' no questions axed.'

"Wen Sam come home f'm de fiel' dat night, I tole him 'bout ole marse gwine steal 'im, an' Sam run erway. His time wuz mos' up, an' he swo' dat w'en he wuz twenty-one he would come back an' he'p me run erway, er else save up de money ter buy my freedom. An' I know he'd 'a' done it, fer he thought a heap er me, Sam did. But w'en he come back he did n' fin' me, fer I wuz n' dere. Ole marse had heerd dat I warned Sam, so he had me whip' an' sol' down de ribber.

"Den de wah broke out, an' w'en it wuz ober de cullud folks wuz scattered. I went back ter de ole home; but Sam wuz n' dere, an' I could n' l'arn nuffin' 'bout 'im. But I knowed he'd be'n dere to look fer me an' had n' foun' me, an' had gone erway ter hunt fer me.

"I's be'n lookin' fer 'im eber sense," she added simply, as though twenty-five years were but a couple of weeks, "an' I knows he's be'n lookin' fer me. Fer he sot a heap er sto' by me, Sam did, an' I know he's be'n huntin' fer me all dese years,—'less'n he's be'n sick er sump'n, so he could n' work, er out'n his head, so he could n' 'member his promise. I went back down de ribber, fer I 'lowed he'd gone down dere lookin' fer me. I's be'n ter Noo Orleans, an' Atlanty, an' Charleston, an' Richmon'; an' w'en I'd be'n all ober de Souf I come ter de Norf. Fer I knows I'll fin' 'im some er dese days," she added softly, "er he'll fin' me, an' den we'll bofe be as happy in freedom as we wuz in de ole days befo' de wah." A smile stole over her withered countenance as she paused a moment, and her bright eyes softened into a faraway look.

This was the substance of the old woman's story. She had wandered a little here and there. Mr. Ryder was looking at her curiously when she finished.

"How have you lived all these years?" he asked.

"Cookin', suh. I's a good cook. Does you know anybody w'at needs a good cook, suh? I's stoppin' wid a cullud fam'ly roun' de corner yonder 'tel I kin git a place."

"Do you really expect to find your husband? He may be dead long ago."

She shook her head emphatically. "Oh no, he ain' dead.   De signs an' de tokens tells me. I dremp three nights runnin' on'y dis las' week dat I foun' him."

"He may have married another woman. Your slave marriage would not have prevented him, for you never lived with him after the war, and without that your marriage does n't count."

"Would n' make no diff'ence wid Sam. He would n' marry no yuther 'ooman 'tel he foun' out 'bout me. I knows it," she added. "Sump'n's be'n tellin' me all dese years dat I's gwine fin' Sam 'fo' I dies."

"Perhaps he's outgrown you, and climbed up in the world where he would n't care to have you find him."

"No, indeed, suh," she replied, "Sam ain' dat kin' er man. He wuz good ter me, Sam wuz, but he wuz n' much good ter nobody e'se, fer he wuz one er de triflin'es' han's on de plantation. I 'spec's ter haf ter suppo't 'im w'en I fin' 'im, fer he nebber would work 'less'n he had ter. But den he wuz free, an' he did n' git no pay fer his work, an' I don' blame 'im much. Mebbe he's done better sence he run erway, but I ain' 'spectin' much."

"You may have passed him on the street a hundred times during the twenty-five years, and not have known him; time works great changes."

She smiled incredulously. "I'd know 'im 'mongs' a hund'ed men. Fer dey wuz n' no yuther merlatter man like my man Sam, an' I could n' be mistook. I' toted his picture roun' wid me twenty-five years."

"May I see it?" asked Mr. Ryder. "It might help me to remember whether I have seen the original."

As she drew a small parcel from her bosom he saw that it was fastened to a string that went around her neck. Removing several wrappers, she brought to light an old-fashioned daguerreotype in a black case. He looked long and intently at the portrait. It was faded with time, but the features were still distinct, and it was easy to see what manner of man it had represented.

He closed the case, and with a slow movement handed it back to her.

"I don't know of any man in town who goes by that name," he said, "nor have I heard of any one making such inquiries. But if you will leave me your address, I will give the matter some attention, and if I find out anything I will let you know."

She gave him the number of a house in the neighborhood, and went away, after thanking him warmly.

He wrote the address on the fly-leaf of the volume of Tennyson, and, when she had gone, rose to his feet and stood looking after her curiously. As she walked down the street with mincing step, he saw several persons whom she passed turn and look back at her with a smile of kindly amusement. When she had turned the corner, he went upstairs to his bedroom, and stood for a long time before the mirror of his dressing-case, gazing thoughtfully at the reflection of his own face.

III

At eight o'clock the ballroom was a blaze of light and the guests had begun to assemble; for there was a literary programme and some routine business of the society to be gone through with before the dancing. A black servant in evening dress waited at the door and directed the guests to the dressing-rooms.

The occasion was long memorable among people of the city; not alone for the dress and display, but for the high average intelligence and culture that distinguished the gathering as a whole. There were a number of school-teachers, several young doctors, three or four lawyers, some professional singers, an editor, a lieutenant in the United States army spending his furlough in the city, and others in various polite callings; these were colored, though most of them would not have attracted even a casual glance because of any marked difference from white people. Most of the ladies were in evening costume, and dress coats and dancing pumps were the rule among the men. A band of string music, stationed in an alcove behind a row of palms, played popular airs while the guests were gathering.

The dancing began at half past nine. At eleven o'clock supper was served. Mr. Ryder had left the ballroom some little time before the intermission, but reappeared at the supper table. The spread was worthy of the occasion, and the guests did full justice to it. When the coffee had been served, the toastmaster, Mr. Solomon Sadler, rapped for order. He made a brief introductory speech, complimenting host and guests, and then presented in their order the toasts of the evening. They were responded to with a very fair display of after-dinner wit.

"The last toast," said the toast-master, when he reached the end of the list, "is one which must appeal to us all. There is no one of us of the sterner sex who is not at some time dependent upon woman,—in infancy for protection, in manhood for companionship, in old age for care and comforting. Our good host has been trying to live alone, but the fair faces I see around me to-night prove that he too is largely dependent upon the gentler sex for most that makes life worth living,— the society and love of friends,—and rumor is at fault if he does not soon yield entire subjection to one of them. Mr. Ryder will now respond to the toast,—The Ladies."

There was a pensive look in Mr. Ryder's eyes as he took the floor and adjusted his eyeglasses. He began by speaking of woman as the gift of Heaven to man, and after some general observations on the relations of the sexes he said: "But perhaps the quality which most distinguishes woman is her fidelity and devotion to those she loves. History is full of examples, but has recorded none more striking than one which only to-day came under my notice."

He then related, simply but effectively, the story told by his visitor of the afternoon. He gave it in the same soft dialect, which came readily to his lips, while the company listened attentively and sympathetically. For the story had awakened a responsive thrill in many hearts. There were some present who had seen, and others who had heard their fathers and grandfathers tell, the wrongs and sufferings of this past generation, and all of them still felt, in their darker moments, the shadow hanging over them. Mr. Ryder went on:—

"Such devotion and confidence are rare even among women. There are many who would have searched a year, some who would have waited five years, a few who might have hoped ten years; but for twenty-five years this woman has retained her affection for and her faith in a man she has not seen or heard of in all that time.

"She came to me to-day in the hope that I might be able to help her find this long-lost husband. And when she was gone I gave my fancy rein, and imagined a case I will put to you.

Suppose that this husband, soon after his escape, had learned that his wife had been sold away, and that such inquiries as he could make brought no information of her whereabouts. Suppose that he was young, and she much older than he; that he was light, and she was black; that their marriage was a slave marriage, and legally binding only if they chose to make it so after the war. Suppose, too, that he made his way to the North, as some of us have done, and there, where he had larger opportunities, had improved them, and had in the course of all these years grown to be as different from the ignorant boy who ran away from fear of slavery as the day is from the night. Suppose, even, that he had qualified himself, by industry, by thrift, and by study, to win the friendship and be considered worthy the society of such people as these I see around me to-night, gracing my board and filling my heart with gladness; for I am old enough to remember the day when such a gathering would not have been possible in this land. Suppose, too, that, as the years went by, this man's memory of the past grew more and more indistinct, until at last it was rarely, except in his dreams, that any image of this bygone period rose before his mind. And then suppose that accident should bring to his knowledge the fact that the wife of his youth, the wife he had left behind him,— not one who had walked by his side and kept pace with him in his upward struggle, but one upon whom advancing years and a laborious life had set their mark,— was alive and seeking him, but that he was absolutely safe from recognition or discovery, unless he chose to reveal himself. My friends, what would the man do? I will presume that he was one who loved honor, and tried to deal justly with all men. I will I even carry the case further, and suppose that perhaps he had set his heart upon another, whom he had hoped to call his own. What would he do, or rather what ought he to do, in such a crisis of a lifetime?

"It seemed to me that he might hesitate, and I imagined that I was an old friend, a near friend, and that he had come to me for advice; and I argued the case with him. I tried to discuss it impartially. After we had looked upon the matter from every point of view, I said to him, in words that we all know:—

'This above all: to thine own self be true,
And it must follow, as the night the day,
Thou canst not then be false to any man.'

Then, finally, I put the question to him, 'Shall you acknowledge her?'

"And now, ladies and gentlemen, friends and companions, I ask you, what should he have done?"

There was something in Mr. Ryder's voice that stirred the hearts of those who sat around him. It suggested more than mere sympathy with an imaginary situation; it seemed rather in the nature of a personal appeal. It was observed, too, that his look rested more especially upon Mrs. Dixon, with a mingled expression of renunciation and inquiry.

She had listened, with parted lips and streaming eyes. She was the first to speak: "He should have acknowledged her."

"Yes," they all echoed, "he should have acknowledged her."

"My friends and companions," responded Mr. Ryder, "I thank you, one and all. It is the answer I expected, for I knew your hearts."

He turned and walked toward the closed door of an adjoining room, while every eye followed him in wondering curiosity. He came back in a moment, leading by the hand his visitor of the afternoon, who stood startled and trembling at the sudden plunge into this scene of brilliant gayety. She was neatly dressed in gray, and wore the white cap of an elderly woman.

"Ladies and gentlemen," he said, "this is the woman, and I am the man, whose story I have told you. Permit me to introduce to you the wife of my youth."

WILLIAM DEAN HOWELLS:
Criticism and Assessment:

William Dean Howells was an accomplished novelist, editor, literary and social critic in the late nineteenth and early twentieth centuries. His influence on American literature was based on his reputation in fiction and scholarship, and on his positions, first as editor of *Atlantic Monthly*, then literary columnist for *Harper's Monthly* and frequent contributor to *The North American Review*. His commitment to social reform, his interest in the race issue, and his sharing an Ohio origin explain his interest in Dunbar and Chesnutt. The three essays that follow document his assistance to the two black writers as well as the limits of this assistance. The first two essays are reprinted in their entirety; in the third essay the comments on Chesnutt are excerpted.

Introduction to *Lyrics of Lowly Life*
1896

I think I should scarcely trouble the reader with a special appeal in behalf of this book, if it had not specially appealed to me for reasons apart from the author's race, origin, and condition. The world is too old now, and I find myself too much of its mood, to care for the work of a poet because he is black, because his father and mother were slaves, because he was, before and after he began to write poems, an elevator-boy. These facts would certainly attract me to him as a man, if I knew him to have a literary ambition, but when it came to his literary art, I must judge it irrespective of these facts, and enjoy or endure it for what it was in itself.

It seems to me that this was my experience with the poetry of Paul Laurence Dunbar when I found it in another form, and in justice to him I cannot wish that it should be otherwise with his readers here. Still, it will legitimately interest those who like to know the causes, or, if these may not be known, the sources, of things, to learn that the father and mother of the first poet of his race in our language were Negroes without admixture of white blood. The father escaped from slavery in Kentucky to freedom in Canada, while there was still no hope of freedom otherwise; but the mother was freed by the events of the civil war, and came North to Ohio, where their son was born at Dayton, and grew up with such chances and mischances for mental training as everywhere befall the children of the poor. He has told me that his father picked up the trade of a plasterer, and when he had taught himself to read, loved chiefly to read history. The boy's mother shared his passion for literature, with a special love of poetry, and after the father died she struggled on in more than the poverty she had shared with him. She could value the faculty which her son showed first in prose sketches and attempts at fiction, and she was proud of the praise and kindness they won him among the people of the town, where he has never been without the warmest and kindest friends.

In fact from every part of Ohio and from several cities of the adjoining States, there came letters in cordial appreciation of the critical recognition which it was my pleasure no less than my duty to offer Paul Dunbar's work in another place. It seemed to me a happy omen for him that so many people who had known him, or known of him, were glad of a stranger's good word; and it was gratifying to see that at home he was esteemed for the things he had done rather than because as the son of Negro slaves he had done them. If a prophet is often without honor in his own country, it surely is nothing against him when he has it. In this case it deprived me of the glory of a discoverer; but that is sometimes a barren joy, and I am always willing to forego it.

What struck me in reading Mr. Dunbar's poetry was what had already struck his friends in Ohio and Indiana, in Kentucky and Illinois. They had felt, as I felt, that however gifted his race had proven itself in music, in oratory, in several of the other arts, here was the first instance of an American Negro who had evinced innate distinction in literature. In my criticism of his book I had alleged Dumas in France, and I had forgetfully failed to allege the far greater Pushkin in Russia; but these were both mulattoes, who might have been supposed to derive their qualities from white blood vastly more artistic than ours, and who were the creatures of an environment more favorable to their literary development. So far as I could remember, Paul Dunbar was the only man of pure African blood and of American civilization to feel the Negro life aesthetically and express it lyrically. It seemed to me that this had come to its most modern consciousness in him, and that his brilliant and unique achievement was to have studied the American Negro objectively, and to have represented him as he found him to be, with humor, with sympathy, and yet with what the reader must instinctively feel to be entire truthfulness. I said that a race which had come to this effect in any member of it, had attained civilization in him, and I permitted myself the imaginative prophecy that the hostilities and the prejudices which had so long constrained his race were destined to vanish in the arts; that these were to be the final proof that God had made of one blood all nations of men. I thought his merits positive and not comparative; and I held that if his black poems had been written by a white man, I should not have found them less admirable. I accepted them as an evidence of the essential unity of the human race, which does not think or feel black in one and white in another, but humanly in all.

Yet it appeared to me then, and it appears to me now, that there is a precious difference of temperament between the races which it would be a great pity ever to lose, and that this is best preserved and most charmingly suggested by Mr. Dunbar in those pieces of his where he studies the moods and traits of his race in its own accent of our English. We call such pieces dialect pieces for want of some closer phrase, but they are really not dialect so much as delightful personal attempts and failures for the written and spoken language. In nothing is his essentially refined and delicate art so well shown as in these pieces, which, as I ventured to say, described the range between appetite and emotion, with certain lifts far beyond and above it, which is the range of the race. He reveals in these a finely ironical perception of the Negro's limitations, with a tenderness for them which I think so very rare as to be almost quite new. I should say, perhaps, that it was this humorous quality which Mr. Dunbar had added to our literature, and it would be this which would most distinguish him, now and hereafter. It is something that one feels in nearly all the dialect pieces; and I hope that in the present collection he has kept all of these in his earlier volume, and added others to them. But the contents of this book are wholly of his own choosing, and I do not know how much or little he may have preferred the poems in literary English. Some of these I thought very good, and even more than very good, but not distinctively his contribution to the body of American poetry. What I mean is that several people might have written them; but I do not know any one else at present who could quite have written the dialect pieces. These are divinations and reports of what passes in the hearts and minds of a lowly people whose poetry had hitherto been inarticulately expressed in music, but now finds, for the first time in our tongue, literary interpretation of a very artistic completeness.

I say the event is interesting, but how important it shall be can be determined only by Mr. Dunbar's future performance. I cannot undertake to prophesy concerning this; but if he should do nothing more than he has done, I should feel that he had made the strongest claim for the Negro in English literature that the Negro has yet made. He has at least produced something that, however we may critically disagree about it, we cannot well refuse to enjoy; in more than one piece he has produced a work of art.

"Mr. Charles W. Chesnutt's Stories"
The Atlantic Monthly
May 1900

The critical reader of the story called "The Wife of his Youth," which appeared in these pages two years ago, must have noticed uncommon traits in what was altogether a remarkable piece of work. The first was the novelty of the material; for the writer dealt not only with people who were not white, but with people who were not black enough to contrast grotesquely with white people,—who in fact were of that near approach to the ordinary American in race and color which leaves, at the last degree, every one but the connoisseur in doubt whether they are Anglo-Saxon or Anglo-African. Quite as striking as this novelty of the material was the author's thorough mastery of it, and his unerring knowledge of the life he had chosen in its peculiar racial characteristics. But above all, the story was notable for the passionless handling of a phase of our common life which is tense with potential tragedy; for the attitude, almost ironical, in which the artist observes the play of contesting emotions in the drama under his eyes; and for his apparently reluctant, apparently helpless consent to let the spectator know his real feeling in the matter. Any one accustomed to study methods in fiction, to distinguish between good and bad art, to feel the joy which the delicate skill possible only from a love of truth can give, must have known a high pleasure in the quiet self-restraint of the performance; and such a reader would probably have decided that the social situation in the piece was studied wholly from the outside, by an observer with special opportunities for knowing it, who was, as it were, surprised into final sympathy.

Now, however, it is known that the author of this story is of Negro blood,—diluted, indeed, in such measure that if he did not admit this descent few would imagine it, but still quite of that middle world which lies next, though wholly outside, our own. Since his first story appeared he has contributed several others to these pages, and he now makes a showing palpable to criticism in a volume called *The Wife of his Youth, and Other Stories of the Color Line*; a volume of Southern sketches called *The Conjure Woman*; and a short life of Frederick Douglass, in the Beacon Series of biographies. The last is a simple, solid, straight piece of work, not remarkable above many other biographical studies by people entirely white, and yet important as the work of a man not entirely white treating of a great man of his inalienable race. But the volumes of fiction are remarkable above many, above most short stories by people entirely white, and would be worthy of unusual notice if they were not the work of a man not entirely white.

It is not from their racial interest that we could first wish to speak of them, though that must have a very great and very just claim upon the critic. It is much more simply and directly, as works of art, that they make their appeal, and we must allow the force of this quite independently of the other interest. Yet it cannot always be allowed. There are times in each of the stories of the first volume when the simplicity lapses, and the effect is as of a weak and uninstructed touch. There are other times when the attitude, severely impartial and studiously aloof, accuses itself of a little pompousness. There are still other times when the literature is a little too ornate for beauty, and the diction is journalistic, reporteristic. But it is right to add that these are the exceptional times, and that for far the greatest part Mr. Chesnutt seems to know quite as well what he wants to do in a given case as Maupassant, or Tourguénief, or Mr. James, or Miss Jewett, or Miss Wilkins, in other given cases, and has done it with an art of kindred quiet and force. He belongs, in other words, to the good school, the only school, all aberrations from nature being so much truancy and anarchy. He sees his people very clearly, very justly, and he shows them as he sees them, leaving the reader to divine the depth of his feeling for them. He touches all the stops, and with equal delicacy in stories of real tragedy and comedy and pathos, so that it would be hard to say which is the finest in such admirably rendered effects as "The Web of Circumstance," "The Bouquet," and "Uncle Wellington's Wives." In some others the comedy degenerates into satire, with a look in the reader's direction which the author's friend must deplore.

As these stories are of our own time and country, and as there is not a swashbuckler of the seventeenth century, or a sentimentalist of this, or a princess of an imaginary kingdom, in any of them, they will possibly not reach half a million readers in six months, but in twelve months possibly more readers will remember them than if they had reached the half million. They are new and fresh and strong, as life always is, and fable never is; and the stories of *The Conjure Woman* have a wild, indigenous poetry, the creation of sincere and original imagination, which is imparted with a tender humorousness and a very artistic reticence. As far as his race is concerned, or his sixteenth part of a race, it does not greatly matter whether Mr. Chesnutt invented their motives, or found them, as he feigns, among his distant cousins of the Southern cabins. In either case, the wonder of their beauty is the same; and whatever is primitive and sylvan or campestral in the reader's heart is touched by the spells thrown on the simple black lives in these enchanting tales. Character, the most precious thing in fiction, is as faithfully portrayed, against the poetic background as in the setting of the *Stories of the Color Line.*

Yet these stories, after all, are Mr. Chesnutt's most important work, whether we consider them merely as realistic fiction, apart from their author, or as studies of that middle world of which he is naturally and voluntarily a citizen. We had known the nethermost world of the grotesque and comical Negro and the terrible and tragic Negro though the white observer on the outside, and black character in its lyrical moods we had known from such an inside witness as Mr. Paul Dunbar; but it had remained for Mr. Chesnutt to acquaint us with those regions where the paler shades dwell as hopelessly, with relation to ourselves, as the blackest Negro. He has not shown the dwellers there as very different from ourselves. They have within their own circles the same social ambitions and prejudices; they intrigue and truckle and crawl, and are snobs, like ourselves, both of the snobs that snub and the snobs that are snubbed. We may choose to think them droll in their parody of pure white society, but perhaps it would be wiser to recognize that they are like us because they are of our blood by more than a half, or three quarters, or nine tenths. It is not, in such cases, their Negro blood that characterizes them; but it is their Negro blood that excludes them, and that will imaginably fortify them and exalt them. Bound in that sad solidarity from which there is no hope of entrance into polite white society for them, they may create a civilization of their own, which need not lack the highest quality. They need not be ashamed of the race from which they have sprung, and whose exile they share; for in many of the arts it has already shown, during a single generation of freedom, gifts which slavery apparently only obscured. With Mr. Booker Washington the first American orator of our time, fresh upon the time of Frederick Douglass; with Mr. Dunbar among the truest of our poets; with Mr. Tanner, a black American, among the only three Americans from whom the French government ever bought a picture, Mr. Chesnutt may well be willing to own his color.

But that is his personal affair. Our own more universal interest in him arises from the more than promise he has given in a department of literature where Americans hold the foremost place. In this there is, happily, no color line; and if he has it in him to go forward on the way which he has traced for himself, to be true to life as he has known it, to deny himself the glories of the cheap success which awaits the charlatan in fiction, one of the places at the top is open to him. He has sounded a fresh note, boldly, not blatantly, and he has won the ear of the more intelligent public.

From "A Psychological Counter-Current in Recent Fiction"
North American Review
December 1901

I wish that I could at all times praise as much the literature of an author who speaks for another colored race, not so far from us as the Japenese [sic.], but of as much claim upon our conscience, if not our interest. Mr. Chesnutt, it seems to me, has lost literary quality in acquiring literary quantity, and though his book, *The Marrow of Tradition*, is of the same strong material as his earlier books, it is less simple throughout, and therefore less excellent in manner. At his worst, he is no worse than the higher average of the ordinary novelist, but he ought always to be very much better, for he began better, and he is of that race which has, first of all, to get rid of the cakewalk, if it will not suffer from a smile far more blighting than any frown. He is fighting a battle, and it is not for him to pick up the cheap graces and poses of the jouster. He does, indeed, cast them all from him when he gets down to his work, and in the dramatic climaxes and closes of his story he shortens his weapons and deals his blows so absolutely without flourish that I have nothing but admiration for him. *The Marrow of Tradition*, like everything else he has written, has to do with the relations of the blacks and whites, and in that republic of letters where all men are free and equal he stands up for his own people with a courage which has more justice than mercy in it. The book is, in fact, bitter, bitter. There is no reason in history why it should not be so, if wrong is to be repaid with hate, and yet it would be better if it was not so bitter. I am not saying that he is so inartistic as to play the advocate; whatever his minor foibles may be, he is an artist whom his stepbrother Americans may well be proud of; but while he recognizes pretty well all the facts in the case, he is too clearly of a judgment that is made up. One cannot blame him for that; what would one be one's self? If the tables could once be turned, and it could be that it was the black race which violently and lastingly triumphed in the bloody revolution at Wilmington, North Carolina, a few years ago, what would not we excuse to the white man who made the atrocity the argument of his fiction?

Mr. Chesnutt goes far back of the historic event in his novel, and shows us the sources of the cataclysm which swept away a legal government and perpetuated an insurrection, but he does not paint the blacks all good, or the whites all bad. He paints them as slavery made them on both sides, and if in the very end he gives the moral victory to the blacks—if he suffers the daughter of the black wife to have pity on her father's daughter by his white wife, and while her own child lies dead from a shot fired in the revolt, gives her husband's skill to save the life of her sister's child—it cannot be said that either his aesthetics or ethics are false. Those who would question either must allow, at least, that the Negroes have had the greater practice in forgiveness, and that there are many probabilities to favor his interpretation of the fact. No one who reads the book can deny that the case is presented with great power, or fail to recognize in the writer a portent of the sort of Negro equality against which no series of hangings and burnings will finally avail.

III
AFRICAN AMERICAN LITERATURE IN TRANSITION

During the early twentieth century African American literature was in transition from the essentially nineteenth century work of Dunbar and Chesnutt to what would become the Harlem Renaissance. Despite their successes, Dunbar and Chesnutt remained essentially nineteenth century in their outlook and style. Their audience expected to be entertained by dialect and by comedy; when they veered into more serious material, they lost their audience. Simply put, the literary marketplace was not ready for them. In the early twentieth century a number of new black writers emerged, less dependent on the stereotyped expectations of the white market, and therefore able to produce literature in a slightly freer environment. Their work was more realistic, in content and theme if not in style, and they did not have to retreat when they failed to achieve commercial or critical success. The shift in literary style and taste that followed the first World War provided greater opportunity for experiment with content and theme. This fit well with the increasing efforts of black writers to explore racial themes and the black experience.

The first two of these new black writers were W.E.B. Du Bois and James Weldon Johnson. Both were better know for activities other than literature. During the first decade of the twentieth century Du Bois, a professor at Atlanta University, had become known for his historical and sociological studies of race, and for his efforts to challenge the racial status quo in the United States. In 1905 he became one of the founding members and leaders of the Niagara Movement, which sought a more aggressive, more assertive leadership for African Americans. In 1909 and 1910 he participated in the organization of the National Association for the Advancement of Colored People, a biracial, white dominated civil rights organization. At the beginning of the second decade of the century, Du Bois left Atlanta and relocated to New York, where he served as an officer in the new NAACP and as editor of its monthly magazine, *The Crisis*. With the death of Booker T. Washington in 1915, Du Bois became the most prominent and visible black leader in the United States. Starting in the early twentieth century he wrote and occasionally publish poetry. In 1911 he published his first novel, *The Quest of the Silver Fleece*. The novel was brought out by A.C. McClurg and Company, the Chicago publisher that also published *The Souls of Black Folk*. Du Bois always saw literature as a secondary activity. Not that he did not take it seriously, but it was never his intention to make if his profession, and always, even in his literary writings, the political message was most important.

James Weldon Johnson like Du Bois spent most of his life earning his living through endeavors other than writing. In contrast to Du Bois he was more serious about his writing, and certainly considered art separate from politics and perhaps more elevated. For a brief period he did consider writing as a career. After achieving some success as a lawyer and educator in Florida, Johnson began to dabble in poetry, and especially song-writing. In 1902 he joined his brother Rosamond and Bob Cole in New York and began writing songs for their successful vaudeville act. Although this work brought economic success, Johnson quit, determined to produce more serious work. He studied literature at Columbia, became politically active with the Booker T. Washington faction in New York, and continued writing poetry. In 1907 his political connections resulted in a consular post, first in Venezuela, then in Nicaragua. These positions gave his free time for his writing; he published several poems and in 1912 completed his novel, *The Autobiography of an Ex-Colored Man*. Johnson returned to New York in 1913, and two years later became Field Secretary for the NAACP. Here he combined political and civil rights work with his interest in literature. He would continue to write poetry, but spent more and more of his energy promoting black literature. In 1921 he published his anthology, *The Book of American Negro Poetry*, which outlined his views of the importance of African American literature.

In the post-war period two younger black writers emerged who anticipated the explosion in literary energy that would occur a few years later. Jamaican Claude McKay had already published two volumes of dialect poetry before he came to the United States in 1912 to study agriculture. Instead he discovered socialism and Du Bois's *The Souls of Black Folk*. By 1915 he was in Harlem determined to become a writer. His political connections led him to the radicals—Garvey, for a time, then the socialists and Communists in Harlem, and then downtown to the radicals of Greenwich Village. His literary contacts were also downtown, although his writing more and more focused on race and on Harlem. In 1920, while in England, he published his third volume of poetry, *Spring in New Hampshire*, and followed that in 1922 with his first volume of Harlem poetry, *Harlem Shadows*. In 1922, before the Renaissance was fully underway, he left the United States for the Soviet Union, then France and North Africa. On the basis of his poetry, and later his novels, McKay became an important though absent player in the Renaissance.

Jean Toomer, perhaps the most gifted of the young writers at the eve of the Renaissance, grew up in Washington, D.C. in the home of his aristocratic grandfather, P.B.S. Pinchback, former lieutenant governor of Reconstruction Louisiana, and prominent black Republican politician. By the time Toomer was born, the Pinchback fortunes, both political and financial, were in decline. Nevertheless, he enjoyed a financially comfortable childhood. He completed high school, and then drifted through several colleges, with no clear career goals in mind. In 1920 the twenty-six-year-old Toomer returned to his grandparents's household, determined to become a writer. He spent a little over two years at this, including about four months in rural Georgia at a temporary teaching job. This brief venture into the South impressed him immensely, and he became determined to give voice to the black experience. Ironically his literary connections were largely among whites, especially Waldo Frank, who became his mentor and friend. Though his exposure to the black South was limited, Toomer drew heavily on the region, both in his poems and his highly acclaimed novel 1923 *Cane*. In spite of the critical success of this novel, Toomer did not pursue a literary career, and more importantly, backed away from his racial identity. He spent most of the rest of his life on a spiritual quest, engaged first with the French mystic Georges Gurdjieff, then with Quakerism. Nevertheless, on the strength of his one major work, Toomer is still celebrated as a major talent of the Harlem Renaissance.

These four writers brought African American literature to the beginnings of the Harlem Renaissance. Except for Toomer, all would be important participants in the movement.

W.E.B. Du Bois
Poems

Although known primarily for his historical, sociological, political and other non-fiction writings, Du Bois also wrote and published poetry and fiction. The two poems presented here illustrate both his strengths in poetry, and the relationship between his art and his racial politics. "A Litany at Atlanta" is a prose poem, modern in style, in which Du Bois responded to the 1906 Atlanta race riot. The riot occurred while he was out of the city. He wrote the poem during his long train ride back to Atlanta, still uncertain of the fate of his wife and child. The experience hardened his attitude against the South. "The Song of the Smoke" was considered by many to be a precursor to the poetry of the Harlem Renaissance, some twenty years later, both in its freer style and in its strong message of racial pride. Both poems illustrated Du Bois's religious doubts.

"A Litany Of Atlanta"
Done at Atlanta, in the Day of Death, 1906.

O Silent God, Thou whose voice afar in mist and mystery hath left our ears anhungered in these fearful days—
Hear us, good Lord!

Listen to us, Thy children: our faces dark with doubt, are made a mockery in Thy sanctuary. With uplifted hands we front Thy heaven, O God, crying:
We beseech Thee to hear us, good Lord!

We are not better than our fellows, Lord, we are but weak and human men. When our devils do deviltry, curse Thou the doer and the deed: curse them as we curse them, do to them all and more than ever they have done to innocence and weakness, to womanhood and home.
Have mercy upon us, miserable sinners!

And yet whose is the deeper guilt? Who made these devils? Who nursed them in crime and fed them on injustice? Who ravished and debauched their mothers and their grandmothers? Who bought and sold their crime, and waxed fat and rich on public iniquity?
Thou knowest, good God!

Is this Thy justice, O Father, that guile be easier than innocence, and the innocent crucified for the guilt of the untouched guilty?

Justice, O judge of men!

Wherefore do we pray? Is not the God of the fathers dead? Have not seers seen in Heaven's halls Thine hearsed and lifeless form stark amidst the black and rolling smoke of sin, where all along bow bitter forms of endless dead?

Awake, Thou that sleepest!

Thou art not dead, but flown afar, up hills of endless light, through blazing corridors of suns, where worlds do swing of good and gentle men, of women strong and free—far from the cozenage, black hypocrisy and chaste prostitution of this shameful speck of dust!

Turn again, O Lord, leave us not to perish in our sin!

From lust of body and lust of blood,
Great God, deliver us!

From lust of power and lust of gold,
Great God, deliver us!

From the leagued lying of despot and of brute,
Great God, deliver us!

A city lay in travail, God our Lord, and from her loins sprang twin Murder and Black Hate. Red was the midnight; clang, crack and cry of death and fury filled the air and trembled underneath the stars when church spires pointed silently to Thee. And all this was to sate the greed of greedy men who hide behind the veil of vengeance!

Bend us Thine ear, O Lord!

In the pale, still morning we looked upon the deed. We stopped our ears and held our leaping hands, but they—did they not wag their heads and leer and cry with bloody jaws: *Cease from Crime!* The word was mockery, for thus they train a hundred crimes while we do cure one.

Turn again our captivity, O Lord!

Behold this maimed and broken thing; dear God, it was an humble black man who toiled and sweat to save a bit from the pittance paid him. They told him: *Work and Rise.* He worked. Did this man sin? Nay, but some one told how some one said another did—one whom he had never seen nor known. Yet for that man's crime this man lieth maimed and murdered, his wife naked to shame, his children, to poverty and evil.

Hear us, O Heavenly Father!

Doth not this justice of hell stink in Thy nostrils, O God? How long shall the mounting flood of innocent blood roar in Thine ears and pound in our hearts for vengeance? Pile the pale frenzy of blood-crazed brutes who do such deeds high on Thine altar, Jehovah Jireh, and burn it in hell forever and forever!

Forgive us, good Lord; we know not what we say!

Bewildered we are, and passion-tost, mad with the madness of a mobbed and mocked and murdered people; straining at the armposts of Thy Throne, we raise our shackled hands and charge Thee, God, by the bones of our stolen fathers, by the tears of our dead mothers, by the very blood of Thy crucified Christ: *What meaneth this?* Tell us the Plan; give us the Sign!

Keep not Thou silence, O God!

Sit no longer blind, Lord God, deaf to our prayer and dumb to our dumb suffering. Surely Thou too art not white, O Lord, a pale, bloodless, heartless thing?

Ah! Christ of all the Pities!

Forgive the thought! Forgive these wild, blasphemous words. Thou art still the God of our black fathers, and in Thy soul's soul sit some soft darkenings of the evening, some shadowings of the velvet night.

But whisper—speak—call, great God, for Thy silence is white terror to our hearts! The way, O God, show us the way and point us the path.

Whither? North is greed and South is blood; within, the coward, and without, the liar. Whither? To death?

Amen! Welcome dark sleep!

Whither? To life? But not this life, dear God, not this. Let the cup pass from us, tempt us not beyond our strength, for there is that clamoring and clawing within, to whose voice we would not listen, yet shudder lest we must, and it is red, Ah! God! It is a red and awful shape.

Selah!

In yonder East trembles a star.

Vengeance is mine; I will repay, saith the Lord!

Thy will, O Lord, be done!

Kyrie Eleison!

Lord, we have done these pleading, wavering words.

We beseech Thee to hear us, good Lord!

We bow our heads and hearken soft to the sobbing of women and little children.

We beseech Thee to hear us, good Lord!

Our voices sink in silence and in night.

Hear us, good Lord!

In night, O God of a godless land!

Amen!

In silence, O Silent God.

Selah!

"The Song of the Smoke"
1907

I am the Smoke King,
I am black!
I am swinging in the sky,
I am wringing worlds awry;
   I am the thought of the throbbing mills;
   I am the soul of the soul-toil kills,
   Wraith of the ripple of trading rills;
Up I'm curling from the sod;
I am whirling home to God.
   I am the Smoke King
   I am black.

I am the Smoke King,
I am black!
I am wreathing broken hearts,
I am sheathing love's light darts;
   Inspiration of iron times
   Wedding the toil of toiling climes,
   Shedding the blood of bloodless crimes—
Lurid lowering 'mid the blue,
Torrid towering toward the true,
   I am the Smoke King,
   I am black.

I am the Smoke King,
I am black!
I am darkening with song,
I am hearkening to wrong!
   I will be black as blackness can—
   The blacker the mantle, the mightier the man!
   For blackness was ancient ere whiteness began.
I am daubing God in night,
I am swabbing Hell in white:
   I am the Smoke King
   I am black.

I am the Smoke King,
I am black!
I am cursing ruddy morn,
I am hearsing hearts unborn:
   Souls unto me are as stars in a night,
   I whiten my black men—I blacken my white!
   What's the hue of a hide to a man in his might!
Hail! Great, gritty, grimy hands—
Sweet Christ, pity toiling lands!
   I am the Smoke King
   I am black.

W.E.B DU BOIS
The Quest of the Silver Fleece: A Novel
1911

Du Bois published his first novel after writing it, off and on, for five years. The novel was ambitious, complex, and convoluted. It examined cotton, and the financing of the cotton industry; race, from the perspective of both whites and blacks; and gender, especially the role of women in the post-Victorian era. The chapter presented here introduces the two major African American characters, Zora and Bles.

Chapter V
"Zora"

Zora, child of the swamp, was a heathen hoyden of twelve wayward, untrained years. Slight, straight, strong, full-blooded, she had dreamed her life away in willful wandering through her dark and sombre kingdom until she was one with it in all its moods; mischievous, secretive, brooding; full of great and awful visions, steeped body and soul in wood-lore. Her home was out of doors, the cabin of Elspeth her port of call for talking and eating. She had not known, she had scarcely seen, a child of her own age until Bles Alwyn had fled from her dancing in the night, and she had searched and found him sleeping in the misty morning light. It was to her a strange new thing to see a fellow of like years with herself, and she gripped him to her soul in wild interest and new curiosity. Yet this childish friendship was so new and incomprehensible a thing to her that she did not know how to express it. At first she pounced upon him in mirthful, almost impish glee, teasing and mocking and half scaring him, despite his fifteen years of young manhood.

"Yes, they is devils down yonder behind the swamp," she would whisper, warningly, when, after the first meeting, he had crept back again and again, half fascinated, half amused to greet her; "I'se seen 'em, I'se heard 'em, 'cause my mammy is a witch."

The boy would sit and watch her wonderingly as she lay curled along the low branch of the mighty oak, clinging with little curved limbs and flying fingers. Possessed by the spirit of her vision, she would chant, low-voiced, tremulous, mischievous:

"One night a devil come to me on blue fire out of a big red flower that grows in the south swamp; he was tall and big and strong as anything, and when he spoke the trees shook and the stars fell. Even mammy was afeared; and it takes a lot to make mammy afeared, 'cause she's a witch and can conjure. He said, 'I'll come when you die—I'll come when you die, and take the conjure off you,' and then he went away on a big fire."

"Shucks!" the boy would say, trying to express scornful disbelief when, in truth, he was awed and doubtful. Always he would glance involuntarily back along the path behind him. Then her low birdlike laughter would rise and ring through the trees.

So passed a year, and there came the time when her wayward teasing and the almost painful thrill of her tale-telling nettled him and drove him away. For long months he did not meet her, until one day he saw her deep eyes fixed longingly upon him from a thicket in the swamp. He went and greeted her. But she said no word, sitting nested among the greenwood with passionate, proud silence, until he had sued long for peace; then in sudden new friendship she had taken his hand and led him through the swamp, showing him all the beauty of her swamp-world— great shadowy oaks and limpid pools, lone, naked trees and sweet flowers; the whispering and flitting of wild things, and the winging of furtive birds. She had dropped the impish mischief of her way, and up from beneath it rose a wistful, visionary tenderness; a mighty half-confessed, half-concealed, striving for unknown things. He seemed to have found a new friend.

And to-day, after he had taken Miss Taylor home and supped, he came out in the twilight under the new moon and whistled the tremulous note that always brought her.

"Why did you speak so to Miss Taylor?" he asked, reproachfully. She considered the matter a moment.

"You don't understand," she said. "You can't never understand. I can see right through people. You can't. You never had a witch for a mammy—did you?"

"No."

"Well, then, you see I have to take care of you and see things for you."

"Zora," he said thoughtfully, "you must learn to read."

"What for?"

"So that you can read books and know lots of things."

"Don't white folks make books?"

"Yes—most of the books."

"Pooh! I knows more than they do now—a heap more."

"In some ways you do; but they know things that give them power and wealth and make them rule."

"No, no. They don't really rule; they just thinks they rule. They just got things,—heavy, dead things. We black folks is got the *spirit*. We'se lighter and cunninger; we fly right through them; we go and come again just as we wants to. Black folks is wonderful."

He did not understand what she meant; but he knew what he wanted and he tried again.

"Even if white folks don't know everything they know different things from us, and we ought to know what they know."

This appealed to her somewhat.

"I don't believe they know much," she concluded; "but I'll learn to read and just see."

"It will be hard work," he warned. But he had come prepared for acquiescence. He took a primer from his pocket and, lighting a match, showed her the alphabet.

"Learn those," he said.

"What for?" she asked, looking at the letters disdainfully.

"Because that's the way," he said, as the light flared and went out.

"I don't believe it," she disputed, disappearing in the wood and returning with a pine-knot. They lighted it and its smoky flame threw wavering shadows about. She turned the leaves till she came to a picture which she studied intently.

"Is this about this?" she asked, pointing alternately to reading and picture.

"Yes. And if you learn—"

"Read it," she commanded. He read the page.

"Again," she said, making him point out each word. Then she read it after him, accurately, with more perfect expression. He stared at her. She took the book, and with a nod was gone.

It was Saturday and dark. She never asked Bles to her home—to that mysterious black cabin in mid-swamp. He thought her ashamed of it, and delicately refrained from going. So to-night she slipped away, stopped and listened till she heard his footsteps on the pike, and then flew homeward. Presently the old black cabin loomed before her with its wide flapping door. The old woman was bending over the fire, stirring some savory mess, and a yellow girl with a white baby on one arm was placing dishes on a rickety wooden table when Zora suddenly and noiselessly entered the door.

"Come, is you? I 'lowed victuals would fetch you," grumbled the hag.

But Zora deigned no answer. She walked placidly to the table, where she took up a handful of cold corn-bread and meat, and then went over and curled up by the fire.

Elspeth and the girl talked and laughed coarsely, and the night wore on.

By and by loud laughter and tramping came from the road—a sound of numerous footsteps. Zora listened, leapt to her feet and started to the door. The old crone threw an epithet after her; but she flashed through the lighted doorway and was gone, followed by the oath and shouts from the approaching men. In the hut night fled with wild song and revel, and day dawned again. Out from some fastness of the wood crept Zora. She stopped and bathed in a pool and combed her close-clung hair, then entered silently to breakfast.

Thus began in the dark swamp that primal battle with the Word. She hated it and despised it, but her pride was in arms and her one great life friendship in the balance. She fought her way with a dogged persistence that brought word after word of praise and interest from Bles. Then, once well begun, her busy, eager mind flew with a rapidity that startled; the stories especially she devoured—tales of strange things and countries and men gripped her imagination and clung to her memory.

"Did n't I tell you there was lots to learn?" he asked once.

"I knew it all," she retorted; "every bit. I'se thought it all before; only the little things is different—and I like the little, strange things."

Spring ripened to summer. She was reading well and writing some.

"Zora," he announced one morning under their forest oak, "you must go to school."

She eyed him, surprised.

"Why?"

"You've found some things worth knowing in this world, have n't you, Zora?"

"Yes," she admitted.

"But there are more—many, many more—worlds on worlds of things—you have not dreamed of."

She stared at him, open-eyed, and a wonder crept upon her face battling with the old assurance. Then she looked down at her bare brown feet and torn gown.

"I've got a little money, Zora," he said quickly. But she lifted her head.

"I'll earn mine," she said.

"How?" he asked doubtfully.

"I'll pick cotton."

"Can you?"

"Course I can."

"It's hard work."

She hesitated.

"I don't like to work," she mused. "You see, mammy's pappy was a king's son, and kings don't work. I don't work; mostly I dreams. But I can work, and I will—for the wonder things—and for you."

So the summer yellowed and silvered into fall. All the vacation days Bles worked on the farm, and Zora read and dreamed and studied in the wood, until the land lay white with harvest. Then, without warning, she appeared in the cotton-field beside Bles, and picked.

It was hot, sore work. The sun blazed; her bent and untrained back pained, and the soft little hands bled. But no complaint passed her lips; her hands never wavered, and her eyes met his steadily and gravely. She bade him good-night, cheerily, and then stole away to the wood, crouching beneath the great oak, and biting back the groans that trembled on her lips. Often, she fell supper-less to sleep, with two great tears creeping down her tired cheeks.

When school-time came there was not yet money enough, for cotton-picking was not far advanced. Yet Zora would take no money from Bles, and worked earnestly away.

Meantime there occurred to the boy the momentous question of clothes. Had Zora thought of them? He feared not. She knew little of clothes and cared less. So one day in town he dropped into Caldwell's "Emporium" and glanced hesitantly at certain ready-made dresses. One caught his eye. It came from the great Easterly mills in New England and was red—a vivid red. The glowing warmth of this cloth of cotton caught the eye of Bles, and he bought the gown for a dollar and a half.

He carried it to Zora in the wood, and unrolled it before her eyes that danced with glad tears. Of course, it was long and wide; but he fetched needle and thread and scissors, too. It was a full month after school had begun when they, together back in the swamp, shadowed by the foliage, began to fashion the wonderful garment. At the same time she laid ten dollars of her first hard-earned money in his hands.

"You can finish the first year with this money," Bles assured her, delighted, "and then next year you must come in to board; because, you see, when you're educated you won't want to live in the swamp."

"I wants to live here always."

"But not at Elspeth's."

"No-o—not there, not there." And a troubled questioning trembled in her eyes, but brought no answering thought in his, for he was busy with his plans.

"Then, you see, Zora, if you stay here you'll need a new house, and you'll want to learn how to make it beautiful."

"Yes, a beautiful, great castle here in the swamp," she dreamed; "but," and her face fell, "I can't get money enough to board in; and I don't want to board in—I wants to be free."

He looked at her, curled down so earnestly at her puzzling task, and a pity for the more than motherless child swept over him. He bent over her, nervously, eagerly, and she laid down her sewing and sat silent and passive with dark, burning eyes.

"Zora," he said, "I want you to do all this—for me."

"I will, if you wants me to," she said quietly, but with something in her voice that made him look half startled into her beautiful eyes and feel a queer flushing in his face. He stretched his hand out and taking hers held it lightly till she quivered and drew away, bending again over her sewing.

Then a nameless exaltation rose within his heart. "Zora," he whispered, "I've got a plan."

"What is it?" she asked, still with bowed head. "Listen, till I tell you of the Golden Fleece."

Then she too heard the story of Jason. Breathless she listened, dropping her sewing and leaning forward, eager-eyed. Then her face clouded.

"Do you s'pose mammy's the witch?" she asked dubiously.

"No; she wouldn't give her own flesh and blood to help the thieving Jason."

She looked at him searchingly.

"Yes, she would, too," affirmed the girl, and then she paused, still intently watching him. She was troubled, and again a question eagerly hovered on her lips. But he continued:

"Then we must escape her," he said gayly. "See! yonder lies the Silver Fleece spread across the brown back of the world; let's get a bit of it, and hide it here in the swamp, and comb it, and tend it, and make it the beautifullest bit of all. Then we can sell it, and send you to school."

She sat silently bent forward, turning the picture in her mind. Suddenly forgetting her trouble, she bubbled with laughter, and leaping up clapped her hands.

"And I knows just the place!" she cried eagerly, looking at him with a flash of the old teasing mischief—"down in the heart of the swamp—where dreams and devils lives."

Up at the school-house Miss Taylor was musing. She had been invited to spend the summer with Mrs. Grey at Lake George, and such a summer!—silken clothes and dainty food, motoring and golf, well-groomed men and elegant women. She would not have put it in just that way, but the vision came very close to spelling heaven to her mind. Not that she would come to it vacant-minded, but rather as a trained woman, starved for companionship and wanting something of the beauty and ease of life. She sat dreaming of it here with rows of dark faces before her, and the singsong wail of a little black reader with his head aslant and his patched kneepants.

The day was warm and languorous, and the last pale mist of the Silver Fleece peeped in at the windows. She tried to follow the third-reader lesson with her finger, but persistently off she went, dreaming, to some exquisite little parlor with its green and gold, the clink of dainty china and hum of low voices, and the blue lake in the window; she would glance up, the door would open softly and—

Just here she did glance up, and all the school glanced with her. The drone of the reader hushed. The door opened softly, and upon the threshold stood Zora. Her small feet and slender ankles were black and bare; her dark, round, and broad-browed head and strangely beautiful face were poised almost defiantly, crowned with a misty mass of waveless hair, and lit by the velvet radiance of two wonderful eyes. And hanging from shoulder to ankle, in formless, clinging folds, blazed the scarlet gown.

JAMES WELDON JOHNSON:
Poems

The two poems presented here are among the best known from Johnson's writing before the Harlem Renaissance. The first, "Lift Ev'ry Voice and Sing," he wrote in 1900 for a school celebration of Lincoln's birthday. His brother, Rosamond, set it to music, and the song soon won widespread fame as the "Negro National Anthem." Today it is still sung on formal occasions or celebrations in the African American community. Johnson wrote the second poem, "Fifty Years," to celebrate the fiftieth anniversary of emancipation. Both poems share a positive assessment of African American progress and advancement; both also acknowledge the difficulty and suffering that African Americans had to endure.

"Lift Ev'ry Voice and Sing"
1900

Lift ev'ry voice and sing,
Till earth and heaven ring,
Ring with the harmonies of Liberty;
Let our rejoicing rise
High as the list'ning skies,
Let it resound loud as the rolling sea.
Sing a song full of the faith that the dark past has taught us,
Sing a song full of the hope that the present has brought us;
Facing the rising sun of our new day begun,
Let us march on till victory is won.

Stony the road we trod,
Bitter the chast'ning rod,
Felt in the days when hope unborn had died;
Yet with a steady beat,
Have not our weary feet
Come to the place for which our fathers sighed?
We have come over a way that with tears has been watered,
We have come, treading our path through the blood of the slaughtered,
Out from the gloomy past,
Till now we stand at last
Where the white gleam of our bright star is cast.

God of our weary years,
God of our silent tears,
Thou who hast brought us thus far on the way;
Thou who hast by Thy might,
Led us into the light,

Keep us forever in the path, we pray.
Lest our feet stray from the places, our God, where we met Thee,
Lest our hearts, drunk with the wine of the world, we forget Thee;
Shadowed beneath Thy hand;
May we forever stand,
True to our God,
True to our native land.

"Fifty Years"
1913

Today Is the Fiftieth Anniversary of Lincoln's Emancipation Proclamation

O brothers mine, to-day we stand
Where half a century sweeps our ken,
Since God, through Lincoln's ready hand
Struck off our bonds and made us men.

Just fifty years—a Winter's day—
As runs the history of a race;
Yet, as we look back o'er the way,
How distant seems our starting-place!

Look farther back! Three centuries!
To where a naked, shivering score;
Snatched from their haunts across the seas;
Stood, wild-eyed, on Virginia's shore.

Far, far the way that we have trod,
From heathen kraals and jungle dens,
To freedmen, freemen, sons of God,
Americans and Citizens.

A part of His unknown design,
We've lived within a mighty age;
And we have helped to write a line
On history's most wondrous page.

A few black bondmen strewn along
The borders of our eastern coast.
Now grown a race, ten million strong,
An upward, onward, marching host.

Then let us here erect a stone,
To mark the place, to mark the time;
A witness to God's mercies shown,
A pledge to hold this day sublime.

And let that stone an altar be
Whereon thanksgivings we may lay—
Where we, in deep humility,
For faith and strength renewed may pray,

With open hearts ask from above
New zeal, new courage and new pow'rs,
That we may grow more worthy of
This country and this land of ours.

For never let the thought arise
That we are here on sufferance bare;
Outcasts, asylumed 'neath these skies,
And aliens without part or share.

This land is ours by right of birth,
This land is ours by right of toil;
We helped to turn its virgin earth,
Our sweat is in its fruitful soil.

Where once the tangled forest stood,
Where flourished once rank weed and thorn;
Behold the path-traced, peaceful wood,
The cotton white, the yellow corn.

To gain these fruits that have been earned,
To hold these fields that have been won,
Our arms have strained, our backs have burned;
Bent bare beneath a ruthless sun.

That Banner, which is now the type
Of victory on field and flood—
Remember, its first crimson stripe
Was dyed by Attucks' willing blood.

And never yet has come the cry—
When that fair flag has been assailed
For men to do, for men to die,
That have we faltered or have failed.

We've helped to bear it, rent and torn,
Through many a hot-breath'd battle breeze;
Held in our hands, it has been borne
And planted far across the seas.

And, never yet, O haughty Land
Let us, at least, for this be praised—

Has one black, treason-guided hand
Ever against that flag been raised.

Then should we speak but servile words,
Or shall we hang our heads in shame?
Stand back of new-come foreign hordes,
And fear our heritage to claim?

No! Stand erect and without fear,
And for our foes let this suffice—
We've bought a rightful sonship here,
And we have more than paid the price.

And yet, my brothers, well I know
The tethered feet, the pinioned wings,
The spirit bowed beneath the blow,
The heart grown faint from wounds and stings;

The staggering force of brutish might,
That strikes and leaves us stunned and dazed;
The long, vain waiting through the night
To hear some voice for justice raised.

Full well I know the hour when hope
Sinks dead, and 'round us everywhere
Hangs stifling darkness, and we grope
With hands uplifted in despair.

Courage! Look out, beyond, and see
The far horizon's beckoning span!
Faith in your God-known destiny!
We are a part of some great plan.

Because the tongues of Garrison
And Phillips now are cold in death,
Think you their work can be undone?
Or quenched the fires lit by their breath?

Think you that John Brown's spirit stops?
That Lovejoy was but idly slain?
Or do you think those precious drops
From Lincoln's heart were shed in vain?

That for which millions prayed and sighed,
That for which tens o thousands fought,
For which so many freely died,
God cannot let it come to naught.

JAMES WELDON JOHNSON:
The Autobiography of an Ex-Colored Man
1912

During his lengthy and varied literary career James Weldon Johnson wrote only one novel. At the time that he wrote and published the work, he was serving in the United States Foreign Service. For this reason, and perhaps for others, the book was published anonymously, and generated considerable speculation about the identity of the author. The novel anticipated the work of the Harlem Renaissance by its direct discussion of race, especially the social and psychological aspects of racial identity, and by its descriptions of black life. Most reviewers responded to it favorably, but many took it at face value and treated it as an autobiography rather than fiction. Despite the reviews and the gossip about its unknown author, the book sold very poorly until it was reissued during the Harlem Renaissance. The selection presented here is from Chapter 1, which introduces the main character, indicates the situation of his birth and childhood, and describes his realization of his racial identity. This sudden awareness of racial difference is a common element in African American literature.

Anonymous [James Weldon Johnson]
The Autobiography of an Ex-Colored Man

Chapter I

I know that in writing the following pages I am divulging the great secret of my life, the secret which for some years I have guarded far more carefully than any of my earthly possessions; and it is a curious study to me to analyze the motives which prompt me to do it. I feel that I am led by the same impulse which forces the un-found-out criminal to take somebody into his confidence, although he knows that the act is likely, even almost certain, to lead to his undoing. I know that I am playing with fire, and I feel the thrill which accompanies that most fascinating pastime; and, back of it all, I think I find a sort of savage and diabolical desire to gather up all the little tragedies of my life, and turn them into a practical joke on society.

And, too, I suffer a vague feeling of unsatisfaction, of regret, of almost remorse, from which I am seeking relief, and of which I shall speak in the last paragraph of this account.

I was born in a little town of Georgia a few years after the close of the Civil War. I shall not mention the name of the town; because there are people still living there who could be connected with this narrative. I have only a faint recollection of the place of my birth. . . .

I have a dim recollection of several people who moved in and about . . . [our] little house, but I have a distinct mental image of only two: one, my mother; and the other, a tall man with a small, dark mustache. I remember that his shoes or boots were always shiny, and that he wore a gold chain and a great gold watch with which he was always willing to let me play. My admiration was almost equally divided between the watch and chain and the shoes. He used to come to the house evenings, perhaps two or three times a week; and it became my appointed duty whenever he came to bring him a pair of slippers and to put the shiny shoes in a particular corner; he often gave me in return for this service a bright coin, which my mother taught me to promptly drop in a little tin bank. I remember distinctly the last time this tall man came to the little house in Georgia; that evening before I went to bed he took me up in his arms and squeezed me very tightly; my mother stood behind his chair wiping tears from her eyes. I remember how I sat upon his knee and watched him laboriously drill a hole through a ten-dollar gold piece, and then tie the coin around my neck with a string. I have worn that gold piece around my neck the greater part of my life, and still possess it, but more than once I have wished that some other way had been found of attaching it to me besides putting a hole through it.

On the day after the coin was put around my neck my mother and I started on what seemed to me an endless journey. I knelt on the seat and watched through the train window the corn- and cotton-fields pass swiftly by until I fell asleep. When I fully awoke, we were being driven through the streets of a large city—Savannah. I sat up and blinked at the bright lights. At Savannah we boarded a steamer which finally landed us in New York. From New York we went to a town in Connecticut, which became the home of my boyhood.

My mother and I lived together in a little cottage which seemed to me to be fitted up almost luxuriously; there were horse-hair covered chairs in the parlor, and a little square piano; there was a stairway with red carpet on it leading to a half second story; there were pictures on the walls, and a few books in a glass-doored case. My mother dressed me very neatly, and I developed that pride which well-dressed boys generally have. She was careful about my associates, and I myself was quite particular. As I look back now I can see that I was a perfect little aristocrat. My mother rarely went to anyone's house, but she did sewing, and there were a great many ladies coming to our cottage. If I was round they would generally call me, and ask me my name and age and tell my mother what a pretty boy I was. Some of them would pat me on the head and kiss me.

My mother was kept very busy with her sewing; sometimes she would have another woman helping her. I think she must have derived a fair income from her work. I know, too, that at least once each month she received a letter; I used to watch for the postman, get the letter, and run to her with it; whether she was busy or not, she would take it and instantly thrust it into her bosom. I never saw her read one of these letters. I knew later that they contained money and what was to her more than money. As busy as she generally was, she found time, however, to teach me my letters and figures and how to spell a number of easy words. Always on Sunday evenings she opened the little square piano and picked out hymns. . . .

At a very early age I began to thump on the piano alone, and it was not long before I was able to nick out a few tunes. When I was seven years old, I could play by ear all of the hymns and songs that my mother knew. I had also learned the names of the notes in both clefs, but I preferred not to be hampered by notes. About this time several ladies for whom my mother sewed heard me play and they persuaded her that I should at once be put under a teacher; so arrangements were made for me to study the piano with a lady who was a fairly good musician; at the same time arrangements were made for me to study my books with this lady's daughter. . . .

And so for a couple of years my life was divided between my music and my school-books. Music took up the greater part of my time. I had no playmates, but amused myself with games—some of them my own invention—which could be played alone. I knew a few boys whom I had met at the church which I attended with my mother, but I had formed no close friendships with any of them. Then, when I was nine years old, my mother decided to enter me in the public school, so all at once I found myself thrown among a crowd of boys of all sizes and kinds; some of them seemed to me like savages. I shall never forget the bewilderment, the pain, the heart-sickness, of that first day at school. I seemed to be the only stranger in the place; every other boy seemed to know every other boy. I was fortunate enough, however, to be assigned to a teacher who knew me; my mother made her dresses. She was one of the ladies who used to pat me on the head and kiss me. She had the tact to address a few words directly to me; this gave me a certain sort of standing in the class and put me somewhat at ease.

Within a few days I had made one staunch friend and was on fairly good terms with most of the boys. I was shy of the girls, and remained so; even now a word or look from a pretty woman sets me all a-tremble. This friend I bound to me with hooks of steel in a very simple way. He was a big awkward boy with a face full of freckles and a head full of very red hair. . . . I felt that "Red Head"— as I involuntarily called him—and I were to be friends. I do not doubt that this feeling was strengthened by the fact that I had been quick enough to see that a big, strong boy was a friend to be desired at a public school; and, perhaps, in spite of his dullness, "Red Head" had been able to discern that I could be of service to him. At any rate there was a simultaneous mutual attraction. . . .

There were some black and brown boys in the school, and several of them were in my class. One of the boys strongly attracted my attention from the first day I saw him. His face was as black as night, but shone as though it were polished; he had sparkling eyes, and when he opened his mouth, he displayed glistening white teeth. It struck me at once as appropriate to call him "Shiny Face," or "Shiny Eyes," or "Shiny Teeth," and I spoke of him often by one of these names to the other boys. These terms were finally merged into "Shiny," and to that name he answered good-naturedly during the balance of his public school days.

"Shiny" was considered without question to be the best speller, the best reader, the best penman—in a word, the best scholar, in the class. . . . Yet it did not take me long to discover that, in spite of his standing as a scholar, he was in some way looked down upon.

The other black boys and girls were still more looked down upon. Some of the boys often spoke of them as "niggers." Sometimes on the way home from school a crowd would walk behind them repeating:

> "Nigger, nigger, never die,
> Black face and shiny eye."

On one such afternoon one of the black boys turned suddenly on his tormentors and hurled a slate; it struck one of the white boys in the mouth, cutting a slight gash in his lip. At sight of the blood the boy who had thrown the slate ran, and his companions quickly followed. We ran after them pelting them with stones until they separated in several directions. I was very much wrought up over the affair, and went home and told my mother how one of the "niggers" had struck a boy with a slate. I shall never forget how she turned on me. "Don't you ever use that word again," she said, "and don't you ever bother the colored children at school. You ought to be ashamed of yourself." I did hang my head in shame, not because she had convinced me that I had done wrong, but because I was hurt by the first sharp word she had ever given me.

My school-days ran along very pleasantly. I stood well in my studies, not always so well with regard to my behavior. I was never guilty of any serious misconduct, but my love of fun sometimes got me into trouble. I remember, however, that my sense of humor was so sly that most of the trouble usually fell on the head of the other fellow. My ability to play on the piano, at school exercises was looked upon as little short of marvelous in a boy of my age. I was not chummy with many of my mates, but, on the whole, was about as popular as it is good for a boy to be.

One day near the end of my second term at school the principal came into our room and, after talking to the teacher, for some reason said: "I wish all of the white scholars to stand for a moment." I rose with the others. The teacher looked at me and, calling my name, said: "You sit down for the present, and rise with the others." I did not quite understand her, and questioned: "Ma'm?" She repeated, with a softer tone in her voice: "You sit down now, and rise with the others." I sat down dazed. I saw and heard nothing. When the others were asked to rise, I did not know it. When school was dismissed, I went out in a kind of stupor. A few of the white boys jeered me, saying: "Oh, you're a nigger too." I heard some black children say: "We knew he was colored." "Shiny" said to them: "Come along, don't tease him," and thereby won my undying gratitude.

I hurried on as fast as I could, and had gone some distance before I perceived that "Red Head" was walking by my side. After a while he said to me: "Le' me carry your books." I gave him my strap without being able to answer. When we got to the gate, he said as he handed me my books: "Say, you know my big red agate? I can't shoot with it any more. I'm going to bring it to school for you tomorrow." I took my books and ran into the house. As I passed through the hallway, I saw that my mother was busy with one of her customers; I rushed up into my own little room, shut the door, and went quickly to where my looking-glass hung on the wall. For an instant I was afraid to look, but when I did, I looked long and earnestly. I had often heard people say to my mother: "What a pretty boy you have!" I was accustomed to hear remarks about my beauty; but now, for the first time, I became conscious of it and recognized it. I noticed the ivory whiteness of my skin, the beauty of my mouth, the size and liquid darkness of my eyes, and how the long, black lashes that fringed and shaded them produced an effect that was strangely fascinating even to me. I noticed the softness and glossiness of my dark hair that fell in waves over my temples, making my forehead appear whiter than it really was. How long I stood there gazing at my image I do not know. When I came out and reached the head of the stairs, I heard the lady who had been with my mother going out. I ran downstairs and rushed to where my mother was sitting, with a piece of work in her hands. I buried my head in her lap and blurted out: "Mother, mother, tell me, am I a nigger?" I could not see her face, but I knew the piece of work dropped to the floor and I felt her hands on my head. I looked up into her face and repeated: "Tell me, mother, am I a nigger?" There were tears in her eyes and I could see that she was suffering for me. And then it was that I looked at her critically for the first time. I had thought of her in a child-ish way only as the most beautiful woman in the world; now I looked at her search-ing for defects. I could see that her skin was almost brown, that her hair was not so soft as mine, and that she did differ in some way from the other ladies who came to the house; yet, even so, I could see that she was very beautiful, more beautiful than any of them. She must have felt that I was examining her, for she hid her face in my hair and said with difficulty: "No, my darling, you are not a nigger." She went on: "You are as good as anybody; if anyone calls you a nigger, don't notice them." But the more she talked, the less was I reassured, and I stopped her by asking: "Well, mother, am I white? Are you white?" She answered trem-blingly: "No, I am not white, but you—your father is one of the greatest men in the country—the best blood of the South is in you—" This suddenly opened up in my heart a fresh chasm of misgiving and fear, and I almost fiercely demanded: "Who is my father? Where is he?" She stroked my hair and said: "I'll tell you about him some day." I sobbed: "I want to know now." She answered: "No, not now."

Perhaps it had to be done, but I have never forgiven the woman who did it so cruelly. It may be that she never knew that she gave me a sword-thrust that day in school which was years in healing.

CLAUDE MCKAY
Poems

Claude McKay published his first two poems in the United States in 1917 in Waldo Frank's avant-garde literary magazine, *Seven Arts*. "The Harlem Dancer" was one of these. It revealed how McKay, in just two years, had absorbed enough Harlem street life to write sensitively about it; it also underscored that his per-spective was through the eyes of an outsider, a Jamaican, who saw brief images of home in the gritty streets of New York. The selections here reflect well McKay's poetry. He combined a radical militancy with a formalistic language and style, as in "If We Must Die," his powerful response to the 1919 race riots; he also demon-strated in "America" the complexities of the feelings of a black man and an im-migrant towards his adopted home, and in "Harlem Shadows" his application of a class-conscious interpretation of a prostitute.

"The Harlem Dancer"
1917

Applauding youths laughed with young prostitutes
And watched her perfect, half-clothed body sway;
Her voice was like the sound of blended flutes
Blown by black players upon a picnic day.
She sang and danced on gracefully and calm,
The light gauze hanging loose about her form;
To me she seemed a proudly-swaying palm
Grown lovelier for passing through a storm.
Upon her swarthy neck black shiny curls

Luxuriant fell; and tossing coins in praise,
The wine-flushed, bold-eyed boys, and even the girls,
Devoured her shape with eager, passionate gaze;
But looking at her falsely-smiling face,
I knew her self was not in that strange place.

"Harlem Shadows"
1918

I hear the halting footsteps of a lass
   In Negro Harlem when the night lets fall
Its veil. I see the shapes of girls who pass
   To bend and barter at desire's call.
Ah, little dark girls who in slippered feet
Go prowling through the night from street to street!

Through the long night until the silver break
   Of day the little gray feet know no rest;
Through the lone night until the last snow-flake
   Has dropped from heaven upon the earth's white breast,
The dusky, half-clad girls of tired feet
Are trudging, thinly shod, from street to street.

Ah, stem harsh world, that in the wretched way
   Of poverty, dishonor and disgrace,
Has pushed the timid little feet of clay,
   The sacred brown feet of my fallen race!
Ah, heart of me, the weary, weary feet
In Harlem wandering from street to street.

"If We Must Die"
1919

If we must die, let it not be like hogs
Hunted and penned in an inglorious spot,
While round us bark the mad and hungry dogs,
Making their mock at our accursed lot.
If we must die, O let us nobly die,
So that our precious blood may not be shed
In vain; then even the monsters we defy
Shall be constrained to honor us though dead!
O kinsmen! we must meet the common foe!
Though far outnumbered let us show us brave,
And for their thousand blows deal one deathblow!
What though before us lies the open grave?
Like men we'll face the murderous, cowardly pack,
Pressed to the wall, dying, but fighting back!

"Spring In New Hampshire"
(To J.L.J.F.E.)
1920

Too green the springing April grass,
    Too blue the silver-speckled sky,
For me to linger here, alas,
    While happy winds go laughing by,
Wasting the golden hours indoors,
Washing windows and scrubbing floors.

Too wonderful the April night,
    Too faintly sweet the first May flowers,
The stars too gloriously bright,
    For me to spend the evening hours,
When fields are fresh and streams are leaping
Wearied, exhausted, dully sleeping.

"The Tropics In New York"
1920

Bananas ripe and green, and ginger-root,
    Cocoa in pods and alligator pears,
And tangerines and mangoes and grape fruit,
    Fit for the highest prize at parish fairs,

Set in the window, bringing memories
    Of fruit-trees laden by low-singing rills,
And dewy dawns, and mystical blue skies
    In benediction over nun-like hills.

My eyes grew dim, and I could no more gaze;
    A wave of longing through my body swept,
And, hungry for the old, familiar ways,
    I turned aside and bowed my head and wept.

"America"
1921

Although she feeds me bread of bitterness,
And sinks into my throat her tiger's tooth,
Stealing my breath of life, I will confess
I love this cultured hell that tests my youth!
Her vigor flows like tides into my blood,
Giving me strength erect against her hate.
Her bigness sweeps my being like a flood.
Yet as a rebel fronts a king in state,
I stand within her walls with not a shred

Of terror, malice, not a word of jeer.
Darkly I gaze into the days ahead,
And see her might and granite wonders there,
Beneath the touch of Time's unerring hand,
Like priceless treasures sinking in the sand.

JEAN TOOMER
Cane
1923

The publication of *Cane* in 1923 hit the African American literary community like a lightening bolt. Nothing like this had been seen before. *Cane* was modern and it was experimental. It contained a series of prose pieces, some short sketches, others more like short stories; poems were placed between the prose selections. There was no plot in a traditional sense; rather the book flowed from the South to the North, raising the question: in which region was African American destiny to be found? Toomer also was an accomplished writer who used language sparsely, but brilliantly, with rich vivid descriptions. He addressed all the taboos of race simply and matter-of-factly. The book was enthusiastically acclaimed and helped stimulate other young black writers. But Toomer did not take part in the emerging Renaissance. *Cane* was his only work of any note. The selection presented here consists of the opening two sketches and the associated poems.

Jean Toomer
Cane

"Karintha"

Her skin is like dusk on the eastern horizon,
O cant you see it, O cant you see it,
Her skin is like dusk on the eastern horizon
. . . When the sun goes down.

Men had always wanted her, this Karintha, even as a child, Karintha carrying beauty, perfect as dusk when the sun goes down. Old men rode her hobby-horse upon their knees. Young men danced with her at frolics when they should have been dancing with their grownup girls. God grant us youth, secretly prayed the old men. The young fellows counted the time to pass before she would be old enough to mate with them. This interest of the male, who wishes to ripen a growing thing too soon, could mean no good to her.

Karintha, at twelve, was a wild flash that told the other folks just what it was to live. At sunset, when there was no wind, and the pinesmoke from over by the sawmill hugged the earth, and you couldnt see more than a few feet in front, her sudden darting past you was a bit of vivid color, like a black bird that flashes in light. With the other children one could hear, some distance off, their feet flopping in the two-inch dust. Karintha's running was a whir. It had the sound of the red dust that sometimes makes a spiral in the road. At dusk, during the hush just after the sawmill had closed down, and before any of the women had started their supper-getting-ready songs, her voice, highpitched, shrill, would put one's ears to itching. But no one ever thought to make her stop because of it. She stoned the cows, and beat her dog, and fought the other children. . . Even the preacher, who caught her at mischief, told himself that she was as innocently lovely as a November cotton flower. Already, rumors were out about her. Homes in Georgia are most often built on the two-room plan. In one, you cook and eat, in the other you sleep, and there love goes on. Karintha had seen or heard, perhaps she had felt her parents loving. One could but imitate one's parents, for to follow them was the way of God. She played "home" with a small boy who was not afraid to do her bidding. That started the whole thing. Old men could no longer ride her hobby-horse upon their knees. But young men counted faster.

> Her skin is like dusk,
> O cant you see it,
> Her skin is like dusk,
> When the sun goes down.

Karintha is a woman. She who carries beauty, perfect as dusk when the sun goes down. She has been married many times. Old men remind her that a few years back they rode her hobbyhorse upon their knees. Karintha smiles, and indulges them when she is in the mood for it. She has contempt for them. Karintha is a woman. Young men run stills to make her money. Young men go to the big cities and run on the road. Young men go away to college. They all want to bring her money. These are the young men who thought that all they had to do was to count time. But Karintha is a woman, and she has had a child. A child fell out of her womb onto a bed of pine-needles in the forest. Pine-needles are smooth and sweet. They are elastic to the feet of rabbits. . . A sawmill was nearby. Its pyramidal sawdust pile smouldered. It is a year before one completely burns. Meanwhile, the smoke curls up and hangs in odd wraiths about the trees, curls up, and spreads itself out over the valley. . . Weeks after Karintha returned home the smoke was so heavy you tasted it in water. Some one made a song:

> Smoke is on the hills. Rise up.
> Smoke is on the hills, O rise
> And take my soul to Jesus.

Karintha is a woman. Men do not know that the soul of her was a growing thing ripened too soon. They will bring their money; they will die not having found it out. . . Karintha at twenty, carrying beauty, perfect as dusk when the sun goes down. Karintha. . .

> Her skin is like dusk on the eastern horizon,
> O cant you see it, O cant you see it,
> Her skin is like dusk on the eastern horizon
> . . . When the sun goes down.

> Goes down. . .

"Reapers"

Black reapers with the sound of steel on stones
Are sharpening scythes. I see them place the hones
In their hip-pockets as a thing that's done,
And start their silent swinging, one by one.
Black horses drive a mower through the weeds,
And there, a field rat, startled, squealing bleeds,
His belly close to ground. I see the blade,
Blood-stained, continue cutting weeds and shade.

"November Cotton Flower"

Boll-weevil's coming, and the winter's cold,
Made cotton-stalks look rusty, seasons old,
And cotton, scarce as any southern snow,
Was vanishing; the branch, so pinched and slow,
Failed in its function as the autumn rake;
Drouth fighting soil had caused the soil to take
All water from the streams; dead birds were found
In wells a hundred feet below the ground
Such was the season when the flower bloomed.
Old folks were startled, and it soon assumed
Significance. Superstition saw
Something it had never seen before:
Brown eyes that loved without a trace of fear,
Beauty so sudden for that time of year.

"Becky"

Becky was the white woman who had two Negro sons. She's dead; they've gone away. The pines whisper to Jesus. The Bible flaps its leaves with an aimless rustle on her mound.

Becky had one Negro son. Who gave it to her? Damn buck nigger, said the white folks' mouths. She wouldnt tell. Common, God-forsaken, insane white shameless wench, said the white folks' mouths. Her eyes were sunken, her neck stringy, her breasts fallen, till then. Taking their words, they filled her, like a bubble rising—then she broke. Mouth setting in a twist that held her eyes, harsh, vacant, staring. . . Who gave it to her? Low-down nigger with no self-respect, said the black folks' mouths. She wouldnt tell. Poor Catholic poor-white crazy woman, said the black folks' mouths. White folks and black folks built her cabin, fed her and her growing baby, prayed secretly to God who'd put His cross upon her and cast her out.

When the first was born, the white folks said they'd have no more to do with her. And black folks, they too joined hands to cast her out. . . The pines whispered to Jesus. . The railroad boss said not to say he said it, but she could live, if she wanted to, on the narrow strip of land between the railroad and the road. John Stone, who owned the lumber and the bricks, would have shot the man who told he gave the stuff to Lonnie Deacon, who stole out there at night and built the cabin. A single room held down to earth. . . O fly away to Jesus . . . by a leaning chimney. . .

Six trains each day rumbled past and shook the ground under her cabin. Fords, and horseand mule-drawn buggies went back and forth along the road. No one ever saw her. Trainmen, and passengers who'd heard about her, threw out papers and food. Threw out little crumpled slips of paper scribbled with prayers, as they passed her eye-shaped piece of sandy ground. Ground islandized between the road and railroad track. Pushed up where a blue-sheen God with listless eyes could look at it. Folks from the town took turns, unknown, of course, to each other, in bringing corn and meat and sweet potatoes. Even sometimes snuff. . . O thank y Jesus. . . Old David Georgia, grinding cane and boiling syrup, never went her way without some sugar sap. No one ever saw her. The boy grew up and ran around. When he was five years old as folks reckoned it, Hugh Jourdon saw him carrying a baby. "Becky has another son," was what the whole town knew. But nothing was said, for the part of man that says things to the likes of that had told itself that if there was a Becky, that Becky now was dead.

The two boys grew. Sullen and cunning. . . O pines, whisper to Jesus; tell Him to come and press sweet Jesus-lips against their lips and eyes. . . It seemed as though with those two big fellows there, there could be no room for Becky. The part that prayed wondered if perhaps she'd really died, and they had buried her. No one dared ask. They'd beat and cut a man who meant nothing at all in mentioning that they lived along the road. White or colored? No one knew, and least of all themselves. They drifted around from job to job. We, who had cast out their mother because of them, could we take them in? They answered black and white folks by shooting up two men and leaving town. "Godam the white folks; godam the niggers," they shouted as they left town. Becky? Smoke curled up from her chimney; she must be there. Trains passing shook the ground. The ground shook the leaning chimney. Nobody noticed it. A creepy feeling came over all who saw that thin wraith of smoke and felt the trembling of the ground. Folks began to take her food again. They quit it soon because they had a fear. Becky if dead might be a hant, and if alive—it took some nerve even to mention it. . . O pines, whisper to Jesus. . .

It was Sunday. Our congregation had been visiting at Pulverton, and were coming home. There was no wind. The autumn sun, the bell from Ebenezer Church, listless and heavy. Even the pines were stale, sticky, like the smell of food that makes you sick. Before we turned the bend of the road that would show us the Becky cabin, the horses stopped stock-still, pushed back their ears, and nervously whinnied. We urged, then whipped them on. Quarter of a mile away thin smoke curled up from the leaning chimney. . . O pines, whisper to Jesus. . . Goose-flesh came on my skin though there still was neither chill nor wind. Eyes left their sockets for the cabin. Ears burned and throbbed. Uncanny eclipse! fear closed my mind. We were just about to pass. . . Pines shout to Jesus! . . the ground trembled as a ghost train rumbled by. The chimney fell into the cabin. Its thud was like a hollow report, ages having passed since it went off. Barlo and I were pulled out of our seats. Dragged to the door that had swung open. Through the dust we saw the bricks in a mound upon the floor. Becky, if she was there, lay under them. I thought I heard a groan. Barlo, mumbling something, threw his Bible on the pile. (No one has ever touched it.) Somehow we got away. My buggy was still on the road. The last thing that I remember was whipping old Dan like fury; I remember nothing after that—that is, until I reached town and folks crowded round to get the true word of it.

> Becky was the white woman who had two Negro sons. She's dead; they've gone away. The pines whisper to Jesus. The Bible flaps its leaves with an aimless rustle on her mound.

Criticism and Assessment
A review of *The Autobiography of an Ex-Colored Man*
New York Times, May 26, 1912

"An Ex-Colored Man"

A curious and in some respects a startling tale is this narration of the life experiences of a colored man, who forsook his own race and joined the white. It bears some evidences of truth. Nevertheless, it is necessary to consider the possibility that it may be merely the product of some whimsical imagination. Yet there is nothing in it that violates probability, and the book carries the publishers' assurance of good faith. And whether or not it is accepted on its face value, there remains the very interesting fact that it does make an astute, dispassionate study of the race problem in the United States from the standpoint of a man who has lived on both sides of it.

The author describes himself as being of a complexion so white and of features so Caucasian that the slight admixture of Negro blood in his veins has never been guessed except when he chooses to identify himself with his mother's race. His youth was lived in a Connecticut village, in school, where his race was known, but where it made no social difference. His young manhood he spent as a Negro in the South in a tobacco factory, and in New York City, where he passed much time in gambling dens as a crap player and musical entertainer. An eccentric millionaire, who sometimes visited the "club" which was his particular haunt, admired his piano playing because it lifted him out of the environment into which he had sunk, carried him off to Europe, where they lived a long time, journeying about in leisurely fashion as friends and companions. But the author had musical ambitions, and his few drops of Negro blood kept calling to him to acknowledge his race and to do something that would add to its glory. So he came back, went South again as a Negro, and traveled about in rural districts gathering material for his scheme of taking up ragtime music and evolving it into a classic. Then by chance he witnessed the burning alive of a brutal Negro. This so revolted him—the thought of belonging to a race that had to submit to such treatment—that he decided to throw off for all time the label of inferiority. He came again to New York, where he has lived ever since as a white man. He says that he has made money, won a good position among cultured and refined people, and married a beautiful white woman of this circle, not, however, without telling her his true status. In all material ways he has succeeded. But at the end of his story he admits that when he thinks of "that small but gallant band of colored men who are publicly fighting the cause of their race," he feels "small and selfish." "They are men," he says, "who are making history and a race. I, too, might have taken part in a work so glorious. . . . I cannot repress the thought that I have chosen the lesser part; that I have sold my birthright for a mess of pottage."

However true or untrue may be the personal side of the story, the observations upon the condition of the Negro race in the South and of the attitude of the whites toward it are full of interest. He discusses, quite dispassionately, the way in which the ever-present "Negro question" narrows the mental, political, and financial activities of the white race, and in this respect considers "the condition of the whites more to be deplored than that of the blacks." His view of "the tremendous struggle" between the two races is that of the man who has been behind the embankments on both sides and understands what each is fighting for. But his sympathies are evidently with his mother's people, though his words are calm and judicial. "The battle was first waged," he says, "over the right of the Negro to be classed as a human being with a soul; later, as to whether he had sufficient intellect to master even the rudiments of learning; and to-day it is being fought out over his social recognition." The black man, he declares, fights passively, and the white man is using in the contest his best energies. "The South to-day," he concludes, "stands panting and almost breathless from its exertions."

James Weldon Johnson
The Book of American Negro Poetry
1922

Preface

There is, perhaps, a better excuse for giving an Anthology of American Negro Poetry to the public than can be offered for many of the anthologies that have recently been issued. The public, generally speaking, does not know that there are American Negro poets—to supply this lack of information is, alone, a work worthy of somebody's effort.

Moreover, the matter of Negro poets and the production of literature by the colored people in this country involves more than supplying information that is lacking. It is a matter which has a direct bearing on the most vital of American problems.

A people may become great through many means, but there is only one measure by which its greatness is recognized and acknowledged. The final measure of the greatness of all peoples is the amount and standard of the literature and art they have produced. The world does not know that a people is great until that people produces great literature and art. No people that has produced great literature and art has ever been looked upon by the world as distinctly inferior.

The status of the Negro in the United States is more a question of national mental attitude toward the race than of actual conditions. And nothing will do more to change that mental attitude and raise his status than a demonstration of intellectual parity by the Negro through the production of literature and art.

Is there likelihood that the American Negro will be able to do this? There is, for the good reason that he possesses the innate powers. He has the emotional endowment, the originality and artistic conception, and, what is more important, the power of creating that which has universal appeal and influence.

I make here what may appear to be a more startling statement by saying that the Negro has already proved the possession of these powers by being the creator of the only things artistic that have yet sprung from American soil and been universally acknowledged as distinctive American products.

These creations by the American Negro may be summed up under four heads. The first two are the Uncle Remus stories, which were collected by Joel Chandler Harris, and the "spirituals" or slave songs, to which the Fisk Jubilee Singers made the public and the musicians of both the United States and Europe listen. The Uncle Remus stories constitute the greatest body of folk lore that America has produced, and the "spirituals" the greatest body of folk song. I shall speak of the "spirituals" later because they are more than folk songs, for in them the Negro sounded the depths, if he did not scale the heights, of music.

The other two creations are the cakewalk and ragtime. We do not need to go very far back to remember when cakewalking was the rage in the United States, Europe and South America. Society in this country and royalty abroad spent time in practicing the intricate steps. Paris pronounced it the "poetry of motion." The popularity of the cakewalk passed away but its influence remained. The influence can be seen today on any American stage where there is dancing.

. . . .

As for Ragtime, I go straight to the statement that it is by which America is known the world over. It has been all-conquering. Everywhere it is "American music."

. . . .

This power of the Negro to suck up the national spirit from the soil and create something artistic and original, which, at the same time, possesses the note of universal appeal, is due to a remarkable racial gift of adaptability; it is more than adaptability, it is a transfusive quality. And the Negro has exercised this transfusive quality not only here in America, where the race lives in large numbers, but in European countries, where the number has been almost infinitesimal.

. . . .

Paul Laurence Dunbar stands out as the first poet from the Negro race in the United States to show a combined mastery over poetic material and poetic technique, to reveal innate literary distinction in what he wrote, and to maintain a high level of performance. He was the first to rise to a height from which he could take a perspective view of his own race. He was the first to see objectively its humor, its superstitions, its shortcomings; the first to feel sympathetically its heart-wounds, its yearnings, its aspirations, and to voice them all in a purely literary form.

Dunbar's fame rests chiefly on his poems in Negro dialect. This appraisal of him is, no doubt, fair; for in these dialect poems he not only carried his art to the highest point of perfection, but he made a contribution to American literature unlike what any one else had made, a contribution which, perhaps, no one else could have made. Of course, Negro dialect poetry was written before Dunbar wrote, most of it by white writers; but the fact stands out that Dunbar was the first to use it as a medium for the true interpretation of Negro character and psychology. And yet, dialect poetry does not constitute the whole or even the bulk of Dunbar's work. In addition to a large number of poems of a very high order done in literary English, he was the author of four novels and several volumes of short stories.

Indeed, Dunbar did not begin his career as a writer of dialect. I may be pardoned for introducing here a bit of reminiscence. My personal friendship with Paul Dunbar began before he had achieved recognition, and continued to be close until his death. When I first met him he had published a thin volume, *Oak and Ivy,* which was being sold chiefly through his own efforts. *Oak and Ivy* showed no distinctive Negro influence, but rather the influence of James Whitcomb Riley. At this time Paul and I were together every day for several months. He talked to me a great deal about his hopes and ambitions. In these talks he revealed that he had reached a realization of the possibilities of poetry in the dialect, together with a recognition of the fact that it offered the surest way by which he could get a hearing. Often he said to me: "I've got to write dialect poetry; it's the only way I can get them to listen to me." I was with Dunbar at the beginning of what proved to be his last illness. He said to me then: "I have not grown. I am writing the same things I wrote ten years ago, and am writing them no better." His self-accusation was not fully true; he had grown, and he had gained a surer control of his art, but he had not accomplished the greater things of which he was constantly dreaming; the public had held him to the things for which it had accorded him recognition. If Dunbar had lived he would have achieved some of those dreams, but even while he talked so dejectedly to me he seemed to feel that he was not to live. He died when he was only thirty-three.

. . . .

It may be surprising to many to see how little of the poetry being written by Negro poets today is being written in Negro dialect. The newer Negro poets show a tendency to discard dialect; much of the subject-matter which went into the making of traditional dialect poetry, 'possums, watermelons, etc., they have discarded altogether, at least, as poetic material. This tendency will, no doubt, be regretted by the majority of white readers; and, indeed, it would be a distinct loss if the American Negro poets threw away this quaint and musical folk speech as a medium of expression. And yet, after all, these poets are working through a problem not realized by the reader, and, perhaps, by many of these poets themselves not realized consciously. They are trying to break away from, not Negro dialect itself, but the limitations on Negro dialect imposed by the fixing effects of long convention. The Negro in the United States has achieved or been placed in a certain artistic niche. When he is thought of artistically, it is as a happy-go-lucky, singing, shuffling, banjo-picking being or as a more or less pathetic figure. The picture of him is in a log cabin amid fields of cotton or along the levees. Negro dialect is naturally and by long association the exact instrument for voicing this phase of

Negro life; and by that very exactness it is an instrument with but two full stops, humor and pathos. So even when he confines himself to purely racial themes, the Aframerican poet realizes that there are phases of Negro life in the United States which cannot be treated in the dialect either adequately or artistically. Take, for example, the phases rising out of life in Harlem, that most wonderful Negro city in the world. I do not deny that a Negro in a log cabin is more picturesque than a Negro in a Harlem flat, but the Negro in the Harlem flat is here, and he is but part of a group growing every where in the country, a group whose ideals are becoming increasingly more vital than those of the traditionally artistic group, even if its members are less picturesque.

What the colored poet in the United States needs to do is something like what Synge did for the Irish; he needs to find a form that will express the racial spirit by symbols from within rather than by symbols from without, such as the mere mutilation of English spelling and pronunciation. He needs a form that is freer and larger than dialect, but which will still hold the racial flavor; a form expressing the imagery, the idioms, the peculiar turns of thought, and the distinctive humor and pathos, too, of the Negro, but which will also be capable of voicing the deepest and highest emotions and aspirations, and allow of the widest range of subjects and the widest scope of treatment.

Negro dialect is at present a medium that is not capable of giving expression to the varied conditions of Negro life in America, and much less is it capable of giving the fullest interpretation of Negro character and psychology. This is no indictment against the dialect as dialect, but against the mold of convention in which Negro dialect in the United States has been set. In time these conventions may become lost, and the colored poet in the United States may sit down to write in dialect without feeling that his first line will put the general reader in a frame of mind which demands that the poem be humorous or pathetic. In the meantime, there is no reason why these poets should not continue to do the beautiful things that can be done, and done best, in the dialect.

. . . .

Not many of the writers here included, except Dunbar, are known at all to the general reading public; and there is only one of these who has a widely recognized position in the American literary world, William Stanley Braithwaite. Mr. Braithwaite is not only unique in this respect, but he stands unique among all the Aframerican writers the United States has yet produced. He has gained his place, taking as the standard and measure for his work the identical standard and measure applied to American writers and American literature. He has asked for no allowances or rewards, either directly or indirectly, on account of his race.

. . . .

But the group of the new Negro poets, whose work makes up the bulk of this anthology, contains names destined to be known. Claude McKay, although still quite a young man, has already demonstrated his power, breadth and skill as a poet. Mr. McKay's breadth is as essential a part of his equipment as his power and skill. He demonstrates mastery of the three when as a Negro poet he pours out the bitterness and rebellion in his heart in those two sonnet-tragedies, "If We Must Die" and "To the White Fiends," in a manner that strikes terror; and when as a cosmic poet he creates the atmosphere and mood of poetic beauty in the absolute, as he does in "Spring in New Hampshire" and "The Harlem Dancer." Mr. McKay gives evidence that he has passed beyond the danger which threatens many of the new Negro poets—the danger of allowing the purely polemical phases of the race problem to choke their sense of artistry.

. . . .

I offer this collection without making apology or asking allowance. I feel confident that the reader will find not only an earnest for the future, but actual achievement. The reader cannot but be impressed by the distance already covered. It is a long way from the plaints of George Horton to the invectives of Claude McKay, from the obviousness of Frances Harper to the complexness of Anne Spencer. Much ground has been covered, but more will yet be covered. It is this side of prophecy to declare that the undeniable creative genius of the Negro is destined to make a distinctive and valuable contribution to American poetry.

W.E.B. Du Bois
Review of Cane

From W.E.B. Du Bois and Alain Locke, "The Younger Literary Movement,"

The Crisis
February 1924

There have been times when we writers of the older set have been afraid that the procession of those who seek to express the life of the American Negro was thinning and that none were coming forward to fill the footsteps of the fathers. Dunbar is dead; Chesnutt is silent; and Kelly Miller is mooning after false gods while Brawley and Woodson are writing history rather than literature. But even as we ask "Where are the young Negro artists to mold and weld this mighty material about us?"—even as we ask, they come.

There are two books before me, which, if I mistake not, will mark an epoch: a novel by Jessie Fauset and a book of stories and poems by Jean Toomer. There are besides these, five poets writing: Langston Hughes, Countee Cullen, Georgia Johnson, Gwendolyn Bennett and Claude McKay. Finally, Negro men are appearing as essayists and reviewers, like Walter White and Eric Walrond. (And even as I write comes the news that a novel by Mr. White has just found a publisher.) Here then is promise sufficient to attract us. . . .

The world of black folk will some day arise and point to Jean Toomer as a writer who first dared to emancipate the colored world from the conventions of sex. It is quite impossible for most Americans to realize how straight-laced and conventional thought is within the Negro World, despite the very unconventional acts of the group. Yet this contradiction is true. And Jean Toomer is the first of our writers to hurl his pen across the very face of our sex conventionality. In

"Cane", one has only to take his women characters *seriatim* to realize this: Here is Karintha, an innocent prostitute; Becky, a fallen white woman; Carma, a tender Amazon of unbridled desire; Fern, an unconscious wanton; Esther, a woman who looks age and bastardy in the face and flees in despair; Louise, with a white and a black lover; Avey, unfeeling and unmoral; and Doris, the cheap chorus girl. These are his women, painted with a frankness that is going to make his black readers shrink and criticize; and yet they are done with a certain splendid, careless truth.

Toomer does not impress me as one who knows his Georgia but he does know human beings; and, from the background which he has seen slightly and heard of all his life through the lips of others, he paints things that are true, not with Dutch exactness, but rather with an impressionist's sweep of color. He is an artist with words but a conscious artist who offends often by his apparently undue striving for effect. On the other hand his powerful book is filled with felicitous phrases— Karintha, "carrying beauty perfect as the dusk when the sun goes down",—

> "Hair—
> Silver-grey
> Like streams of stars"

Or again, "face flowed into her eyes—flowed in soft creamy foam and plaintive ripples". His emotion is for the most part entirely objective. One does not feel that he feels much and yet the fervor of his descriptions shows that he has felt or knows what feeling is. His art carries much that is difficult or even impossible to understand. The artist, of course, has a right deliberately to make his art a puzzle to the interpreter (the whole world is a puzzle) but on the other hand I am myself unduly irritated by this sort of thing. I cannot, for the life of me, for instance see why Toomer could not have made the tragedy of Carma something that I could understand instead of vaguely guess at; "Box Seat" muddles me to the last degree and I am not sure that I know what "Kabnis" is about. All of these essays and stories, even when I do not understand them, have their strange flashes of power, their numerous messages and numberless reasons for being. But still for me they are partially spoiled. Toomer strikes me as a man who has written a powerful book but who is still watching for the fullness of his strength and for that calm certainty of his art which will undoubtedly come with years.

IV
THE ORIGINS OF
THE HARLEM RENAISSANCE
1924–1926

In the mid-1920s the literary and artistic stirrings of the previous decade coalesced into the literary and cultural event known as the Harlem Renaissance. The social and political developments that affected the African American community in the early twentieth century provided the context and influenced the nature of the movement. The Renaissance was enriched by the transformation of Harlem to the "capital" of black America. It benefited from the presence of the new publishing houses and political and literary journals that flourished in New York in the 1920s. Most of these were downtown operations, but several of the journals were Harlem-based and controlled by blacks. African Americans intellectuals also contributed to the Renaissance. They attempted to define its aesthetic and content; they encouraged and promoted black creative artists; but their most important service was to connect black artists and white publishers, patrons, and critics. By 1926 the Harlem Renaissance was well underway.

The first sign of the emerging Renaissance was the increase in the amount of work published by African Americans—particularly the novels and poetry. In 1924 two novels appeared: Jessie Fauset's *There Is Confusion* and Walter White's *The Fire in the Flint*. Fauset was both a writer and the literary editor of the NAACP's monthly magazine, *The Crisis*. She would write three additional novels, which made her the most productive Harlem Renaissance novelist. Walter White also was connected with the NAACP. Beginning in 1918 he served the organization as Assistant Executive Secretary. Fascinated by the arts and culture, as well as by the talents of Du Bois, James Weldon Johnson, and others of his associates at the NAACP, White deviated briefly from his civil rights work and produced his 1924 novel, and another two years later. In 1924 another book was expected from poet Claude McKay, but the Jamaican's first attempt at a novel was never published. Within two years, however, seven additional books appeared by writers connected with the new literary movement.

This increase in literary activity in 1924 mobilized black intellectuals into action. Determined to nurture this new writing they intervened to support and promote the emerging Harlem Renaissance.

The first of these efforts established a link among three major players in the literary Renaissance—the black literary and political intelligentsia, the white publishers and critics, and the young black writers. The occasion was the dinner that

Charles S. Johnson of the Urban League hosted on March 21, 1924 to recognize the new literary talent in the black community and to present it to New York's white literary establishment. Out of this dinner came the March 1925 "Harlem issue" of the avant-garde literary magazine *Survey Graphic*, edited by Alain Locke and devoted to defining the aesthetic of black literature and art. Locke expanded this work into a full-length study, *The New Negro*, which featured the work of black writers, poets, and artists, as well as essays by scholars on all aspects of the African American creative arts and the role of these arts and the artists in both exploring the African American experience and addressing the realities of race in America. *The New Negro* was the first and the most comprehensive of a series of anthologies and collections that both presented black writing to the public and attempted to define the parameters of the Renaissance.

Along with the *Survey Graphic* issue and *The New Negro*, black literary promoters organized literary contests and literary prizes, both to draw attention to black art and literature and to provide financial rewards for talented writers and artists. Most notable in this endeavor were the two New York based civil rights organizations, the NAACP and the Urban League, and their journals, *The Crisis*, edited by W.E.B. Du Bois, and *Opportunity*, edited by Charles S. Johnson. In the early 1920s both periodicals opened their pages to black poets and writers; in 1925 both established literary prizes to outstanding black writers. Suspended after several years, these efforts contributed greatly to drawing attention to black literature during the early years of the Harlem Renaissance.

The next event that stimulated the growth and the popularity of black literature was the publication in early 1926 of the white novelist Carl Van Vechten's *Nigger Heaven*. This controversial novel, which quickly became a best seller, had a major influence on the Harlem Renaissance. It both reflected and helped stimulate the unprecedented white fascination with Harlem, African Americans, and their art and culture. *Nigger Heaven*, a spectacularly popular exposé of Harlem life, helped, create the "Negro vogue" that drew thousands of sophisticated New Yorkers to Harlem's exotic night life and stimulated the national market for African American literature and music. Some black critics praised Van Vechten for writing an honest novel about African American urban life; others blasted him for concentrating on the exotic, the deviant, and the criminal elements of Harlem's back streets and cabarets, and ignoring the honest, hardworking, respectable majority. Even worse he was accused of seducing young black writers into following his example and catering to the appetite of white publishers and white readers for similar renderings of black life. The result, warned these critics, would reinforce negative stereotypes of blacks as immoral, sex-crazed, violence-prone, or criminal.

Then came an event that symbolized the coalescence of a core of young writers and artists into a movement. In the fall of 1926 a group of black writers produced their own literary magazine, *Fire!!* With *Fire!!* the poet Langston Hughes, writers Wallace Thurman and Zora Neale Hurston, artist Aaron Douglas, along with other young writers and artists declared their intent to assume ownership of the literary Renaissance. In part *Fire!!* was a reaction against efforts, well intentioned or otherwise, of white and black critics to take charge and define the movement. Instead, the *FIRE!!* group was determined to take charge of the movement and develop their own literary venue, independent of both the white literary establishment and the black political demands. *Fire!!* was not a commercial success—it failed financially after only one issue. But the spirit of independence it represented continued to define the aspirations of the movement, if not the reality.

JESSE FAUSET
There Is Confusion
1924

Jessie Fauset was one of the most successful novelists of the Harlem Renaissance and among its influential promoters. Her four novels established her credentials as prolific, and her role as literary editor of *The Crisis* in the early 1920s gave her the opportunity to promote and influence the emerging Harlem Renaissance. Her first novel, *There Is Confusion*, is deceptive. It is easy to dismiss it as a shallow, melodramatic romance of middle-class black life. But the novelist used this form to address head-on issues of race and gender. The driving force is a strong woman who is determined not to let the obstacles of race or the weaknesses of others prevent her from achieving her goals. The two chapters presented here depict the struggle between Joanna Marshall and Peter Bye. Joanna is headstrong In pursuit of her singing career and uncompromising in her vision of success. Peter is torn by his bitterness and his pride—ready to seize racial prejudice as an excuse to abandon his medical studies.

Chapter XVII

They enjoyed the opera and sang snatches of it coming home as they walked to the subway. Once in the express train, however, Joanna lapsed into sadness.

"I don't think my voice is as big as that prima donna's, but those dancing girls! I should have been right up there with them! Oh, Peter, I believe I'm the least bit discouraged."

She told him of her trips with Bertully. "I didn't mind those girls calling me 'nigger.' That was sheer ill-breeding. Remember what we used to say when we were children when they called us names?" She recited it: "'Sticks and stones may break my bones, but names will never hurt me.' What I minded was that they couldn't dream of my being accepted. Thought I had a nerve even to ask it."

She mounted the steps. "Come in, Peter."

After dinner they sat in the back parlor and Joanna went on with her story, Peter listening closely.

"I'm glad you're telling me about this, Joanna," he said seriously. "Now you'll understand my case better. You know how I feel about white people and their everlasting unfairness. As though the world and all that in it is belonged to them! I tell you, Jan, I'm sick of the whole business,—college, my everlasting grind, my poverty, this confounded prejudice. If I want to get a chance to study a certain case and it's in a white hospital you'd think I'd committed a crime. As though diseases picked out different races! I'm a good surgeon, I'll swear I am, but I've got so I don't care whether I get my degree or not. You can't imagine all the petty unfairness about me. Only the other day the barber refused to shave me in the college barber-shop. Your own cousin, John Talbert, is a Zeta Gamma man if ever there was one—that's the equivalent to Phi Beta Kappa in his school, you know.

Do you think he got it? No, they black-balled him out."

Joanna sat silent, stunned by this avalanche. And to think she had precipitated it!

"Arabelle Morton's sister, Selma," Peter went on morosely, "took her Master's degree last year. The candidates sat in alphabetical order. Selma sat in her seat wondering whom the chair on the left of her belonged to—it was vacant. At the last moment a girl came in, a Miss Nelson, who had been in one or two of her classes. Selma knew she was a Southerner. 'Oh, I just can't sit there,' Selma heard her say, not too much under her breath. And some friend of hers went to the Professor in charge of the exercises and he let her change her place, though it threw the whole line out of order."

He paused, still brooding.

"Another colored girl—can't think of her name—paid for a seat in one of the Seminary rooms. The white girl next to her, apparently a very pleasant person, had her books all over her own desk space and this one, too. They were the best seats in the room. The colored girl asked her to move them. She just looked at her. Then this Miss—Miss Taylor, that was her name, took it from one authority to another, finally to the professor in charge of the Library. He assigned her another seat. Said the girl had been there four years, and that anyway, she—the white girl—resented the colored girl's manner toward her. The damned petty injustice!"

"But, Peter," Joanna argued, "you wouldn't let that interfere with your whole career, change your whole life?"

"Why shouldn't I? There're plenty of pleasanter ways to earn a living. Why should I take any more of their selfish dog-in-the-manger foolishness? I can make all the money I want with Tom Mason. If you aren't satisfied for me to be an accompanist, I could go into partnership with him and we could form and place orchestras. It's a perfectly feasible plan, Joanna. Why shouldn't I pick the job that comes handiest, since the world owes me a living?"

He frowned, meditating. "Isn't it funny, I felt just then as though I'd been through all this before. It's just as though I'd heard myself say that very thing some other time. Well, what do you say, Joanna?"

"That I don't want a coward and a shirker for a husband. As though that weren't the thing those white people—those mean ones—wanted! Not all white people are that way. Both of us know it, Peter. And it's up to us, to you and me, Peter Bye, to show them we can stick to our last as well as anybody else. If they can take the time to be petty, we can take the time to walk past it. Oh, we must fight it when we can, but we mustn't let it hold us back. Buck up, Peter, be a man. You've got to be one if you're going to marry me."

He shrugged his shoulders. "May I light a cigarette?" But she noticed he did it with trembling fingers. "Just as you say, Joanna."

She rose and faced him, this new Peter—this old Peter if she did but know it, with the early shiftlessness, the irresoluteness of his father, Meriwether Bye, the ancient grudge of his grandfather, Isaiah Bye, rearing up, bearing full and perfect fruit in his heart. Both rage and despair possessed her, as she saw the beautiful fabric of their future felled wantonly to the ground. For the sake of a few narrow pedants!

"Peter, Peter, we've got to make our own lives. We can't let these people ruin us." She felt her knees trembling under her. "We're both tired and beside ourselves. Come and see me to-morrow, will you?"

What should she say to him now, she wondered next day after a long white night. And once she had only to raise her finger and he was willing, glad to do her bidding. Could it be that after all these years she had failed to touch his pride, worse yet that he had no pride? She had been longing so for a cessation from all this bickering, so that they might have time for a touch of tenderness. But she could not afford that now. His love for her was her strongest hold over him. She was sure she could bring him back to reason. Perhaps she had been a little severe last night, calling him a coward.

"I musn't lose my temper," she told herself. Yet that was the very thing she did. The matter took such a sudden, such a grotesque turn.

He came in about eleven, his handsome face haggard, his eyes bloodshot. She was astounded at his appearance.

"Peter, you look dreadful!"

He glanced over the top of her head at his reflection in the mirror, lounged to the sofa, threw himself in the corner of it. "Guess I'm due to look a fright after staying up all night. Didn't get to bed till five this morning."

She thought he'd been worrying over their quarrel. "You poor boy, you did-n't need to take it that hard."

He stared at her. "Take what, that hard? Oh, our talk! That didn't keep me awake. I spent the night at 'Jake's.'"

"Jake's" was the cabaret, a cheap one, in which he had played years ago.

She couldn't understand him. "I thought you had plenty of money without playing there."

"I have. I didn't play there. I was a visitor like anybody else, like Harry Por-tor; he spent the night there, too. There was a whole gang of us."

Clearly she must get to the bottom of this. While she had been tossing sleep-less, he had been in a cabaret, dancing with cheap women, laughing, drinking per-haps.

"You mean you deliberately went there to have a good time and stayed all night? You and Harry Portor and the rest drank, I suppose?"

"I don't think Portor did. He's a full-fledged doctor now, though he's hardly any practice yet. But the rest of us did. There's nothing in that, Joanna, fellow's got to get to know the world."

Her anger rose, broke. She lost her dignity.

"I suppose Maggie Ellersley taught you that, too."

"What's that?" His handsome face lowered. "Say, how'd Maggie Ellersley get into this? No, she never taught me anything. But I can tell you what, if a fellow were going with her and went during his holidays to have a spree at a cabaret she wouldn't nag him about it, like you nag me. Yes, about that and about a thousand other things."

She turned into ice. "I'll never nag you again. Here, take this thing!" She drew off the little ring. "I don't want it."

A pin dropping would have crashed in that silence.

His voice came back to him. "You don't mean this, Joanna,—you can't."

"I do. Here, take it."

"You—you mean the engagement is broken?" He ignored her outstretched hand.

She dropped the ring in his pocket. "I mean I can't consider a man for a husband who throws away his career because of the meanness of a few white men. Of a man who sits all night in a low cabaret where every loafer in New York can point him out and say, 'That's the kind of fellow Joanna Marshall goes about with.'"

"Oh, I see, it isn't for my sweet sake, then!"

She pushed him toward the door. "Go, Peter! Go!" On New Year's morning he came back, humble, contrite. "I was a fool, Joanna. I must have been mad. Please forgive me."

"Of course I do, Peter."

He fumbled in his pocket, held out the ring. "Will you take this back?"

"I can't do that."

"When will you?"

"I don't know if ever."

There was a long silence. He came over and put his hand on the back of her chair, afraid to touch her.

"Joanna, I don't deserve your love. But you still do love me?"

She nodded slowly.

His face brightened at that. "But you won't take back the ring?"

"No, Peter, I can't take back the ring."

He knelt and kissed her hands.

"Good-by, sweetheart, I must go to Philadelphia to-day. Happy New Year, Joanna."

She let him go then. None of their other partings had ever been like this. Safe in her room she cried herself sick. "Oh, Peter," she murmured to herself, "come back like the boy I used to know." She wished now that she had been easier with him.

"And yet if I were, he'd let go entirely. Well, it must come out all right." But her heart was heavy.

The very next day she got a letter. Peter must have written her as soon as he arrived in Philadelphia.

"Joanna, I was wrong," he had written contritely, "I confess I had got away somewhat from your manner of thinking, and I suppose I was a little sore, too,— your life seems so full. Sometimes I think there is nothing I can bring you. But I do love you, Joanna. You must always believe that and I think you love me, too. We were meant for each other. I am sure life would hold for us the deepest, most irremediable sorrow if we separated. Whether we are engaged or not, just tell me that you love me still and I can be happy."

Chapter XVIII

If she had only answered the letter then, that very moment!

But she had said to her impulse: "No, I must wait. I can't let him off too easily." Perhaps, too, there was a little sense of satisfaction at having him again at her knees, suing for her favors, but this was secondary. Joanna was really sick at heart to think that her beautiful dreams of success for both of them might not be realized. She wanted to be great herself, but she did not want that greatness to overshadow Peter.

. . . .

Chapter XXII

Ten months later Tom Mason leaned back against the red plush of the car seat and jingled some coins in his pocket.

"Tell you what, Bye, we really are cleaning up. I hadn't expected anything like this run of engagements. Now suppose you beat it along to Mrs. Lea's and find out what special arrangements she wants made for the musicians to-night and I'll go on to Mrs. Lawlor and see about to-morrow."

Peter stared moodily at the flying landscape. "I wish you'd come yourself, Mason. I hate to talk to these white people. Their damned patronizing airs make me sick."

"What do you care about their patronizin'? All I'm interested in is gettin' what I can out of them. When I've made my pile, if I can't spend it here the way I please, Annie and me can pick up and go to South America or France. I hear they treat colored people all right there."

"'Treat colored people all right,'" Peter mimicked. "What business has any one 'treating' us, anyway? The world's ours as much as it is theirs. And I don't want to leave America. It's mine, my people helped make it. These very orchards we're passing now used to be the famous Bye orchards. My grandfather and great-grandfather helped to cultivate them."

"Is that so? Honest?" Tom showed a sudden respectful interest. "How'd they come to lose them?"

"Lose them? They never owned them. The black Byes were slaves of the white Byes."

"Oh, slaves! Oh, you mean they worked in the fields? Well, I guess that's different. Come on, here we are."

Peter flung himself out of the car after Tom and followed him up a tree-lined street. The suburban town stretched calm, peaceful and superior about them. Clearly this was the home of the rich and well-born. It is true that a few ordinary mortals lived here, but mainly to do the bidding of the wealthy. A group of young white girls, passing the two men, glanced at them a little curiously.

"Entertainers for the Lea affair," one of them said, making no effort to keep from being overheard.

Peter stopped short. "That's what I hate," he said fiercely. "Labeled because we're black."

"Ain't you got a grouch, though!" Tom spoke almost admiringly. He told his sister afterwards: "Bye's got this here—now—temper'ment. Never can tell how it's goin' to take him. Seems different since he started keeping company with Maggie, don't you think so?"

Annie admitted she did.

At present Tom patted Peter on the shoulder, and starting him up the drive-way which led to Mrs. Lea's large low white house, went on himself to Mrs. Lawlor.

Mrs. Lea received Peter in a small morning-room. She was pretty, a genuine blonde, with small delicate features and beautiful fluffy hair. But as Peter did not like fair types, his mind simply registered "washed-out," and took no further stock of her looks. What he did notice was that she was dressed in a lacey, too trans-parent floating robe, too low in the neck, and too short in the skirt.

"Something she would wear only before some one for whom she cared very much, or some one whom she didn't think worth considering," he told himself, lowering.

Mrs. Lea, leading him into the ballroom beyond, barely glanced at him. "See, the musicians are to sit behind those palms and the piano will be completely banked with flowers. I'm expecting the decorators every moment. Your men will have to get here very early so as to get behind all this without being seen. I want the effect of music instead of perfume pouring out of the flowers. Do you get the idea—er—what did you say your name was?"

"Yes, I understand," said Peter shortly. "My name is Bye."

"I meant your first name—Bye—why, that's the name of a family in Bryn Mawr, who used to own half of the land about here. There're a Dr. Meriwether Bye and his grandfather, Dr. Meriwether Bye, living in the old Bye house now. Where do you come from?"

"I was born in Philadelphia. like my father and grandfather and his father before him."

She stated the obvious conclusion: "Probably your parents belonged to the Bryn Mawr Byes."

"So my father told me," replied Peter, affecting a composure equal to her own. "His name was Meriwether Bye."

She did not like that. She decided she did not like him either—eyeing his straight, fine figure and meeting his unyielding look. These niggers with their uppish ways! Besides this one looked, looked—indefinably he reminded her of young Meriwether Bye. She spoke to him:

"I don't want you to leave to-night before I get a chance to point you out to young Dr. Bye. He'll be so interested." She looked at Peter again. Yes, he was intelligent enough to get the full force of what she wanted to say. "It's so in keeping with things that the grandson of the man who was slave to his grandfather should be his entertainer to-night."

Peter felt his skin tightening. "I'm afraid you'll be disappointed. I'm a medical student, not an entertainer. I came here for Mr. Mason, who is very busy. You may be sure I'll give him your instructions. Good-day, Mrs. Lea."

He rushed out of the house, down to the station where, without waiting for Tom, he boarded the train. Not far from the West Philadelphia depot he pushed the bell of a certain house, flung open the unlocked door and rushed up a flight of stairs.

In a small room to his left he found the person he was seeking, a short, almost black young fellow who lifted a dejected and then an amazed countenance toward him.

"Am I seeing things? Where'd you blow in from, Pete? Thought you'd chucked us all, the old school and all the rest of it."

"I haven't, I've been a fool, a damned fool, but I'm back to my senses. I'm going back to my classes and I tell you, Ed Morgan, I'll clean up. See here, you've got to do me a favor."

"Name it."

"You know Mason, Tom Mason on Fifteenth Street? I've been playing for him. But I can't stick it any longer. Tom's all right, but I can't stand his customers. Besides, I've got to get back to work. I'm quitting this minute—see. But Tom's got a big dance on, near Bryn Mawr to-night at a Mrs.—Mrs. Lea," he gulped. "Good pay and all that. You can play as well as I can, Ed. Easy stuff, you can read it. You got to do it."

"Do it! Man, lead me to that job. I'm broke, see, stony broke, busted." He turned his pockets inside out. "I was just wondering what I could pawn. And I need instruments—Oh, Lord!"

Peter gave him some money. "Take this, you can pay me any time. Only rush down to Tom's and tell him I can't come. I'm dead—see?—drowned, fallen in the Schuylkill. And see here, old fellow, afterwards we'll have a talk. I want everything, everything, mind you, that you can remember, every note, every bit of paper that bears on the work of these last ten months. And I'll show them—" he seemed to forget Morgan—"with their damned talk of entertainers." Down the stairs he ran, still talking.

"Mad, quite mad," said little Morgan, staring. "Glad he's coming back to work, though. Now, where'd I put that cap?"

Still at white heat, Peter walked the few short blocks to his boarding house. Once inside his room he shut himself in and paced the floor.

"The grandson—that's me—of the man who was his grandfather's slave, should be his—that's Meriwether Bye, young Dr. Meriwether Bye—should be his entertainer, his hired entertainer.

"My grandfather didn't have a chance, but here I am half a century after and I'm still a slave, an entertainer. My grandfather. Let's see, which one of the Byes was that?"

He went to the closet, pushed some books and papers aside and hauled down the old Bye Bible. The leaves, streaked and brown, stuck together. With clumsy, unaccustomed fingers he turned them, until at last between the Old Testament and the Apochrypha he found what he was looking for: "Record of Births and Deaths."

The old, stiff, faded writing with the long German *s*, the work of hands long since still, smote him with a sense of worthlessness. These people, according to their lights, must have considered themselves "people of importance," else why this careful record of dates?

His lean brown finger traced the lines. "Joshua Bye, born about 1780"—heavens, that must have been his great-great-grandfather. No, maybe he was just a "great," for the black Byes, he remembered hearing his father Meriwether say, lived long and married late.

"Isaiah Bye, born 1830—a child of freedom." How proud they had been of that! Yes, that was his grandfather, he remembered now. And he had made a great deal of that freedom. Meriwether had often dwelt with pride on Isaiah's learning, his school, his property, his "half-interest," Meriwether had said grandiloquently, in a bookshop. Peter could hear his father talking now.

"A child of freedom"—Peter was that but what had he made of it? He wondered what Isaiah in turn had written on the occasion of Meriwether's birth. His finger ran down the page, and found it, stopped.

There it was—"Meriwether," the inscription read, "by *his* fruits shall ye know—*me*."

At first Peter thought it was a mistake. Then gradually it dawned on him—his fine old grandfather, proud of his achievements, seeing his son as a monument to himself, seeing each Bye son doubtless as a monument to each Bye father. Poor

Isaiah, perhaps happy Isaiah, for having died before he realized how worthless, how anything but monumental *his* son had really been, except as a failure. And now he, Peter, was following in that son's footsteps.

He remembered an old daguerreotype of his grandfather that he had seen at his great-uncle Peter's. The face, perfectly black, looked out from its faded red-plush frame with that immobile look of dignity which only black people can attain. "I have made the most of myself," the proud old face seemed to say. "My father was a slave, but I am a teacher, a leader of men. My son shall be a great healer and my son's son—"

Peter put the open Bible carefully on the table and took out a cigarette. But he held it a long time unlighted.

So far as he could remember he had never had any desire to rise, "to be somebody," as Isaiah, he rightly guessed, would have phrased, it. He saw himself after his mother's death, a small placid boy, perfectly willing to stay out of school. Until he met Joanna. There was his term of service in the butcher-shop and himself again perfectly willing to be the butcher's assistant. Until Joanna's questioning had made him declare for surgery. Once in college his whole impulse had been to get away from it all, not because he hadn't liked the work; he adored it, was fascinated by it. But the obstacles, prejudice, his very real dislike for white people, his poverty, all or any of these had seemed to him sufficient cause for dropping his studies and becoming a musician. Not an artist, but an entertainer, a player in what might be termed "a strolling orchestra," picking up jobs, receiving tips, going down in the servants' dining room for meals. And when Joanna had objected, he thought she was "funny," "bossy."

And as soon as he had broken with her, he had given up striving altogether. He had been nothing without Joanna. He wondered humbly if she had seen something in him which he had not recognized in himself.

How different they had been! After all, Joanna, though she had not had to contend with poverty, had had as hard a fight as he. "She'd have been on the stage long ago if she'd been white," he murmured. "And see how she takes it!"

Well, he would show her and Isaiah, yes, and Mrs. Lea, too, that there was something to him. But chiefly Joanna. Some day he'd go to her and say, "Joanna, what I am, you made me."

His ladylady called up to him:

"Telephone for you, Mr. Bye."

He went downstairs, took down the receiver.

"Hello, this is Mr. Bye, yes, this is Peter. Who's this speaking, please? . . .

"Oh—oh, yes, of course. Why—why, Maggie!"

He had forgotten all about her!

WALTER WHITE
The Fire in the Flint
1924

Walter White, whose novel also came out in 1924, had joined the staff of the NAACP in 1918. In 1930 he replaced the retiring James Weldon Johnson as Executive Director, a post that he held until his death in 1955. The literary talent and activity of the NAACP officers in the early 1920s—Du Bois, Fauset, and Johnson, among others—virtually required that White join in. He worked tirelessly to promote black literary activity, and encouraged by journalist H.L. Mencken, early in the decade he wrote the first of his two Harlem Renaissance novels. White's political talents and interests were greater than his artistic skills, and *The Fire in the Flint* reflects this. Its greatest strength is its open and direct critique of southern racism. The novel's main character, Dr. Kenneth Harper, fresh from a northern medical school and the battlefields of France, is a man of culture and training. He returns to his southern hometown to practice medicine. His knowledge and intellect do not shield him from intensity of southern racism. In the chapter presented here Harper encounters both racism and the hostile ignorance of the local black establishment.

Chapter III

Kenneth came into contact with few others than his own people during the first month after his return to Central City. The first two weeks had been spent in getting his offices arranged with the innumerable details of carpentering, plastering, painting, and disposition of the equipment he had ordered in New York during the days he had spent there on his return from France.

During the early months of 1917, when through every available means propaganda was being used to whip into being America's war spirit, one of the most powerful arguments heard was that of the beneficial effect army life would have on the men who entered the service. Newspapers and magazines were filled with it, orators in church and theatre and hall shouted it, every signboard thrust it into the faces of Americans. Alluring pictures were painted of the growth, physical and mental, that would certainly follow enlistment "to make the world safe for democracy."

To some of those who fought, such a change probably did come, but the mental outlook of most of them was changed but little. The war was too big a thing, too terrible and too searing a catastrophe, to be adequately comprehended by the farmer boys, the clerks, and the boys fresh from school who chiefly made up the fighting forces. Their lives had been too largely confined to the narrow ways to enable them to realize the immensity of the event into which they had been so suddenly plunged. Their most vivid memories were of "that damned second loot" or of *beucoup vin blanc* or, most frequently, of all-too-brief adventures with the *mademoiselles.* With the end of the war and demobilization had come the short periods of hero-worship and then the sudden forgetfulness of those for whom they had fought. The old narrow life began again with but occasional revolts against the monotony of it all, against the blasting of the high hopes held when the war was being fought. Even these spasmodic revolts eventually petered out in vague mutterings among men like themselves who let their inward dissatisfaction dissipate in thin air.

More deep-rooted was this revolt among Negro ex-service men. Many of them entered the army, not so much because they were fired with the desire to fight for an abstract thing like world democracy, but, because they were of a race oppressed, they entertained very definite beliefs that service in France would mean a more decent regime in America, when the war was over, for themselves and all others who were classed as Negroes. Many of them, consciously or subconsciously, had a spirit which might have been expressed like this: "Yes, we'll fight for democracy in France, but when that's over with we're going to expect and we're going to get some of that same democracy for ourselves right here in America." It was because of this spirit and determination that they submitted to the rigid army discipline to which was often added all the contumely that race prejudice could heap upon them.

Kenneth was of that class which thought of these things in a more detached, more abstract, more subconscious manner. During the days when, stationed close to the line, he treated black men brought to the base hospital with arms and legs torn away by exploding shells, with bodies torn and mangled by shrapnel, or with flesh seared by mustard gas, he had inwardly cursed the so-called civilization which not only permitted but made such carnage necessary. But when the nightmare had ended, he rapidly forgot the nausea he had felt, and plunged again into his beloved work. More easily than he would have thought possible, he forgot the months of discomfort and weariness and bloodshed. It came back to him only in fitful memories as of some particularly horrible dream.

To Kenneth, when work grew wearisome or when memories would not down, there came relaxation in literature, an opiate for which he would never cease being grateful to Professor Fuller, his old teacher at Atlanta. It was "Pop" Fuller who, with his benign and paternal manner, his adoration of the best of the world's literature, had sown in Kenneth the seed of that same love. He read and reread *Jean Christophe,* finding in the adventures and particularly in the mental processes of Rolland's hero many of his own reactions towards life. He had read the plays of Bernard Shaw, garnering here and there a morsel of truth though much of Shaw eluded him. Theodore Dreiser's gloominess and sex-obsession he liked though it often repelled him; he admired the man for his honesty and disliked his pessimism or what seemed to him a dolorous outlook on life. He loved the colourful romances of Hergesheimer, considering them of little enduring value but nevertheless admiring his descriptions of affluent life, enjoying it vicariously. Willa Cather's *My Antonia* he delighted in because of its simplicity and power and beauty.

The works of D. H. Lawrence, Kenneth read with conflicting emotions. Mystical, turgid, tortuous phrases, and meaning not always clear. Yet he revelled in Lawrence's clear insight into the bends and backwaters and perplexing twistings of the stream of life. Kenneth liked best of all foreign writers Knut Hamsun. He had read many times *Hunger, Growth of the Soil* and other novels of the Norwegian writer. He at times was annoyed by their lack of plot, but more often he enjoyed them because they had none, reflecting that life itself is never a smoothly turned and finished work of art, its causes and effects, its tears and joys, its loves and hates neatly dovetailing one into another as writers of fiction would have it.

So too did he satisfy his love for the sea in the novels of Conrad—the love so many have who are born and grow to manhood far from the sea. Kenneth loved it with an abiding and passionate love loved, yet feared it for its relentless power and savagery—a love such as a man would have for an alluring, yet tempestuous mistress of fiery and uncertain temper. In Conrad's romances he lived by proxy the life he would have liked had not fear of the water and the circumstances of his life prevented it. Flaubert, Zola, Maupassant be read and reread, finding in the struggles of *Emma Bovary* and *Nana* and other heroines and heroes of the French realists mental counterparts of some of the coloured men and women of his acquaintance in their struggles against the restrictions of stupid and crass and ignorant surroundings. The very dissimilarities of environment and circumstance between his own acquaintances and the characters in the novels he read, seemed to emphasize the narrowness of his own life in the South. So does a bedridden invalid read with keen delight the adventurous and rococo romances of Zane Grey or Jack London.

But perhaps best of all he admired the writing of Du Bois—the fiery, burning philippics of one of his own race against the proscriptions of race prejudice. He read them with a curious sort of detachment—as being something which touched him in a more or less remote way but not as a factor in forming his own opinions as a Negro in a land where democracy often stopped dead at the colour line.

It was in this that Kenneth's attitude towards life was most clearly shown. His was the more philosophic viewpoint on the race question, that problem so close to him. The proscriptions which he and others of his race were forced to endure were inconvenient, yet they were apparently a part of life, one of its annoyances, a thing which had always been and probably would be for all time to come. Therefore, he reasoned, why bother with it any more than one was forced to by sheer necessity? Better it was for him if he attended to his own individual problems, solved them to the best of his ability and as circumstances would permit, and left to those who chose to do it the agitation for the betterment of things in general. If he solved his problems and every other Negro did the same, he often thought, then the thing we call the race problem will be solved. Besides, he reasoned, the whole thing is too big for one man to tackle it, and if he does attack it, more than likely he will go down to defeat in the attempt. And what would be gained? . . .

His office completed, Kenneth began the making of those contacts he needed to secure the patients he knew were coming. In this his mother and Mamie were of invaluable assistance. Everybody knew the Harpers. It was a simple matter for Kenneth to renew acquaintances broken when he had left for school in the North. He joined local lodges of the Grand United Order of Heavenly Reapers and the Exalted Knights of Damon. The affected mysteriousness of his initiation into these fraternal orders, the secret grip, the passwords, the elaborately worded rituals, all of which the other members took so seriously, amused him, but he went through it all with an outwardly solemn demeanour. He knew it was good business to affiliate himself with these often absurd societies which played so large a part in the lives of these simple and illiterate coloured folk. Along with the strenuous emotionalism of their religion, it served as an outlet for their naturally deep feelings.

In spite of the renewal of acquaintances, the careful campaign of winning confidence in his ability as a physician, Kenneth found that the flood of patients did not come as he had hoped. The coloured people of Central City had had impressed upon them by three hundred years of slavery and that which was called freedom after the Emancipation Proclamation was signed, that no Negro doctor, however talented, was quite as good as a white one. This slave mentality, Kenneth now realized, inbred upon generation after generation of coloured folk, is the greatest handicap from which the Negro suffers, destroying as it does that confidence in his own ability which would enable him to meet without fear or apology the test of modern competition.

Kenneth's youthful appearance, too, militated against him. Though twenty-nine years old, he looked not more than a mere twenty-four or twenty-five. "He may know his stuff and be as smart as all outdoors," ran the usual verdict, "but I don't want no boy treating me when I'm sick."

Perhaps the greatest factor contributing to the coloured folks' lack of confidence in physicians of their own race was the inefficiency of Dr. Williams, the only coloured doctor in Central City prior to Kenneth's return. Dr. Williams belonged to the old school and moved on the theory that when he graduated some eighteen years before from a medical school in Alabama, the development of medical knowledge had stopped. He fondly pictured himself as being the most prominent personage of Central City's Negro colony, was pompous, bulbous-eyed, and exceedingly fond of long words, especially of Latin derivation. He made it a rule of his life never to use a word of one syllable if one of two or more would serve as well. Active in fraternal order circles (he was a member of nine lodges), classleader in Central City's largest Methodist church, arbiter supreme of local affairs in general, he filled the role with what he imagined was unsurpassable éclat. His idea of complimenting a hostess was ostentatiously to loosen his belt along about the middle of dinner. Once he had been introduced as the "black William Jennings Bryan," believed it thereafter, and thought it praise of a high order.

He was one of those who say on every possible occasion: "I am kept so terribly busy I never have a minute to myself." Like nine out of ten who say it, Dr. Williams always repeated this stock phrase of those who flatter themselves in this fashion—so necessary to those of small minds who would be thought great—not because it was true, but to enhance his pre-eminence in the eyes of his hearers—and in his own eyes as well.

He always wore coats which resembled morning coats, known in local parlance as "Jim-swingers." He kept his hair straightened, wore it brushed straight back from his forehead like highly polished steel wires, and, with pomades and hair oils liberally applied, it glistened like the patent leather shoes which adorned his ample feet.

His stout form filled the Ford in which he made his professional calls, and it was a sight worth seeing as he majestically rolled through the streets of the town bowing graciously and calling out loud greetings to the acquaintances he espied by the way. Always his bows to white people were twice as low and obsequious as to those of darker skin. Until Kenneth returned, Dr. Williams had had his own way in Central City. Through his fraternal and church connections and lack of competition; he had made a little money, much of it through his position as medical examiner for the lodges to which he belonged. As long as he treated minor ailments—cuts, colic, childbirths, and the like—he had little trouble. But when more serious maladies attacked them, the coloured population sent for the old white physician, Dr. Bennett, instead of for Dr. Williams.

The great amount of time at his disposal irritated Kenneth. He was like a spirited horse, champing at the bit, eager to be off. The patronizing air of his people nettled him—caused him to reflect somewhat bitterly that "a prophet is not without honour save in his own country." And when one has not the gift of prophecy to foretell, or of clairvoyance to see, what the future holds in the way of success, one is not likely to develop a philosophic calm which enables him to await the coming of long-desired results. He was seated one day in his office reading when his mother entered. Closing his book, he asked the reason for her frown.

"You remember Mrs. Bradley—Mrs. Emma Bradley down on Ashley Street—

don't you, Kenneth?" Without waiting for a reply, Mrs. Harper went on: "Well, she's mighty sick. Jim Bradley has had Dr. Bennett in to see what's the matter with her but he don't seem to do her much good."

Kenneth remembered Mrs. Bradley well indeed. The most talkative woman in Central City. It was she who had come to his mother with a long face and dolorous manner when he as a youngster had misbehaved in church. He had learned instinctively to connect Mrs. Bradley's visits with excursions to the little back room accompanied by his mother and a switch cut from the peach-tree in the back yard— a sort of natural cause and effect. Visions of those days rose in his mind and he imagined he could feel the sting of those switches on his legs now.

"What seems to be the trouble with her?" he asked. "It's some sort of stomach-trouble—she's got an awful pain in her side. She says it can't be her appendix because she had that removed up to Atlanta when she was operated on there for a tumour nearly four years ago. Dr. Bennett gave her some medicine but it doesn't help here any. Won't you run down there to see her?"

"I can't, mamma, until I am called in professionally. Dr. Bennett won't like it. It isn't ethical. Besides, didn't Mrs. Bradley say when I came back that she didn't want any coloured doctor fooling with her?"

"Yes, she did, but you mustn't mind that. Just run in to see her as a social call."

Kenneth rose and instinctively took up his bag. Remembering, he put it, down, put on his hat, kissed his mother, and walked down to Mrs. Bradley's. Outside the gate stood Dr. Bennett's mud-splashed buggy, sagging on one side through years of service in carrying its owner's great bulk. Between the shafts stood the old bay horse, its head hung dejectedly as though asleep, which Central City always connected with its driver.

Entering the gate held by one hinge, Kenneth made his way to the little three-room unpainted house which served as home for the Bradleys and their six children. On knocking, the door was opened by Dr. Bennett, who apparently was just leaving. He stood there, his hat on, stained by many storms, its black felt turning a greenish brown through years of service and countless rides through the red dust of the roads leading out of Central City. Dr. Bennett himself was large and flabby. His clothes hung on him in haphazard fashion and looked as though they had never been subjected to the indignity of a tailor's iron. A Sherlock Holmes, or even one less gifted, could read on his vest with little difficulty those things which its wearer had eaten for many meals past. Dr. Bennett's face was red through exposure to many suns, and covered with the bristle of a three days' growth of beard. Small eyes set close together, they belied a bluff good humour which Dr. Bennett could easily assume when there was occasion for it. The corners of the mouth were stained a deep brown where tobacco juice had run down the folds of the flesh.

Behind him stood Jim Bradley with worried face, his ashy black skin showing the effects of remaining all night by the bedside of his wife.

Dr. Bennett looked at Kenneth inquiringly.

"Don't you remember me, Dr. Bennett? I'm Kenneth Harper. "

"Bless my soul, so it is. How're you, Ken? Le's see—it's been nigh on to eight years since you went No'th, ain't it? Heard you was back in town. Hear you goin' to practise here. Come 'round to see me some time. Right glad you're here. I'll be kinder glad to get somebody t' help me treat these niggers for colic or when they get carved up in a crap game. Hope you ain't got none of them No'then ideas 'bout social equality while you was up there. Jus' do like your daddy did, and you'll get along all right down here. These niggers who went over to France and ran around with them Frenchwomen been causin' a lot of trouble 'round here, kickin' up a rumpus, and talkin' 'bout votin' and ridin' in the same car with white folks. But don't you let them get you mixed up in it, 'cause there'll be trouble sho's you born if they don't shut up and git to work. Jus' do like your daddy did, and you'll do a lot to keep the white folks' friendship."

Dr. Bennett poured forth all this gratuitous advice between asthmatic wheezes without waiting for Kenneth to reply. He then turned to Jim Bradley with a parting word of advice.

"Jim, keep that hot iron on Emma's stomach and give her those pills every hour. 'Tain't nothin' but the belly-ache. She'll be all right in an hour or two."

Turning without another word, he half ambled, half shuffled out to his buggy, pulled himself up into it with more puffing and wheezing, and drove away.

Jim Bradley took Kenneth's arm and led him back on to the little porch, closing the door behind him. "I'm pow'ful glad t' see you, Ken. My, but you done growed sence you went up No'th! Befo' you go in dar, I want t' tell you somethin'. Emma's been right po'ly fuh two days. Her stomach's swelled up right sma't and she's been hollering all night. Dis mawning she don't seem jus' right in de haid. I tol' her I was gwine to ast you to come see her, but she said she didn't want no young nigger doctah botherin' with her. But don't you min' her. I wants you to tell me what to do."

Kenneth smiled.

"I'll do what I can for her, Jim. But what about Dr. Bennett?"

"Dat's a' right. He give her some med'cine but it ain't done her no good. She's too good a woman fuh me to lose her, even if she do talk a li'l' too much. You make out like you jus' drap in to pass the time o' day with her."

Kenneth entered the dark and ill-smelling room. Opposite the door a fire smouldered in the fire-place, giving fitful spurts of flame that illumined the room and then died down again. There was no grate, the pieces of wood resting on crude andirons, blackened by the smoke of many fires. Over the mantel there hung a cheap charcoal reproduction of Jim and Emma in their wedding-clothes, made by some local "artist" from an old photograph. One or two nondescript chairs worn shiny through years of use stood before the fire. In one corner stood a dresser on which were various bottles of medicine and of "Madame Walker's Hair Straightener." On the floor a rug, worn through in spots and patched with fragments of other rugs all apparently of different colours, covered the space in front of the bed. The rest of the floor was bare and showed evidences of a recent vigorous scrubbing. The one window was closed tightly and covered over with a cracked shade, long since divorced from its roller, tacked to the upper ledge of the window.

On the bed Mrs. Bradley was rolling and tossing in great pain. Her eyes opened slightly when Kenneth approached the bed and closed again immediately as a new spasm of pain passed through her body. She moaned piteously and held her hands on her side, pressing down hard one hand over the other.

At a sign from Jim, Kenneth started to take her pulse.

"Go way from here and leave me 'lone! Oh, Lawdy, why is I suff'rin' this way? I jus' wish I was daid! Oh—oh—oh!"

This last as she writhed in agony. Kenneth drew back the covers, examined Mrs. Bradley's abdomen, took her pulse. Every sign pointed to an attack of acute appendicitis. He informed Jim of his diagnosis.

"But, Doc, it ain't dat trouble, 'cause Emma says dat was taken out a long time ago."

"I can't help what she says. She's got appendicitis. You go get Dr. Bennett and tell him your wife has got to be operated on right away or she is going to die. Get a move on you now! If it was my case, I would operate within an hour. Stop by my house and tell Bob to bring me an ice bag as quick as he can."

Jim hurried away to catch Dr. Bennett. Kenneth meanwhile did what he could to relieve Mrs. Bradley's suffering. In a few minutes Bob came with the ice bag. Then Jim returned with his face even more doleful than it had been when Kenneth had told him how sick his wife was.

"Doc Bennett says he don't care what you do. He got kinder mad when I told him you said it was 'pendicitis, and tol' me dat if I couldn't take his word, he wouldn't have anything mo' to do with Emma. He seemed kinder mad 'cause you said it was mo' than a stomach-ache. Said he wa'n't goin' to let no young nigger doctor tell him his bus'ness. So, Doc, you'll have t' do what you thinks bes'."

"All right, I'll do it. First thing, I'm going to move your wife over to my office. We can put her up in the spare room. Bob will drive her over in the car. Get something around her and you'd better come on over with her. I'll get Dr. Williams to help me."

Kenneth was jubilant at securing his first surgical case since his return to Central City, though his pleasure was tinged with doubt as to the ethics of the manner in which it had come to him. He did not let that worry him very long, however, but began his preparations for the operation.

First he telephoned to Mrs. Johnson, who, before she married and settled down in Central City, had been a trained nurse at a coloured hospital at Atlanta. She hurried over at once. Neat, quiet, and efficient, she took charge immediately of preparations, sterilizing the array of shiny instruments, preparing wads of absorbent cotton, arranging bandages and catgut and haemostatics.

Kenneth left all this to Mrs. Johnson, for he knew in her hands it would be well done. He telephoned to Dr. Williams to ask that he give the anaesthesia. In his excitement Kenneth neglected to put in his voice the note of asking a great and unusual favour of Dr. Williams. That eminent physician, eminent in his own eyes, cleared his throat several times before replying, while Kenneth waited at the other end of the line. He realized his absolute dependence on Dr. Williams, for he knew no white doctor would assist a Negro surgeon or even operate with a coloured assistant. There was none other in Central City who could give the ether to Mrs. Bradley. It made him furious that Dr. Williams should hesitate so long. At the same time, he knew he must restrain the hot and burning words that he would have used. The pompous one hinted of the pressure of his own work-work that would keep him busy all day. Into his words he injected the note of affront at being asked— he, *the* coloured physician of Central City—to assist a younger man. Especially on that man's first case. Kenneth swallowed his anger and pride, and pleaded with Dr. Williams at least to come over. Finally, the older physician agreed in a condescending manner to do so.

Hurrying back to his office, Kenneth found Mrs. Bradley arranged on the table ready for the operation. Examining her, he found she was in delirium, her eyes glazed, her abdomen hard and distended, and she had a temperature of 105 degrees. He hastily sterilized his hands and put on his gown and cap. As he finished his preparations, Dr. Williams in leisurely manner strolled into the room with a benevolent and patronizing "Howdy, Kenneth, my boy. I won't be able to help you out after all. I've got to see some patients of my own."

He emphasized "my own," for he had heard of the manner by which Kenneth had obtained the case of Mrs. Bradley. Kenneth, pale with anger, excited over his first real case in Central City, stared at Dr. Williams in amazement at his words.

"But, Dr. Williams, you can't do that! Mrs. Bradley here is dying!"

The older doctor looked around patronizingly at the circle of anxious faces. Jim Bradley, his face lined and seamed with toil, the lines deepened in distress at the agony of his wife and the imminence of losing her, gazed at him with dumb pleading in his eyes, pleading without spoken words with the look of an old, faithful dog beseeching its master. Bob looked with a malevolent glare at his pompous sleekness, as though he would like to spring upon him. Mrs. Johnson plainly showed her contempt of such callousness on the part of one who bore the title, however poorly, of physician. In Kenneth's eyes was a commingling of eagerness and rage and bitterness and anxiety. On Emma Bradley's face there was nothing but the pain and agony of her delirious ravings. Dr. Williams seemed to enjoy thoroughly his little moment of triumph. He delayed speaking in order that it might be prolonged as much as possible. The silence was broken by Jim Bradley.

"Doc, won't you please he'p?" he pleaded. "She's all I got!"

Kenneth could remain silent no longer. He longed to punch that fat face and erase from it the supercilious smirk that adorned it.

"Dr. Williams," he began with cold hatred in his voice, "either you are going to give this anaesthesia or else I'm going to go into every church in Central City and tell exactly what you've done here today."

Dr. Williams turned angrily on Kenneth.

"Young man, I don't allow anybody to talk to me like that—least of all, a young whippersnapper just out of school . . ." he shouted.

By this time Kenneth's patience was at an end. He seized the lapels of the other doctor's coat in one hand and thrust his clenched fist under the nose of the now thoroughly alarmed Dr. Williams.

"Are you going to help—or aren't you?" he demanded.

The situation was becoming too uncomfortable for the older man. He could stand Kenneth's opposition but not the ridicule which would inevitably follow the spreading of the news that he had been beaten up and made ridiculous by Kenneth. He swallowed—a look of indecision passed over his face as he visibly wondered if Kenneth really dared hit him—followed by a look of fear as Kenneth drew back his fist as though to strike. Discretion seemed the better course to pursue— he could wait until a later and more propitious date for his revenge—he agreed to help. A look of relief came over Jim Bradley's face. A grin covered Bob's as he saw his brother showing at last some signs of fighting spirit. Without further words Kenneth prepared to operate. . . .

The patient under the ether, Kenneth with sure, deft strokes made an incision and rapidly removed the appendix. Ten—twelve—fifteen minutes, and the work was done. He found Mrs. Bradley's peritoneum badly inflamed, the appendix swollen and about to burst. A few hours' delay and it would have been too late. . . .

The next morning Mrs. Bradley's temperature had gone down to normal. Two weeks later she was sufficiently recovered to be removed to her home. Three weeks later she was on her feet again. Then Kenneth for the first time in his life had no fault to find with the vigour with which Mrs. Bradley could use her tongue. Glorying as only such a woman can in her temporary fame at escape from death by so narrow a margin, she went up and down the streets of the town telling how Kenneth had saved her life. With each telling of the story it took on more embellishments until eventually the simple operation ranked in importance in her mind with the first sewing-up of the human heart.

Kenneth found his practice growing. His days were filled with his work. One man viewed his growing practice with bitterness. It was Dr. Williams, resentful of the small figure he had cut in the episode in Kenneth's office, which had become known all over Central City. Of a petty and vindictive nature, he bided his time until he could force atonement from the upstart who had so presumptuously insulted and belittled him, the Beau Brummel, the leading physician, the prominent coloured citizen. But Kenneth, if he knew of the hatred in the man's heart, was supremely oblivious of it.

The morning after his operation on Mrs. Bradley, he added another to the list of those who did not wish him well. He had taken the bottle of alcohol containing Mrs. Bradley's appendix to Dr. Bennett to show that worthy that he had been right, after all, in his diagnosis. He found him seated in his office. Dr. Bennett, with little apparent interest, glanced at the bottle.

"Humph!" he ejaculated, aiming at the cuspidor and letting fly a thin stream of tobacco juice which accurately met its mark. "You never can tell what's wrong with a nigger anyhow. They ain't got nacheral diseases like white folks. A hoss doctor can treat 'em better'n one that treats humans. I always said that a nigger's more animal than human. . . ."

Kenneth had been eager to discuss the case of Mrs. Bradley with his fellow practitioner. He had not even been asked to sit down by Dr. Bennett. He realized for the first time that in spite of the superiority of his medical training to that of Dr. Bennett's, the latter did not recognize him as a qualified physician, but only as a "nigger doctor." Making some excuse, he left the house. Dr. Bennett turned back to the local paper he had been reading when Kenneth entered, took a fresh chew of tobacco from the plug in his hip pocket, grunted, and remarked: "A damned nigger telling me I don't know medicine!"

THE CIVIC CLUB DINNER
March 21, 1924

On the evening of March 21, 1924 the elite of Harlem's intelligentsia together with many of the most prominent white publishers and literary critics gathered at the Civic Club to celebrate with an informal group of aspiring black writers the publication of Jessie Fauset's new novel and the growing artistic excitement and creativity in Harlem. In many ways this dinner represented the public debut of the Harlem Renaissance. The May issue of *Opportunity* published a description of the event along with a celebratory poem in honor of the occasion by Gwendolyn Bennett, and an address by Carl Van Doren, editor of *Century* magazine.

"The Debut of the Younger School of Negro Writers"
Opportunity
May 1924

Interest among the literati of New York in the emerging group of younger Negro writers found an expression in a recent meeting of the Writers' Guild, an informal group whose membership includes Countee Cullen, Eric Walrond, Langston Hughes, Jessie Fauset, Gwendolyn Bennett, Harold Jackman, Regina Anderson, and a few others. The occasion was a "coming out party," at the Civic Club, on March 21—a date selected around the appearance of the novel "There Is Confusion" by Jessie Fauset. The responses to the invitations sent out were immediate and enthusiastic and the few regrets that came in were genuine.

Although there was no formal, prearranged program, the occasion provoked a surprising spontaneity of expression both from the members of the writers' group and from the distinguished visitors present.

A brief interpretation of the object of the Guild was given by Charles S. Johnson, Editor of *Opportunity*, who introduced Alain Locke, virtual dean of the movement, who had been selected to act as Master of Ceremonies and to interpret the new currents manifest in the literature of this younger school. Alain Locke has been one of the most resolute stimulators of this group, and although he has been writing longer than most of them, he is distinctly a part of the movement. One excerpt reflects the tenor of his remarks. He said: "They sense within their group— meaning the Negro group—a spiritual wealth which if they can properly expound will be ample for a new judgment and re-appraisal of the race."

Horace Liveright, publisher, told about the difficulties, even yet, of marketing books of admitted merit. The value of a book cannot be gauged by the sales. He regarded Jean Toomer's "Cane" as one of the most interesting that he had handled, and yet, less than 500 copies had been sold. In his exhortations to the younger group he warned against the danger of reflecting in one's writings the "inferiority complex" which is so insistently and frequently apparent in an overbalanced emphasis on "impossibly good" fiction types. He felt that to do the best writing it was necessary to give a rounded picture which included bad types as well as good ones since both of these go to make up life.

Dr. W. E. B. Du Bois made his first public appearance and address since his return to this country from Africa. He was introduced by the chairman with soft seriousness as a representative of the "older school." Dr. Du Bois explained that the Negro writers of a few years back were of necessity pioneers, and much of their style was forced upon them by the barriers against publication of literature about Negroes of any sort.

James Weldon Johnson was introduced as an anthologist of Negro verse and one who had given invaluable encouragement to the work of this younger group.

Carl Van Doren, Editor of the *Century*, spoke on the future of imaginative writing among Negroes. His remarks are given in full elsewhere in this issue.

Another young Negro writer, Walter F. White, whose novel "Fire in Flint" has been accepted for publication, also spoke and made reference to the passing of the stereotypes of the Negroes of fiction.

Professor Montgomery Gregory of Howard University, who came from Washington for the meeting, talked about the possibilities of Negroes in drama and told of the work of several talented Negro writers in this field, some of whose plays were just coming into recognition.

Another visitor from Philadelphia, Dr. Albert C. Barnes, art connoisseur and foremost authority in America on primitive Negro art, sketched the growing interest in this art which had had such tremendous influence on the entire modern art movement.

Miss Jessie Fauset was given a place of distinction on the program. She paid her respects to those friends who had contributed to her accomplishments, acknowledging a particular debt to her "best friend and severest critic," Dr. Du Bois.

The original poems read by Countee Cullen were received with a tremendous ovation. Miss Gwendolyn Bennett's poem, dedicated to the occasion, is reproduced. It is called

"To Usward"

Let us be still
As ginger jars are still
Upon a Chinese shelf,
And let us be contained
By entities of Self. . . .

Not still with lethargy and sloth,
But quiet with the pushing of our growth;
Not self-contained with smug identity,
But conscious of the strength in entity.

If any have a song to sing that's different from the rest,
Oh, let him sing before the urgency of Youth's behest!

And some of us have songs to sing Of jungle heat and fires;
And some of us are solemn grown With pitiful desires;
And there are those who feel the pull Of seas beneath the skies;
And some there be who want to croon Of Negro lullabies.
We claim no part with racial dearth, We want to sing the songs of birth!

And so we stand like ginger jars,
Like ginger jars bound round
With dust and age;
Like jars of ginger we are sealed
By nature's heritage.
But let us break the seal of years
With pungent thrusts of song,
For there is joy in long dried tears,
For whetted passions of a throng!

Among the guests present were Paul Kellogg, Editor of the *Survey*; Devere Allen, Editor of *The World Tomorrow*; Freda Kirchwey and Evans Clark of the *Nation*; Mr. and Mrs. Frederick L. Allen of Harper Brothers; Mr. and Mrs. Arthur B. Spingarn; Mr. and Mrs. Horace Liveright; L. Hollingsworth Wood; Mr. and Mrs. Eugene Kinckle Jones; Georgette Carneal; Georgia Douglas Johnson of Washington, D. C.; Louis Weitzenkorn of the New York *World*; A. Granville Dill; Mr. and Mrs. George E. Haynes; Mr. and Mrs. Graham R. Taylor; Mr. and Mrs. John Daniels; A. A. Schomburg; Eva D. Bowles of the Y.W.C.A.; Mr. and Mrs. Jesse Moorland; Mr. and Mrs. Walter Bartlett; Talcott Williams; Mr. and Mrs. Arthur C. Holden; Mr. and Mrs. James H. Hubert; Ottie Graham; Eunice Hunton; Anna L. Holbrook; Crystal Bird; Dr. and Mrs. E. P. Roberts; J. A. Rogers; Cleveland Allen, Mrs. Gertrude McDougal; William Andrews; Mabel Bird; Dr. and Mrs. Matthew Boutte; William Holly; Roger Baldwin; Mary White Ovington; and others, numbering about one hundred and ten.

Of those who could not come Oswald Garrison Villard, Editor of the *Nation,* wrote:

"Nothing would give me greater pleasure than attending the dinner to be given to the young Negro writers on the 21st, but unhappily it is necessary for me to be out of town on that date."

From Herbert Bayard Swope, Editor of the New York *World*:

"I am heartily in sympathy with the purpose of your dinner on the 21st and I should be glad to go were it any other date but that. You have my best wishes for the complete success of your 'coming out' party."

Dorothy Scarborough, author of "In the Land of Cotton," said:

"I think your plan an admirable one, and I send you my heartiest good wishes for the success of all your writers. I have always taken a great interest in the talents which your race possesses, and I rejoice in your every achievement."

George W. Ochs Oakes, Editor of *Current History*, wrote:

"I wish to commend you for the steps that have been taken in this direction and believe that it will do a great deal to stimulate serious intellectual and literary work among the Negroes. I have found evidences of striking literary capacity and fine intellectual expression among the young Negro writers who have contributed to our magazine."

"The Younger Generation of Negro Writers"
Remarks at the Dinner of the Writers Guild, held at the Civic Club
By Carl Van Doren

I have a genuine faith in the future of imaginative writing among Negroes in the United States. This is not due to any mere personal interest in the writers of the race whom I happen to know. It is due to a feeling that the Negroes of the country are in a remarkable strategic position with reference to the new literary age which seems to be impending.

Long oppressed and handicapped, they have gathered stores of emotion and are ready to burst forth with a new eloquence once they discover adequate mediums. Being, however, as a race not given to self-destroying bitterness, they will, I think, strike a happy balance between rage and complacency—that balance in which passion and humor are somehow united in the best of all possible amalgams for the creative artist.

The Negroes, it must be remembered, are our oldest American minority. First slavery and then neglect have forced them into a limited channel of existence. Once they find a voice, they will bring a fresh and fierce sense of reality to their vision of human life on this continent, a vision seen from a novel angle by a part of the population which cannot be duped by the bland optimism of the majority.

Nor will their vision, I think, be that solely of drastic censure and dissent, such as might be expected of them in view of all they have endured from majority rule. Richly gifted by nature with distinctive traits, they will be artists while they are being critics. They will look at the same world that the white poets and novelists and dramatists look at, yet, arraigning or enjoying it, will keep in their modes of utterance the sympathies, the memories, the rhythms of their ancient stock.

That Negro writers must long continue to be propagandists, I do not deny. The wrongs of their people are too close to them to be overlooked. But it happens that in this case the vulgar forms of propaganda are all unnecessary. The facts about Negroes in the United States are themselves propaganda—devastating and unanswerable. A Negro novelist who tells the simple story of any aspiring colored man or woman will call as with a bugle the minds of all just persons, white or black, to listen to him.

But if the reality of Negro life is itself dramatic, there are of course still other elements, particularly the emotional power with which Negroes live—or at least to me seem to live. What American literature decidedly needs at the moment is color, music, gusto, the free expression of gay or desperate moods. If the Negroes are not in a position to contribute these items, I do not know what Americans are.

ALAIN LOCKE
Survey Graphic
Harlem: Mecca of the New Negro
March 1925

During the Civic Club dinner Alain Locke, professor of philosophy at Howard University and one of the promoters and intellectual shepherds of the new literary movement, engaged in a conversation with Paul Kellog, editor of the progressive literary magazine *Survey Graphic*. Kellog, impressed with the quality and extent of the black creativity showcased at the dinner, commissioned Locke, before the evening was over, to edit a New Negro issue of the magazine. As a result the March 1925 *Survey Graphic* was devoted entirely to the new Harlem cultural movement. Included here is an interpretative essay by Locke along with a sampling of the black poetry that appeared in the issue. The artwork of the cover and much of the illustration were created by Winold Reiss, a German-born artist who work combined modernism, African themes, and portraits of Harlem celebrities and ordinary folk

Cover of Harlem issue of *Survey Graphics* by Winold Reiss.

"Youth Speaks"
Alain Locke

We might know the future but for our chronic tendency to turn to age rather than to youth for the forecast. And when youth speaks, the future listens, however the present may shut its ears. Here we have Negro youth, foretelling in the mirror of art what we must see and recognize in the streets of reality tomorrow.

Primarily, of course, it is youth that speaks in the voice of Negro youth, but

the overtones are distinctive; Negro youth speaks out of an unique experience and with a particular representativeness. All classes of a people under social pressure are permeated with a common experience; they are emotionally welded as others cannot be. With them, even ordinary living has epic depth and lyric intensity, and this, their material handicap, is their spiritual advantage. So, in a day when art has run to classes, cliques and coteries, and life lacks more and more a vital common background, the Negro artist, out of the depths of his group and personal experience, has to his hand almost the conditions of a classical art.

Negro genius today relies upon the race-gift as a vast spiritual endowment from which our best developments have come and must come. Racial expression as a conscious motive, it is true, is fading out of our latest art, but just as surely the age of truer, finer group expression is coming in—for race expression does not need to be deliberate to be vital. Indeed at its best it never is. This was the case with our instinctive and quite matchless folk-art, and begins to be the same again as we approach cultural maturity in a phase of art that promises now to be fully representative. The interval between has been an awkward age, where from the anxious desire and attempt to be representative much that was really unrepresentative has come; we have lately had an art that was stiltedly self-conscious, and racially rhetorical rather than racially expressive. Our poets have now stopped speaking for the Negro—they speak as Negroes. Where formerly they spoke to others and tried to interpret, they now speak to their own and try to express. They have stopped posing, being nearer to the attainment of poise.

The younger generation has thus achieved an objective attitude toward life. Race for them is but an idiom of experience, a sort of added enriching adventure and discipline, giving subtler overtones to life, making it more beautiful and interesting, even if more poignantly so. So experienced, it affords a deepening rather than a narrowing of social vision. The artistic problem of the Young Negro has not been so much that of acquiring the outer mastery of form and technique as that of achieving an inner mastery of mood and spirit. That accomplished, there has come the happy release from self-consciousness, rhetoric, bombast, and the hampering habit of setting artistic values with primary regard for moral effect—all those pathetic over-compensations of a group inferiority complex which our social dilemmas inflicted upon several unhappy generations. Our poets no longer have the hard choice between an over-assertive and an appealing attitude. By the same effort, they have shaken themselves free from the minstrel tradition and the fowling-nets of dialect, and through acquiring ease and simplicity in serious expression, have carried the folk-gift to the altitudes of art. There they seek and find art's intrinsic values and satisfactions—and if America were deaf, they would still sing.

But America listens—perhaps in curiosity at first; later, we may be sure, in understanding. But—a moment of patience. The generation now in the artistic vanguard inherits the fine and dearly bought achievement of another generation of creative workmen who have been pioneers and path-breakers in the cultural development and recognition of the Negro in the arts. Though still in their prime, as veterans of a hard struggle, they must have the praise and gratitude that is due them. We have had, in fiction, Chestnutt and Burghardt Du Bois; in drama, Du Bois again and Angelina Grimke; in poetry Dunbar, James Weldon Johnson, Fenton and Charles Bertram Johnson, Everett Hawkins, Lucien Watkins, Cotter, Jameson; and in another file of poets, Miss Grimke, Anne Spencer, and Georgia Douglas Johnson; in criticism and *belles lettres,* Braithwaite and Dr. Du Bois; in painting, Tanner and Scott; in sculpture, Meta Warrick and May Jackson; in acting Gilpin and Robeson; in music, Burleigh. Nor must the fine collaboration of white American artists be omitted; the work of Ridgeley Torrence and Eugene O'Neill in drama, of Stribling, and Shands and Clement Wood in fiction, all of which has helped in the bringing of the materials of Negro life out of the shambles of conventional polemics, cheap romance and journalism into the domain of pure and unbiassed art. Then, rich in this legacy, but richer still, I think, in their own endowment of talent, comes the youngest generation of our Afro-American culture: in music, Diton, Dett, Grant Still, and Roland Hayes; in fiction, Jessie Fauset, Walter White, Claude McKay (a forthcoming book); in drama, Willis Richardson; in the field of the short story, Jean Toomer, Eric Walrond, Rudolf Fisher; and finally a vivid galaxy of young Negro poets, McKay, Jean Toomer, Langston Hughes and Countée Cullen.

These constitute a new generation not because of years only, but because of a new aesthetic and a new philosophy of life. They have all swung above the horizon in the last three years, and we can say without disparagement of the past that in that short space of time they have gained collectively from publishers, editors, critics and the general public more recognition than has ever before come to Negro creative artists in an entire working lifetime. First novels of unquestioned distinction, first acceptances by premier journals whose pages are the ambition of veteran craftsmen, international acclaim, the conquest for us of new provinces of art, the development for the first time among us of literary coteries and channels for the contact of creative minds, and most important of all, a spiritual quickening and racial leavening such as no generation yet felt and known. It has been their achievement also to bring the artistic advance of the Negro sharply into stepping alignment with contemporary artistic thought, mood and style. They are thoroughly modern, some of them ultramodern, and Negro thoughts now wear the uniform of the age.

But for all that, the heart beats a little differently. Toomer gives a folk-lilt and ecstasy to the prose of the American modernists. McKay adds Aesop and irony to the social novel and a peasant clarity and naïveté to lyric thought, Fisher adds Uncle Remus to the art of Maupassant and O. Henry. Hughes puts Biblical ferver into free verse, Hayes carries the gush and depth of folk-song to the old masters, Cullen blends the simple with the sophisticated and puts the vineyards themselves into his crystal goblets. There is in all the marriage of a fresh emotional endowment with the finest niceties of art. Here for the enrichment of American and modern art, among our contemporaries, in a people who still have the ancient key, are some of the things we thought culture had forever lost. Art cannot disdain the gift of a natural irony, of a transfiguring imagination, of rhapsodic Biblical speech, of dynamic musical swing, of cosmic emotion such as only the gifted pagans knew, of a return to nature, not by way of the forced and worn formula of Romanticism, but through the closeness of an imagination that has never broken kinship with nature. Art must accept such gifts, and revaluate the giver.

Not all the new art is in the field of pure art values. There is poetry of sturdy social protest, and fiction of calm, dispassionate social analysis. But reason and realism have cured us of sentimentality: instead of the wail and appeal, there is challenge and indictment. Satire is just beneath the surface of our latest prose, and tonic irony has come into our poetic wells. These are good medicines for the common mind, for us they are necessary antidotes against social poison. Their influence means that at least for us the worst symptoms of the social distemper are passing. And so the social promise of our recent art is as great as the artistic. It has brought with it, first of all, that wholesome, welcome virtue of finding beauty in oneself; the younger generation can no longer be twitted as "cultural nondescripts" or accused of "being out of love with their own nativity." They have instinctive love and pride of race, and, spiritually compensating for the present lacks of America, ardent respect and love for Africa, the motherland. Gradually too under some spiritualizing reaction, the brands and wounds of social persecution are becoming the proud stigmata of spiritual immunity and moral victory. Already enough progress has been made in this direction so that it is no longer true that the Negro mind is too engulfed in its own social dilemmas for control of the necessary perspective of art, or too depressed to attain the full horizons of self and social criticism. Indeed, by the evidence and promise of the cultured few, we are at last spiritually free, and offer through art an emancipating vision to America. But it is a presumption to speak further for those who have spoken and can speak so adequately for themselves.

"Harlem Wine"
Countee Cullen

This is not water running here,
These thick rebellious streams
That hurtle flesh and bone past fear
Down alleyways of dreams.

This is a wine that must flow on
Not caring how or where,
So it has ways to flow upon
Where song is in the air.

So it can woo an artful flute
With loose, elastic lips,
Its measurement of joy compute
With blithe, ecstatic hips.

"Lady, Lady"
Anne Spencer

I saw your face,
Dark as night withholding a star. . .
The chisel fell, or it might have been
You had borne so long the yoke of men.
Lady, Lady, I saw your hands,
Twisted, awry, like crumpled roots,
Bleached poor white in a sudsy tub,

Wrinkled and drawn from your rub-a-dub.
Lady, Lady I saw your heart,
And altared there in its darksome place
Were the tongues of flame the ancients knew
Where the good God sits to spangle through.

"The Black Finger"
Angelina Grimke

I have just seen a most beautiful thing
    Slim and still,
  Against a gold, gold sky,
  A straight black cypress,
    Sensitive,
    Exquisite,
    A black finger
    Pointing upwards.
Why, beautiful still finger, are you black?
And why are you pointing upwards?

"Jazzonia"
Langston Hughes

O, silver tree!
Oh, shining rivers of the soul!

In a Harlem cabaret
Six long-headed jazzers play.
A dancing girl whose eyes are bold
Lifts high a dress of silken gold.

On, singing tree!
Oh, shining rivers of the soul!

Were Eve's eyes
In the first garden
Just a bit too bold?
Was Cleopatra gorgeous
In a gown of gold?

Oh, shining tree!
Oh, silver rivers of the soul!

In a whirling cabaret
Six long-headed jazzers play.

ALAIN LOCKE
The New Negro
1925

A few months after the Harlem issue of *Survey Graphic* Lock expanded his collection of black art and literature into the book, *The New Negro*, published by Albert & Charles Boni, Inc. This anthology contained most of the contents of the *Survey Graphic* issue plus additional literature, essays, illustrations, including several prints by Harlem Renaissance artist Aaron Douglas. Included here are Rudolph Fisher's Harlem short story "The City of Refuge" and the accompanying illustration "Rebirth," by Aaron Douglas.

"Rebirth" by Aaron Douglas in Alain Locke's *The New Negro* (1925)

"The City Of Refuge"
Rudolph Fisher

I

Confronted suddenly by daylight, King Solomon Gillis stood dazed and blinking. The railroad station, the long, white-walled corridor, the impassible slot-machine, the terrifying subway train—he felt as if he had been caught up in the jaws of a steam-shovel, jammed together with other helpless lumps of dirt, swept blindly along for a time, and at last abruptly dumped.

There had been strange and terrible sounds: "New York! Penn Terminal—all change!" "Pohter, hyer, pohter, suh?" Shuffle of a thousand soles, clatter of a thousand heels, innumerable echoes. Cracking rifle-shots—no, snapping turnstiles. "Put a nickel in!" "Harlem? Sure. This side—next train." Distant thunder, nearing. The screeching onslaught of the fiery hosts of hell, headlong, breath-taking. Car doors rattling, sliding, banging open. "Say, wha' d'ye think this is, a baggage car?" Heat, oppression, suffocation—eternity—"Hundred 'n turdy-fif' next!" More turnstiles. Jonah emerging from the whale.

Clean air, blue sky, bright sunlight.

Gillis set down his tan-cardboard extension-case and wiped his black, shining brow. Then slowly, spreadingly, he grinned at what he saw: Negroes at every turn; up and down Lenox Avenue, up and down One Hundred and Thirty-fifth Street; big, lanky Negroes, short, squat Negroes; black ones, brown ones, yellow ones; men standing idle on the curb, women, bundle-laden, trudging reluctantly homeward, children rattle-trapping about the sidewalks; here and there a white face drifting along, but Negroes predominantly, overwhelmingly everywhere. There was assuredly no doubt of his whereabouts. This was Negro Harlem.

Back in North Carolina Gillis had shot a white man and, with the aid of prayer and an automobile, probably escaped a lynching. Carefully avoiding the railroads, he had reached Washington in safety. For his car a Southwest bootlegger had given him a hundred dollars and directions to Harlem; and so he had come to Harlem.

Ever since a travelling preacher had first told him of the place, King Solomon Gillis had longed to come to Harlem. The Uggams were always talking about it; one of their boys had gone to France in the draft and, returning, had never got any nearer home than Harlem. And there were occasional "colored" newspapers from New York: newspapers that mentioned Negroes without comment, but always spoke of a white person as "So-and-so, white." That was the point. In Harlem, black was white. You had rights that could not be denied you; you had privileges, protected by law. And you had money. Everybody in Harlem had money. It was a land of plenty. Why, had not Mouse Uggam sent back as much as fifty dollars at a time to his people in Waxhaw?

The shooting, therefore, simply catalyzed whatever sluggish mental reaction had been already directing King Solomon's fortunes toward Harlem. The land of plenty was more than that now: it was also the city of refuge.

Casting about for direction, the tall newcomer's glance caught inevitably on the most conspicuous thing in sight, a magnificent figure in blue that stood in the middle of the crossing and blew a whistle and waved great white-gloved hands. The Southern Negro's eyes opened wide; his mouth opened wider. If the inside of New York had mystified him, the outside was amazing him. For there stood a handsome, brass-buttoned giant directing the heaviest traffic Gillis had ever seen; halting unnumbered tons of automobiles and trucks and wagons and pushcarts and street-cars; holding them at bay with one hand while he swept similar tons peremptorily on with the other; ruling the wide crossing with supreme self-assurance; and he, too, was a Negro!

Yet most of the vehicles that leaped or crouched at his bidding carried white passengers. One of these overdrove bounds a few feet and Gillis heard the officer's shrill whistle and gruff reproof, saw the driver's face turn red and his car draw back like a threatened pup. It was beyond belief-impossible. Black might be white, but it couldn't be that white!

"Done died an' woke up in Heaven," thought King Solomon, watching, fascinated; and after a while, as if the wonder of it were too great to believe simply by seeing, "Cullud policemans!" he said, half aloud; then repeated over and over, with greater and greater conviction, "Even got cullud policemans—even got cullud—"

"Where y' want to go, big boy?"

Gillis turned. A little, sharp-faced yellow man was addressing him.

"Saw you was a stranger. Thought maybe I could help y' out."

King Solomon located and gratefully extended a slip of paper. "Wha' dis hyeh at, please, suh?"

The other studied it a moment, pushing back his hat and scratching his head. The hat was a tall-crowned, unindented brown felt; the head was brown patent leather, its glistening brush-back flawless save for a suspicious crimpiness near the clean-grazed edges.

"See that second corner? Turn to the left when you get there. Number forty-five's about halfway the block."

"Thank y', suh."

"You from—Massachusetts?"

"No, suh, Nawth Ca'lina."

"Is 'at so? You look like a Northerner. Be with us long?"

"Till I die," grinned the flattered King Solomon.

"Stoppin' there?"

"Reckon I is. Man in Washin'ton 'lowed I'd find lodgin' at dis ad-dress."

"Good enough. If y' don't, maybe I can fix y' up. Harlem's pretty crowded. This is me." He proffered a card.

"Thank y', suh," said Gillis, and put the card in his pocket.

The little yellow man watched him plod flat-footedly on down the street, long awkward legs never quite straightened, shouldered extension-case bending him sidewise, wonder upon wonder halting or turning him about. Presently, as he proceeded, a pair of bright-green stockings caught and held his attention. Tony, the storekeeper, was crossing the sidewalk with a bushel basket of apples. There was a collision; the apples rolled; Tony exploded; King Solomon apologized. The little yellow man laughed shortly, took out a notebook, and put down the address he had seen on King Solomon's slip of paper.

"Guess you're the shine I been waitin' for," he surmised.

As Gillis, approaching his destination, stopped to rest, a haunting notion grew into an insistent idea. "Dat li'l yaller nigger was a sho' 'nuff gen'man to show me de road. Seem lak I knowed him befo'—" He pondered. That receding brow, that sharp-ridged, spreading nose, that tight upper lip over the two big front teeth, that chinless jaw— He fumbled hurriedly for the card he had not looked at and eagerly made out the name.

"Mouse Uggam, sho' 'nuff! Well, dog-gone!"

II

Uggam sought out Tom Edwards, once a Pullman porter, now prosperous proprietor of a cabaret, and told him:

"Chief, I got him: a baby jess in from the land o' cotton and so dumb he thinks ante-bellum's an old woman."

"Wher'd you find him?"

"Where you find all the jay birds when they first hit Harlem—at the subway entrance. This one come up the stairs, batted his eyes once or twice, an' froze to the spot—with his mouth open. Sure sign he's from 'way down behind the sun an' ripe f' the pluckin'."

Edwards grinned a gold-studded, fat-jowled grin. "Gave him the usual line, I suppose?"

"Didn't miss. An' he fell like a ton o' bricks. 'Course I've got him spotted, but damn' if I know jess how to switch 'em on to him."

"Get him a job around a store somewhere. Make out you're befriendin' him. Get his confidence."

"Sounds good. Ought to be easy. He's from my state. Maybe I know him or some of his people."

"Make out you do, anyhow. Then tell him some fairy tale that'll switch your trade to him. The cops'll follow the trade. We could even let Froggy flop into some dumb white cop's hands and 'confess' where he got it. See?"

"Chief, you got a head, no lie."

"Don't lose no time. And remember, hereafter, it's better to sacrifice a little than to get squealed on. Never refuse a customer. Give him a little credit. Humor him along till you can get rid of him safe. You don't know what that guy that died may have said; you don't know who's on to you now. And if they get you—I don't know you."

"They won't get me," said Uggam.

King Solomon Gillis sat meditating in a room half the size of his hencoop back home, with a single window opening into an airshaft.

An airshaft: cabbage and chitterlings cooking; liver and onions sizzling, sputtering; three player-pianos out-plunking each other; a man and woman calling each other vile things; a sick, neglected baby wailing; a phonograph broadcasting blues; dishes clacking; a girl crying heartbrokenly; waste noises, waste odors of a score of families, seeking issue through a common channel; pollution from bottom to top—a sewer of sounds and smells.

Contemplating this, King Solomon grinned and breathed, "Dog-gone!" A little later, still gazing into the sewer, he grinned again. "Green stockin's," he said; "loud green!" The sewer gradually grew darker. A window lighted up opposite, revealing a woman in camisole and petticoat, arranging her hair. King Solomon, staring vacantly, shook his head and grinned yet again. "Even got cullud policemans!" he mumbled softly.

III

Uggam leaned out of the room's one window and spat maliciously into the dinginess of the airshaft. "Damn glad you got him," he commented, as Gillis finished his story. "They's a thousand shines in Harlem would change places with you in a minute jess f' the honor of killin' a cracker."

"But I didn't go to do it. 'Twas a accident."

"That's the only part to keep secret."

"Know whut dey done? Dey killed five o' Mose Joplin's hawses 'fo he lef'. Put groun' glass in de feed-trough. Sam Cheevers come up on three of 'em one night pizenin' his well. Bleesom beat Crinshaw out o' sixty acres o' lan' an' a year's crops. Dass jess how 'tis. Soon's a nigger make a li'l sump'n he better git to leavin'. An' 'fo long ev'ybody's goin' be lef'!"

"Hope to hell they don't all come here."

The doorbell of the apartment rang. A crescendo of footfalls in the hallway culminated in a sharp rap on Gillis's door. Gillis jumped. Nobody but a policeman would rap like that. Maybe the landlady had been listening and had called in the law. It came again, loud, quick, angry. King Solomon prayed that the policeman would be a Negro.

Uggam stepped over and opened the door. King Solomon's apprehensive eyes saw framed therein, instead of a gigantic officer, calling for him, a little blot of a creature, quite black against even the darkness of the hallway, except for a dirty, wide-striped silk shirt, collarless, with the sleeves rolled up.

"Ah hahve bill fo' Mr. Gillis." A high, strongly accented Jamaican voice, with its characteristic singsong intonation, interrupted King Solomon's sigh of relief.

"Bill? Bill fo' me? What kin' o' bill?"

"Wan bushel appels. T'ree seventy-fife."

"Apples? I ain' bought no apples." He took the paper and read aloud, laboriously, "Antonio Gabrielli to K. S. Gillis, Debtor—"

"Mr. Gabrielli say, you not pays him, he send policeman."

"What I had to do wid 'is apples?"

"You bumps into him yesterday, no? Scatter appels everywhere—on de sidewalk, in de gutter. Kids pick up an' run away. Others all spoil. So you pays."

Gillis appealed to Uggam. "How 'bout it, Mouse?"

"He's a damn liar. Tony picked up most of 'em; I seen him. Lemme look at that bill— Tony never wrote this thing. This baby's jess playin' you for a sucker."

"Ain' had no apples, ain' payin' fo' none," announced King Solomon, thus prompted. "Didn't have to come to Harlem to git cheated. Plenty o' dat right wha' I come fum."

But the West Indian warmly insisted. "You cahn't do daht, mon. Whaht you t'ink, 'ey? Dis mon loose 'is appels an' 'is money too?"

"What diff'ence it make to you, nigger?"

"Who you call nigger, mon? Ah hahve you understahn'—"

"Oh, well, white folks, den. What all you got t' do wid dis hyeh, anyhow?"

"Mr. Gabrielli send me to collect bill!"

"How I know dat?"

"Do Ah not bring bill? You t'ink Ah steal tree dollar, 'ey?"

"Three dollars an' sebenty-fi' cent," corrected Gillis. "'Nuther thing: wha' you ever see me befo'? How you know dis is me?"

"Ah see you, sure. Ah help Mr. Gabrielli in de store. When you knocks down de baskette appels, Ah see. Ah follow you. Ah know you comes in dis house."

"Oh, you does? An' how come you know my name an' flat an' room so good How come dat?"

"Ah fin' out. Sometime Ah brings up here vegetables from de store."

"Humph! Mus' be workin' on shares."

"You pays, 'ey? You pays me or de policemon?"

"Wait a minute," broke in Uggam, who had been thoughtfully contemplating the bill. "Now listen, big shorty. You haul hips on back to Tony. We got your menu all right"—he waved the bill—"but we don't eat your kind o' cookin', see?"

The West Indian flared. "Whaht it is to you, 'ey? You can not mind your own business? Ah hahve not spik to you!"

"No, brother. But this is my friend, an' I'll be john-browned if there's a monkey-chaser in Harlem can gyp him if I know it, see? Bes' thing f' you to do is catch air, toot sweet."

Sensing frustration, the little islander demanded the bill back. Uggam figured he could use the bill himself, maybe. The West Indian hotly persisted; he even menaced. Uggam pocketed the paper and invited him to take it. Wisely enough, the caller preferred to catch air.

When he had gone, King Solomon sought words of thanks.

"Bottle it," said Uggam. "The point is this: I figger you got a job."

"Job? No I ain't! Wha' at?"

"When you show Tony this bill, he'll hit the roof and fire that monk."

"What of he do?"

"Then you up 'n ask f' the job. He'll be too grateful to refuse. I know Tony some, an' I'll be there to put in a good word. See?"

King Solomon considered this. "Sho' needs a job, but ain' after stealin' none."

"Stealin'? 'Twouldn't be stealin'. Stealin's what that damn monkey-chaser tried to do from you. This would be doin' Tony a favor, an' gettin' y'self out o' the barrel. What's the hold-back?"

"What make you keep callin' him monkey-chaser?"

"West Indian. That's another thing. Any time y' can knife a monk, do it. They's too damn many of 'em here. They're an achin' pain."

"Jess de way white folks feels 'bout niggers."

"Damn that. How 'bout it? Y' want the job?"

"Hm—well—I'd ruther be a policeman."

"Policeman?" Uggam gasped.

"M-hm. Dass all I wants to be, a policeman, so I kin police all de white folks right plumb in jail!"

Uggam said seriously, "Well, y' might work up to that. But it takes time. An' y've got to eat while y're waitin'." He paused to let this penetrate. "Now, how 'bout this job at Tony's in the meantime? I should think y'd jump at it."

King Solomon was persuaded.

"Hm—well—reckon I does," he said slowly.

"Now y're tootin'!" Uggam's two big front teeth popped out in a grin of genuine pleasure. "Come on. Let's go."

IV

Spitting blood and crying with rage, the West Indian scrambled to his feet. For a moment he stood in front of the store gesticulating furiously and jabbering shrill threats and unintelligible curses. Then abruptly he stopped and took himself off.

King Solomon Gillis, mildly puzzled, watched him from Tony's doorway. "I jess give him a li'l shove," he said to himself, "an' he roll' clean 'cross de sidewalk." And a little later, disgustedly, "Monkey-chaser!" he grunted, and went back to his sweeping.

"Well, big boy, how y' comin' on?"

Gillis dropped his broom. "Hay-o, Mouse. Wha' you been las' two-three days?"

"Oh, around. Gettin' on all right here? Had any trouble?"

"Deed I ain't—'ceptin' jess now I had to throw 'at li'l jigger out."

"Who? The monk?"

"M-hm. He sho' Lawd doan like me in his job. Look like he think I stole it from him, stiddy him tryin' to steal from me. Had to push him down sho' 'nuff 'fo I could git rid of 'im. Den he run off talkin' Wes' Indi'man an' shakin' his fis' at me."

"Ferget it." Uggam glanced about. "Where's Tony?"

"Boss man? He be back direckly."

"Listen—like to make two or three bucks a day extra?"

"Huh?"

"Two or three dollars a day more'n what you're gettin' already?"

"Ain' I near 'nuff in jail now?"

"Listen." King Solomon listened. Uggam hadn't been in France for nothing. Fact was, in France he'd learned about some valuable French medicine. He'd brought some back with him,—little white pills,—and while in Harlem had found a certain druggist who knew what they were and could supply all he could use. Now there were any number of people who would buy and pay well for as much of this French medicine as Uggam could get. It was good for what ailed them, and they didn't know how to get it except through him. But he had no store in which to set up an agency and hence no single place where his customers could go to get what they wanted. If he had, he could sell three or four times as much as he did.

King Solomon was in a position to help him now, same as he had helped King Solomon. He would leave a dozen packages of the medicine—just small envelopes that could all be carried in a coat pocket—with King Solomon every day. Then he could simply send his customers to King Solomon at Tony's store. They'd make some trifling purchase, slip him a certain coupon which Uggam had given them, and King Solomon would wrap the little envelope of medicine with their purchase. Mustn't let Tony catch on, because he might object, and then the whole scheme would go gaflooey. Of course it wouldn't really be hurting Tony any. Wouldn't it increase the number of his customers?

Finally, at the end of each day, Uggam would meet King Solomon some place and give him a quarter for each coupon he held. There'd be at least ten or twelve a day—two and a half or three dollars plumb extra! Eighteen or twenty dollars a week!

"Dog-gone!" breathed Gillis.

"Does Tony ever leave you heer alone?"

"M-hm. Jess started dis mawnin'. Doan nobody much come round 'tween ten an' twelve, so he done took to doin' his buyin' right 'long 'bout dat time. Nobody hyeh but me fo' 'n hour or so."

"Good. I'll try to get my folks to come 'round here mostly while Tony's out, see?"

"I doan miss."

"Sure y' get the idea, now?" Uggam carefully explained it all again. By the time he had finished, King Solomon was wallowing in gratitude.

"Mouse, you sho' is been a friend to me. Why, 'f 't hadn' been fo' you—"

"Bottle it," said Uggam. "I'll be round to your room tonight with enough stuff for to-morrer, see? Be sure 'n be there."

"Won't be nowha' else."

"An' remember, this is all jess between you 'n me."

"Nobody else but," vowed King Solomon.

Uggam grinned to himself as he went on his way. "Dumb Oscar! Wonder how much can we make before the cops nab him? French medicine—Hmph!"

V

Tony Gabrielli, an oblate Neapolitan of enormous equator, wabbled heavily out of his store and settled himself over a soap box.

Usually Tony enjoyed sitting out front thus in the evening, when his helper had gone home and his trade was slackest. He liked to watch the little Gabriellis playing over the sidewalk with the little Levys and Johnsons; the trios and quartettes of brightly dressed, dark-skinned girls merrily out for a stroll; the slovenly gaited, darker men, who eyed them up and down and commented to each other with an unsuppressed "Hot damn!" or "Oh no, now!"

But to-night Tony was troubled. Something was wrong in the store; something was different since the arrival of King Solomon Gillis. The new man had seemed to prove himself honest and trustworthy, it was true. Tony had tested him, as he always tested a new man, by apparently leaving him alone in charge for two or three mornings. As a matter of fact, the new man was never under more vigilant observation than during these two or three mornings. Tony's store was a modification of the front rooms of his flat and was in direct communication with it by way of a glass-windowed door in the rear. Tony always managed to get back into his flat via the side-street entrance and watch the new man through this unobtrusive glass-windowed door. If anything excited his suspicion, like unwarranted interest in the cash register, he walked unexpectedly out of this door to surprise the offender in the act. Thereafter he would have no more such trouble. But he had not succeeded in seeing King Solomon steal even an apple.

What he had observed, however, was that the number of customers that came into the store during the morning's slack hour had pronouncedly increased in the last few days. Before, there had been three or four. Now there were twelve or fifteen. The mysterious thing about it was that their purchases totalled little more than those of the original three or four.

Yesterday and to-day Tony had elected to be in the store at the time when, on the other days, he had been out. But Gillis had not been overcharging or short-changing; for when Tony waited on the customers himself-strange faces all-he found that they bought something like a yeast cake or a five-cent loaf of bread. It was puzzling. Why should strangers leave their own neighborhoods and repeatedly come to him for a yeast cake or a loaf of bread? They were not new neighbors. New neighbors would have bought more variously and extensively and at different times of day. Living near by, they would have come in, the men often in shirtsleeves and slippers, the women in kimonos, with boudoir caps covering their lumpy heads. They would have sent in strange children for things like yeast cakes and loaves of bread. And why did not some of them come in at night when the new helper was off duty?

As for accosting Gillis on suspicion, Tony was too wise for that. Patronage had a queer way of shifting itself in Harlem. You lost your temper and let slip a single *"nègre."* A week later you sold your business.

Spread over his soap box, with his pudgy hands clasped on his preposterous paunch, Tony sat and wondered. Two men came up, conspicuous for no other reason than that they were white. They displayed extreme nervousness, looking about as if afraid of being seen; and when one of them spoke to Tony it was in a husky, toneless, blowing voice, like the sound of a dirty phonograph record.

"Are you Antonio Gabrielli?"

"Yes, sure," Strange behavior for such lusty-looking fellows. He who had spoken unsmilingly winked first one eye then the other, and indicated by a gesture of his head that they should enter the store. His companion looked cautiously up and down the Avenue, while Tony, wondering what ailed them, rolled to his feet and puffingly led the way.

Inside, the spokesman snuffled, gave his shoulders a queer little hunch, and asked, "Can you fix us up, buddy?" The other glanced restlessly about the place as if he were constantly hearing unaccountable noises.

Tony thought he understood clearly now. "Booze, 'ey?" he smiled. "Sorry—I no got."

"Booze? Hell, no!" The voice dwindled to a throaty whisper. "Dope. Coke, milk, dice—anything. Name your price. Got to have it."

"Dope?" Tony was entirely at a loss. "What's a dis, dope?"

"Aw, lay off, brother. We're in on this. Here." He handed Tony a piece of paper. "Froggy gave us a coupon. Come on. You can't go wrong."

"I no got," insisted the perplexed Tony; nor could he be budged on that point.

Quite suddenly the manner of both men changed. "All right," said the first angrily, in a voice as robust as his body. "All right, you're clever, You no got. Well, you will get. You'll get twenty years!"

"Twenty year? Whadda you talk?"

"Wait a minute, Mac," said the second caller. "Maybe the wop's on the level. Look here, Tony, we're officers, see? Policemen." He produced a badge. "A couple of weeks ago a guy was brought in dying for the want of a shot, see? Dope—he needed some dope—like this—in his arm. See? Well, we tried to make him tell us where he'd been getting it, but he was too weak. He croaked next day. Evidently he hadn't had money enough to buy any more.

"Well, this morning a little nigger that goes by the name of Froggy was brought into the precinct pretty well doped up. When he finally came to, he swore he got the stuff here at your store. Of course, we've just been trying to trick you into giving yourself away, but you don't bite. Now what's your game? Know anything about this?"

Tony understood. "I dunno," he said slowly; and then his own problem, whose contemplation his callers had interrupted, occurred to him. "Sure!" he exclaimed. "Wait. Maybeso, I know somet'ing."

"All right. Spill it."

"I got a new man, work-a for me." And he told them what he had noted since King Solomon Gillis came.

"Sounds interesting. Where is this guy?"

"Here in da store—all day."

"Be here to-morrow?"

"Sure. All day."

"All right. We'll drop in to-morrow and give him the eye. Maybe he"s our man."

"Sure. Come ten o'clock. I show you," promised Tony.

VI

Even the oldest and rattiest cabarets in Harlem have sense of shame enough to hide themselves under the ground—for instance, Edwards's. To get into Edwards's you casually enter a dimly lighted corner saloon, apparently—only apparently—a subdued memory of brighter days. What was once the family entrance is now a side entrance for ladies. Supporting yourself against close walls, you crouchingly descend a narrow, twisted staircase until, with a final turn, you find yourself in a glaring, long, low basement. In a moment your eyes become accustomed to the haze of tobacco smoke. You see men and women seated at wire-legged, white-topped tables, which are covered with half-empty bottles and glasses; you trace the slow-jazz accompaniment you heard as you came down the stairs to a pianist, a cornetist, and a drummer on a little platform at the far end of the room. There is a cleared space from the foot of the stairs, where you are standing, to the platform where this orchestra is mounted, and in it a tall brown girl is swaying from side to side and rhythmically proclaiming that she has the world in a jug and the stopper in her hand. Behind a counter at your left sits a fat, bald, tea-colored Negro, and you wonder if this is Edwards—Edwards, who stands in with the police, with the political bosses, with the importers of wines and worse. A white-vested waiter hustles you to a seat and takes your order. The song's tempo changes to a quicker; the drum and the cornet rip out a fanfare, almost drowning the piano; the girl catches up her dress and begins to dance. . .

Gillis's wondering eyes had been roaming about. They stopped.

"Look, Mouse," he whispered. "Look a-yonder!"

"Look at what?"

"Dog-gone if it ain' de self-same gal!"

"Wha' d'ye mean, self-same girl?"

"Over yonder, wi' de green stockin's. Dass de gal made me knock over dem apples fust day I come to town. 'Member? Been wishin' I could see her ev'y sence."

"What for?" Uggam wondered.

King Solomon grew confidential. "Ain' but two things in dis world, Mouse, I really wants. One is to be a policeman. Been wantin' dat ev'y sence I seen dat cullud traffic-cop dat day. Other is to git myself a gal lak dat one over yonder!"

"You'll do it," laughed Uggam, "if you live long enough."

"Who dat wid her?"

"How'n hell do I know?"

"He cullud?"

"Don't look like it. Why? What of it?"

"Hm—nuthin'—"

"How many coupons y' got to-night?"

"Ten." King Solomon handed them over.

"Y'ought to 've slipt 'em to me under the table, but it's all right now, long as we got this table to ourselves. Here's y' medicine for to-morrer."

"Wha'?"

"Reach under the table."

Gillis secured and pocketed the medicine.

"An' here's two-fifty for a good day's work." Uggam passed the money over. Perhaps he grew careless; certainly the passing this time was above the table, in plain sight.

"Thanks, Mouse."

Two white men had been watching Gillis and Uggam from a table near by. In the tumult of merriment that rewarded the entertainer's most recent and daring effort, one of these men, with a word to the other, came over and took the vacant chair beside Gillis.

"Is your name Gillis?"

"'Tain' nuthin' else."

Uggam's eyes narrowed.

The white man showed King Solomon a police officer's badge.

"You're wanted for dope-peddling. Will you come along without trouble?"

"Fo' what?"

"Violation of the narcotic law—dope-selling."

"Who—me?"

"Come on, now, lay off that stuff. I saw what happened just now myself." He addressed Uggam. "Do you know this fellow?"

"Nope. Never saw him before to-night."

"Didn't I just see him sell you something?"

"Guess you did. We happened to be sittin' here at the same table and got to talkin'. After a while I says I can't seem to sleep nights, so he offers me sump'n he says'll make me sleep, all right. I don't know what it is, but he says he uses it himself an' I offers to pay him what it cost him. That's how I come to take it. Guess he's got more in his pocket there now."

The detective reached deftly into the coat pocket of the dumfounded King Solomon and withdrew a packet of envelopes. He tore off a corner of one, emptied a half-dozen tiny white tablets into his palm, and sneered triumphantly. "You'll make a good witness," he told Uggam.

The entertainer was issuing an ultimatum to all sweet mammas who dared to monkey round her loving man. Her audience was absorbed and delighted, with the exception of one couple—the girl with the green stockings and her escort. They sat directly in the line of vision of King Solomon's wide eyes, which, in the calamity that had descended upon him, for the moment saw nothing.

"Are you coming without trouble?"

Mouse Uggam, his friend. Harlem. Land of plenty. City of refuge—city of refuge. If you live long enough—

Consciousness of what was happening between the pair across the room suddenly broke through Gillis's daze like flame through smoke. The man was trying to kiss the girl and she was resisting. Gillis jumped up. The detective, taking the act for an attempt at escape, jumped with him and was quick enough to intercept him. The second officer came at once to his fellow's aid, blowing his whistle several times as he came.

People overturned chairs getting out of the way, but nobody ran for the door. It was an old crowd. A fight was a treat; and the tall Negro could fight.

"Judas Priest!"

"Did you see that?"

"Damn!"

White—both white. Five of Mose Joplin's horses. Poisoning a well. A year's crops. Green stockings—white—white—

"That's the time, papa!"

"Do it, big boy!"

"Good night!"

Uggam watched tensely, with one eye on the door. The second cop had blown for help—

Downing one of the detectives a third time and turning to grapple again with the other, Gillis found himself face to face with a uniformed black policeman.

He stopped as if stunned. For a moment he simply stared. Into his mind swept his own words like a forgotten song, suddenly recalled:

"Cullud policemans!"

The officer stood ready, awaiting his rush. "Even—got—cullud—policemans—"

Very slowly King Solomon's arms relaxed; very slowly he stood erect; and the grin that came over his features had something exultant about it.

THE *OPPORTUNITY* LITERARY CONTEST

In their effort to promote and support literary and artistic creativity a number of African American individuals and institutions organized and funded annual prizes. Among these was the Opportunity Literary Contest instituted by the Urban League and its monthly journal, *Opportunity*. The first contest was announced in September 1924; the awards were published in the May 1925 issue, along with the work of the prizewinners. Prizewinners in this first contest included three of the most significant young African American writers: poets Langston Hughes and Countee Cullen, and short story writer Zora Neale Hurston. While they did not sweep all of the prizes, their work made a very impressive showing. The selections here include the initial announcement of the first Opportunity Literary Contest, the announcement of the prizewinners, and the winning poems of Hughes and Cullen as well as Hurston's short story. Most notably, the first prize in poetry went to "The Weary Blues," Hughes's signature poem noted for its application to literature of the style and texture of the blues.

"An Opportunity for Negro Writers"
Opportunity
September 1924

A new period in creative expression among Negroes is foreshadowed in the notable, even if fugitive and disconnected successes of certain of the generation of Negro writers now emerging. The body of experience and public opinion seem ripe for the development of some new and perhaps distinctive contribution to art, literature, and life. But these contributions demand incentives. The random and obviously inadequate methods of casual inquiry have already disclosed an unexpected amount and degree of writing ability among Negroes which gives promise of further development on a large scale. The ability of these scattered writers has become known largely by the accident of locality. There are undoubtedly others to be discovered. The question of markets has been an agent of inertia in this regard. Even for those of acknowledged competence an almost insuperable discouragement has been the unpopularity of those themes with which Negro writers have been most familiar. This is changing now. The judgment of some of the foremost students of American literature offers encouragement for the future of imaginative writing by Negroes.

There is an extreme usefulness for the cause of inter-racial good-will as well as racial culture and American literature in interpreting the life and longings and emotional experiences of the Negro people to their shrinking and spiritually alien neighbors; of flushing old festers of hate and disgruntlement by becoming triumphantly articulate; of forcing the interest and kindred feeling of the rest of the world by sheer force of the humanness and beauty of one's own story. The old romantic Negro characters of fiction are admittedly *passe*. Negroes have been swept along, even if at the rear of the procession, with the forward movement of the rest of the world. There is an opportunity now for Negroes themselves to replace their out-worn representations in fiction faithfully and incidentally to make themselves better understood.

The purpose, then, of OPPORTUNITY'S literary contest can thus be stated in brief: It hopes to stimulate and encourage creative literary effort among Negroes; to locate and orient Negro writers of ability; to stimulate and encourage interest in the serious development of a body of literature about Negro life, drawing deeply upon these tremendously rich sources; to encourage the reading of literature both by Negro authors and about Negro life, not merely because they are Negro authors but because what they write is literature and because the literature is interesting; to foster a market for Negro writers and for literature by and about Negroes; to bring these writers into contact with the general world of letters to which they have been for the most part timid and inarticulate strangers; to stimulate and foster a type of writing by Negroes which shakes itself free of deliberate propaganda and protest.

"Contest Awards"
Opportunity
May 1925

The winning manuscripts selected from 732 entries in the five divisions of OP-PORTUNITY'S Literary Contest, as announced at the special meeting in New York City on the evening of May 1st, are given below:

The Short Story

First Prize of $100.00 to FOG, by John Matheus, of Institute, West Virginia.

Second Prize of $35.00 to SPUNK, by Zora Neale Hurston, of Jacksonville, Florida.

Third Prize of $15.00 to THE VOODOO'S REVENGE, by Eric D. Walrond, of New York City.

Poetry

First Prize of $40.00 to THE WEARY BLUES, by Langston Hughes, of Washington, D C

Second Prize of $15.00 TO ONE WHO SAID ME *NAY*, by Countee Cullen, of New York City.

Third Place. For the third place there was a tie between the winners of the first and second prizes: A SONG OF SOUR GRAPES, by Countee Cullen, and AMERICA, by Langston Hughes, receiving the same number of votes. The judges decided to award the honor to both and the cash prize to the two contestants receiving Fourth Place.

Cash Price of $5.00 to SOLACE, by Clarissa Scott, of Washington, D. C.

Cash Prize of $5.00 to THE WAYSIDE WELL, by Joseph S. Cotter, of Louisville, Kentucky.

"The Weary Blues"
By Langston Hughes
Awarded First Prize

Droning a drowsy syncopated tune,
Rocking back and forth to a mellow croon,
I heard a Negro play.
Down on Lenox Avenue the other night
By the pale dull pallor of an old gas light
He did a lazy sway . . .
He did a lazy sway . . .
To the tune o' those Weary Blues.
With his ebony hands on each ivory key
He made that poor piano moan with melody.
O Blues!
Swaying to and fro on his rickety stool

He played that sad raggy tune like a musical fool.
Sweet Blues!
Coming from a black man's soul.
O Blues!
In a deep song voice with a melancholy tone
I heard that Negro sing, that old piano moan—
"Ain't got nobody in all this world,
Ain't got nobody but ma self.
I's gwine to quit ma frownin'
And put ma troubles on the shelf."
Thump, thump, thump, went his foot on the floor.
He played a few chords then sang some more—
"I got the Weary Blues
And I can't be satisfied.
Got the Weary Blues
And can't be satisfied—
I ain't happy no mo'
And I wish that I had died."
And far into the night he crooned that tune.
The stars went out and so did the moon.
The singer stopped playing and went to bed
While the Weary Blues echoed through his head.
He slept like a rock or a man that's dead.

"To One Who Said Me Nay"
By Countee Cullen
Awarded Second Prize

This much the gods vouchsafe today:
That we two lie in the clover,
Watching the heavens dip and sway,
With galleons sailing over.

This much is granted for an hour:
That we are young and tender,
That I am bee and you are flower,
Honey-mouthed and swaying slender.

This sweet of sweets is ours now:
To wander through the land,
Plucking an apple from its bough
To toss from hand to hand.

No thing is certain, joy nor sorrow,
Except the hour we know it;
Oh, wear my heart today; tomorrow
Who knows where the winds will blow it?

"Spunk"
By Zora Neale Hurston
Awarded Second Prize

A giant of a brown skinned man sauntered up the one street of the Village and out into the palmetto thickets with a small pretty woman clinging lovingly to his arm.

"Looka theah, folkses!" cried Elijah Mosley, slapping his leg gleefully. "Theah they go, big as life an' brassy as tacks."

All the loungers in the store tried to walk to the door with an air of nonchalance but with small success.

"Now pee-eople!" Walter Thomas gasped, "Will you look at 'em!"

"But that's one thing Ah likes about Spunk Banks—he ain't skeered of nothin' on God's green footstool—*nothin'!* He rides that log down at saw-mill jus' like he struts 'round wid another man's wife—jus' don't give a kitty. When Tes' Miller got cut to giblets on that circle-saw, Spunk steps right up and starts ridin'. The rest of us was skeered to go near it."

A round shouldered figure in overalls much too large, came nervously in the door and the talking ceased. The men looked at each other and winked.

"Gimme some soda-water. Sass'prilla Ah reckon," the new-comer ordered, and stood far down the counter near the open pickled pig-feet tub to drink it.

Elijah nudged Walter and turned with mock gravity to the newcomer.

"Say Joe, how's everything up yo' way? How's yo' wife?"

Joe started and all but dropped the bottle he held in his hands. He swallowed several times painfully and his lips trembled.

"Aw 'Lige, you oughtn't to do nothin' like that," Walter grumbled. Elijah ignored him.

"She jus' passed heah a few minutes ago goin' thata way," with a wave of his hand in the direction of the woods.

Now Joe knew his wife had passed that way. He knew that the men lounging in the general store had seen her, moreover, he knew that the men knew he knew. He stood there silent for a long moment staring blankly, with his Adam's apple twitching nervously up and down his throat. One could actually see the pain he was suffering, his eyes, his face, his hands and even the dejected slump of his shoulders. He set the bottle down upon the counter. He didn't bang it, just eased it out of his hand silently and fiddled with his suspender buckle.

"Well, Ah'm goin' after her today. Ah'm goin' an' fetch her back. Spunk's done gone too fur."

He reached deep down into his trouser pocket and drew out a hollow ground razor, large and shiny, and passed his moistened thumb back and forth over the edge.

"Talkin' like a man, Joe. Course that's yo' fambly affairs, but Ah like to see grit in anybody."

Joe Kanty laid down a nickel and stumbled out into the street.

Dusk crept in from the woods. Ike Clarke lit the swinging oil lamp that was almost immediately surrounded by candle-flies. The men laughed boisterously behind Joe's back as they watched him shamble woodward.

"You oughtn't to said whut you did to him, Lige—look how it worked him up," Walter chided.

"And Ah hope it did work him up. Tain't even decent for a man to take and take like he do."

"Spunk will sho' kill him."

"Aw, Ah doan't know. You never kin tell. He might turn him up an' spank him fur gettin' in the way, but Spunk wouldn't shoot no unarmed man. Dat razor he carried outa heah ain't gonna run Spunk down an' cut him, an' Joe ain't got the nerve to go up to Spunk with it knowing he totes that Army 45. He makes that break outa heah to bluff us. He's gonna hide that razor behind the first likely palmetto root an' sneak back home to bed. Don't tell me nothin' 'bout that rabbit-foot colored man. Didn't he meet Spunk an' Lena face to face one day las' week an' mumble sumthin' to Spunk 'bout lettin' his wife alone?"

"What did Spunk say?" Walter broke in—"Ah like him fine but taint right the way he carries on wid Lena Kanty, jus' cause Joe's timid 'bout fightin.'"

"You wrong theah, Walter. 'Tain't cause Joe's timid at all, it's cause Spunk wants Lena. If Joe was a passle of wile cats Spunk would tackle the job just the same. He'd go after *anything* he wanted the same way. As Ah wuz sayin' a minute ago, he tole Joe right to his face that Lena was his. 'Call her,' he says to Joe. 'Call her and see if she'll come. A woman knows her boss an' she answers when he calls.' 'Lena, ain't I yo' husband?' Joe sorter whines out. Lena looked at him real disgusted but she don't answer and she don't move outa her tracks. Then Spunk reaches out an' takes hold of her arm an' says: 'Lena, youse mine. From now on Ah works for you an' fights for you an' Ah never wants you to look to nobody for a crumb of bread, a stitch of close or a shingle to go over yo' head, but me long as Ah live. Ah'll git the lumber foh owah house tomorrow. Go home an' git yo' things together!'"

"'Thass mah house' Lena speaks up. 'Papa gimme that.'

"Well," says Spunk, "doan give up whut's yours, but when youse inside don't forgit youse mine, an' let no other man git outa his place wid you!"

"Lena looked up at him with her eyes so full of love that they wuz runnin' over an' Spunk seen it an' Joe seen it too, and his lip started to tremblin' and his Adam's apple was galloping up and down his neck like a race horse. Ah bet he's wore out half a dozen Adam's apples since Spunk's been on the job with Lena. That's all he'll do. He'll be back heah after while swallowin' an' workin' his lips like he wants to say somethin' an' can't."

"But didn't he do nothin' to stop 'em?"

"Nope, not a frazzlin' thing—jus' stood there. Spunk took Lena's arm and walked off jus' like nothin' ain't happened and he stood there gazin' after them till they was outa sight. Now you know a woman don't want no man like that. I'm jus' waitin' to see whut he's goin' to say when he gits back."

II

But Joe Kanty never came back, never. The men in the store heard the sharp report of a pistol somewhere distant in the palmetto thicket and soon Spunk came walking leisurely, with his big black Stetson set at the same rakish angle and Lena clinging to his arm, came walking right into the general store. Lena wept in a frightened manner.

"Well," Spunk announced calmly, "Joe come out there wid a meatax an' made me kill him."

He sent Lena home and led the men back to Joe—Joe crumple and limp with his right hand still clutching his razor.

"See mah back? Mah closs cut clear through. He sneaked up an' tried to kill me from the back, but Ah got him, an' got him good, first shot," Spunk said.

The men glared at Elijah, accusingly.

"Take him up an' plant him in 'Stoney lonesome'," Spunk said in a careless voice. "Ah didn't wanna shoot him but he made me do it. He's a dirty coward, jumpin' on a man from behind."

Spunk turned on his heel and sauntered away to where he knew his love wept in fear for him and no man stopped him. At the general store later on, they all talked of locking him up until the sheriff should come from Orlando, but no one did anything but talk.

A clear case of self-defense, the trial was a short one, and Spunk walked out of the court house to freedom again. He could work again, ride the dangerous log-carriage that fed the singing, snarling, biting, circle-saw; he could stroll the soft dark lanes with his guitar. He was free to roam the woods again; he was free to return to Lena. He did all of these things.

III

"What you reckon, Walt?" Elijah asked one night later. "Spunk's gittin' ready to marry Lena!"

"Naw! Why Joe ain't had time to git cold yit. Nohow Ah didn't figger Spunk was the marryin' kind."

"Well, he is," rejoined Elijah. "He done moved most of Lena's things—and her along wid 'em—over to the Bradley house. He's buying it. Jus' like Ah told yo' all right in heah the night Joe wuz kilt. Spunk's crazy 'bout Lena. He don't want folks to keep on talkin' 'bout her-thass reason he's rushin' so. Funny thing 'bout that bobcat, want it?"

Whut bob-cat, 'Lige? Ah ain't heared 'bout none."

"Ain't cher? Well, night befo' las' was the fust night Spunk an' Lena moved together an' jus' as they was goin' to bed, a big black bob-cat, black all over, you hear me, *black,* walked round and round that house and howled like forty, an' when Spunk got his gun an' went to the winder to shoot it, he says it stood right still an' looked him in the eye, an' howled right at him. The thing got Spunk so ner-voused up he couldn't shoot. But Spunk says twan't no bob-cat nohow. He says it was Joe done sneaked back from Hell!"

"Humph!" sniffed Walter, "he oughter be nervous after what he done. Ah reckon Joe come back to dare him to marry Lena, or to come out an' fight. Ah bet he'll be back time and agin, too. Know what Ah think? Joe wuz a braver man than Spunk."

There was a general shout of derision from the group.

"Thass a fact," went on Walter. "Lookit whut he done; took a razor an' went out to fight a man he knowed toted a gun an' wuz a crack shot, too; 'nother thing Joe wuz skeered of Spunk, skeered plumb stiff! But he went jes' the same. It took him a long time to get his nerve up. 'Tain't nothin' for Spunk to fight when he ain't skeered of nothin'. Now, Joe's done come back to have it out wid the man that's got all he ever had. Y'll know Joe ain't never had nothin' nor wanted nothin' besides Lena. It musta been a h'ant cause ain' nobody never seen no black bobcat."

"'Nother thing," cut in one of the men, "Spunk waz cussin' a blue streak today 'cause he 'lowed dat saw wuz wobblin'—almos' got 'im once. The machinist come, looked it over an' said it wuz alright. Spunk musta been leanin' t'wards it some. Den he claimed somebody pushed 'im but 'twant nobody close to 'im. Ah wuz glad when knockin' off time come. I'm skeered of dat man when he gits hot. He'd beat you full of button holes as quick as he's look atcher."

IV

The men gathered the next evening in a different mood, no laughter. No badinage this time.

"Look Lige, you goin' to set up wid Spunk?"

"Naw, Ah reckon not, Walter. Tell yuh the truth, Ah'm a lil bit skittish. Spunk died too wicket—died cussin' he did. You know he thought he wuz done outa life."

"Good Lawd, who'd he think done it?"

"Joe."

"Joe Kanty? How come?"

"Walter, Ah b'leeve Ah will walk up thata way an' set. Lena would like it Ah reckon."

But whut did he say, Lige?"

Elijah did not answer' until they had left the lighted store and were strolling down the dark street.

"Ah wuz loadin' a wagon wid scantlin' right near the saw when Spunk fell on the carriage but 'fore Ah could git to him the saw got him in the body—awful sight. Me an' Skint Miller got him off but it was too late. Anybody could see that. The fust thing he said wuz: 'He pushed me, Lige—the dirty hound pushed me in the back!'—He was spittin' blood at ev'ry breath. We laid him on the sawdust pile with his face to the East so's he could die easy. He helt mah han' till the last, Walter, and said: 'It was Joe, 'Lige—the dirty sneak shoved me . . . he didn't dare come to mah face . . . but Ah'll git the son-of-a-wood louse soon's Ah get there an' make hell too hot for him. . . . Ah felt him shove me. . . . !' Thass how he died."

If spirits kin fight, there's a powerful tussle goin' on somewhere ovah Jordan 'cause Ah b'leeve Joe's ready for Spunk an' ain't skeered anymore—yas, Ah b'leeve Joe pushed 'im mahself."

They had arrived at the house. Lena's lamentations were deep and loud. She had filled the room with magnolia blossoms that gave off a heavy sweet odor. The keepers of the wake tipped about whispering in frightened tones. Everyone in the Village was there, even old Jeff Kanty, Joe's father, who a few hours before would have been afraid to come within ten feet of him, stood leering triumphantly down upon the fallen giant as if his fingers had been the teeth of steel that laid him low.

The cooling board consisted of three sixteen-inch boards on saw horses, a dingy sheet was his shroud. The women ate heartily of the funeral baked meats and wondered who would be Lena's next. The men whispered coarse conjectures between guzzles of whiskey.

Advertising Art for Carl Van Vechten's *Nigger Heaven* by Aaron Douglas

CARL VAN VECHTEN
Nigger Heaven
1926

Nigger Heaven, one of the most important and infamous novels of the Harlem Renaissance was the work of a white artist— Carl Van Vechten, the white novelist, photographer, and promoter of black literature. Van Vechten was accused of creating the white appetite for exposés of the seamy underside of Harlem life and redirecting much of the Renaissance in this direction. Certainly the popular success and the controversy surrounding *Nigger Heaven* contributed to the demand for black writing, but as the chapter below indicates, Van Vechten did not focus exclusively on the lower elements of Harlem life. The title also generated criticism. "Nigger heaven," was Harlem slang for the segregated balconies of New York theaters; Van Vechten applied the phrase satirically to Harlem itself, the segregated district situated "above" white Manhattan. Chapter Two presents a picture of Harlem's young, middle class, intellectual community that most critics thought Van Vechten ignored.

Two

With Olive Hamilton, who worked as a responsible secretary-stenographer for a white lawyer on Wall Street—Olive herself was seven-eighths white—Mary occupied an apartment on the sixth storey of a building on Edgecombe Avenue, that pleasant thoroughfare facing the rocky cliff surmounted by City College. Neither of the girls earned very much money, but their salaries were supplemented by occasional welcome cheques from their families which made it possible for them to live comfortably, especially as Olive was an excellent cook. Mary could fry an egg and boil coffee, but here her culinary capacities ended.

Each of the girls had her own bedroom; the use of the sitting-room they shared. The sitting-room, though small, was pleasant. The furniture included an upholstered couch, several easy chairs, a desk, a table with an electric lamp, and a phonograph. Blue-flowered chintz curtains hung at the window. The walls were brightened by framed reproductions of paintings by Bellini and Carpaccio which Mary had collected during a journey through Italy.

Olive's personal taste inclined to the luxurious. Her dressing-table was hung in lace over pink satin and her bed was covered with a spread of the same materials. On the dressing-table was laid out a toilet-set of carved ivory, an extravagance which had cost her a great deal of economy in other directions. A bottle of Narcisse Noir stood near the toilet-set. Framed, on a table, and on the walls, were many photographs of friends. A French worsted doll lay dejected in one corner.

Mary's taste was more sober. There was only one picture in her room, a reproduction of the Monna Lisa. Her bed-cover was plain white; her dressing-table austere and generally devoid of articles, save for inexpensive brush, comb, and mirror. On the shelves of a bookcase were ranged volumes by James Branch Cabell, Anatole France, Jean Cocteau, Louis Bromfield, Aldous Huxley, Sherwood Anderson, Somerset Maugham, Edmond Gosse, Elinor Wylie, James Huneker, and others. Several Negro writers were represented by inscribed copies: Charles W. Chesnutt by The Conjure Woman, James Weldon Johnson by Fifty Years, Jean Toomer by Cane, Claude McKay by Harlem Shadows, W. E. B. Du Bois by The Souls of Black Folk, Walter White by The Fire in the Flint, Jessie Fauset by There is Confusion. In addition, on her writing-table stood a photograph of her father, in a silver frame, and usually a row of a dozen or so of the latest books which she had borne home from

the library in an effort to keep abreast with the best of the modern output, an altruistic endeavour which enabled her to offer her patrons advice when they were in doubt, as so often she found they were.

Mary's life was simple but full: she found she had very little time to spare. Six days a week, and one evening, she worked in the library. Leaving the library usually in the afternoon around five, she often went to the Park for a walk. Then she came home, changed her dress, and read or mended her clothes while Olive cooked dinner. In the evening, frequently there would be callers: the girls knew all the young men and women in the Harlem literary circles, most of the young school-teachers, doctors, lawyers, and dentists. To some extent they mingled with, but did not entertain, the richer social set that lived in the splendid row of houses Stanford White had designed on One hundred and thirty-ninth Street, or in other pleasant localities. These people occasionally invited Mary or Olive to large dinner- or bridge-parties. The girls also encountered them at dances. It had become, Olive observed cynically to Mary, quite the thing for these more affluent folk to take up with the young intellectuals since their work had begun to appear in the Atlantic Monthly, Vanity Fair, the American Mercury, and the New Republic. The young intellectuals accepted these hitherto unfamiliar attentions without undue humility, at the same time laughing a good deal about them among themselves. Times had changed indeed when brains, rather than money, a lighter colour, or straight hair, was the password to social favour. The limits of the Blue Vein Circle were being extended.

The girls took in most of the good plays and musical entertainments, revues and song recitals alike, downtown, usually sitting in the balcony to save expense, although Olive was light enough and Mary's features were sufficiently Latin so that they were not rudely received when they asked at the box-office for places in the orchestra. Once or twice, however, when they had been escorted to the theatre by some man of darker colour, they had been caused some humiliation and embarrassment. On one such occasion, after the usher had seated them, the house-manager had descended the aisle to demand a view of their stubs. On examination, he informed them that a mistake had been made, assuring them that their seats were for another night. He refused, moreover, to relinquish the stubs and escorted them to the lobby where he stated that he would willingly exchange them for balcony tickets, as the orchestra for this particular evening had been sold out. The lesson was learned. Thereafter Olive always took charge of the stubs and, if a view of them were requested, held them up so that the figures might be deciphered, but refused to permit them to leave her fingers.

Occasionally, caught in the lower part of town at an inconvenient hour, the question arose as to where one might eat. Olive alone was white enough to be spared any anxiety on this count, and even Mary, accompanied by Olive, succeeded in passing, but when their companion had unmistakably African features, difficulties arose. Once, indeed, when their escort had been a very black Negro of international reputation they had been ejected from a hotel dining-room. The head-waiter who was acquainted with Olive and was quite aware that she had Negro blood, explained that he himself had no objection to serving coloured people, but that X—was so undeniably black that the patrons of the restaurant might object to his proximity. The taboo, it appeared, was solely one of colour, and there were, it sometimes occurred to Mary, the highest advantages, both social and economic, in being near white or yellow, or, if dark, possessed of Spanish features and glib enough with words in some foreign tongue to convince the waiter that one belonged to a dark European race, but, unfortunately, as Olive knew well to her cost—she had once been insulted by a policeman because a black man had accompanied her to a Negro restaurant—in certain public places in Harlem the reverse difficulty arose.

With one young man in particular, Howard Allison, the girls were accustomed to discuss these and allied problems which touched their very existence. Allison's father had been born a slave. He was nine years old when he was freed. Later he had become an itinerant preacher. By scrimping, his family had managed to send Howard to Harvard, and afterwards to Columbia Law School. He had just begun to practise his profession; as yet he was quite destitute of clients. Handsome and tall, dark brown in colour, he had personal reasons for being seriously interested in the perplexing phases of the Negro problem.

One night he came in after dinner—Olive, expecting him, had prepared a large pot of coffee—with Richard Fort Sill, a young man who was so white that, like Olive, below the line he was never taken for a Negro.

They became expansive over the coffee and cigarettes.

Of course, Howard was saying, it isn't so bad for us as it was for those who came before. We at least have Harlem.

Sill began to snicker. The Mecca of the New Negro! The City of Refuge! he cried derisively.

I don't know that we even have Harlem, Olive argued, so many white people come up here now to the cabarets. Why, in one or two places they've actually tried to do a little jim crowing!

Think of it! Howard replied. It isn't, he went on, that we want to mingle with the whites—I mean that we don't want to much more than we are already compelled to—but it is a bore to have them all over our places while we are excluded from their theatres and restaurants merely on account of our colour, theatres and restaurants which admit Chinese and Hindus—if I wore a turban or a burnous I could go anywhere—and prostitutes of any nationality. Why, a white prostitute can go places where a coloured preacher would be refused admittance.

True enough, Counsellor, Sill drawled. There's no social line drawn in jail anyway. Probably Marcus Garvey is treated just as well as his fellow convicts. . . . He was lounging in a chair with his hand hanging so far over one arm that his cigarette almost singed the rug. . . . It all comes down, he went on, to that question the ofays are always asking each other: would you like your sister to marry a Negro? You must realize, my dear coloured brethren, that social equality means a mingling of the sexes of the two races. Sill's tone was tinged with a bitter irony.

Well, Howard laughed, the buckras should have thought of that earlier, before you were born, Dick. How did you get as white as you are?

The Southern explanation is that Sherman marched to the sea.

They all laughed.

He must have had a considerable and very vital army, was Olive's comment. You know as well as I do that practically every other ofay in the South has a coloured half-brother and you know how many successful intermarriages there have been, especially in the West Indies. It strikes me as particularly amusing what they have to say, these ofays, about the geniuses of our race. Oh yes, they admit that Pushkin was a genius, that Dumas was a genius, but it was because they had white blood! Apparently miscegenation is a very fine thing indeed after it has happened, but for God's sake don't let it happen!

You know very well, Mary inserted, as she set down her empty cup, that the best people of our race object to mixed marriages more strenuously than the whites do. I believe if the social barriers were let down there would be fewer of them than there are now.

And if the barriers were let down, another great factor would be eliminated, Howard asserted, the present advantage of being as near white as possible. Why, the white Negro—you , Dick, or Olive—can go anywhere, to any hotel or theatre, without being challenged. You know the number of us that have gone even farther than that.

Buda Green is passing, Olive put in. I met her on Fifth Avenue last Sunday. She was with a white man and she tipped me a wink. Later, she called me up and told me all about it. You can't blame her. I couldn't do it, though. No matter what happens, I stick to my race.

Mary noted that a more intense expression had come into Dick Sill's face.

You say that, he said, but I wonder how much you mean. Think how much easier it is to get jobs if you don't acknowledge your race. Why, even in the Negro theatre they won't engage dark girls. In *their* world, the white world, they won't even give you a look-in at anything good if you're not somewhere near their colour. Ollie, do you think for one moment you'd be engaged as a private secretary if you were black? You know you wouldn't. And the same thing is true of me. Well, I've thought it all out and I'm going to pass!

Dick! The trio cried out simultaneously.

Yes, he went on defiantly. Not today or tomorrow perhaps, but sooner or later I'm going to pass, go over the line, and marry a white woman. It serves them jolly well right for forcing us to. I'd like to start a movement for all us near whites to pass. In a short time there wouldn't be any Negro problem. There wouldn't even be any Negroes.

Well, a good many have preceded you, Howard said. I've heard there are about eight thousand in New York alone.

I couldn't do it, Olive asserted. I just couldn't do it. Somehow I feel my race.

What race? cried Dick. What race do you feel? If you lived in Brazil and had one drop of white blood you'd be considered white. Here the reverse is true. What's the coloured race ever done for you? Dick, now thoroughly worked up, demanded. What?

Well, they haven't done anything particularly for or against me, but somehow in spirit I belong to them. I know that. I don't *feel* white. What you do is your business, just as it's Buda's business. I just couldn't do it myself, that's all.

Mary was conciliatory. We go round and round like squirrels in a cage and we never get anywhere, she said. Is there any solution? Sometimes I like to think there is, and sometimes I don't really care. Do you know, when we keep away from this subject, we have so much pleasure among ourselves that I sometimes think it isn't very important . . . she hesitated . . . if a thoughtless white person occasionally is rude. You can laugh all you like, Dick, but Harlem is a sort of Mecca. In some ways it's even an advantage to be coloured. Certainly on the stage it's no handicap. It's almost an asset. And now the white editors are beginning to regard Negroes as interesting novelties, like white elephants or black roses. They'll print practically anything our coloured writers send in. . . .

That won't last. Dick interrupted her fiercely. The time is coming and soon enough, at that, when the Negro artist will have to compete with the white artist on an equal plane if he expects to make any impression. I think the ofays must begetting tired of saying "Pretty good for a Nigger."

Howard had been meditating. I believe, he said at last, a trifle sententiously, Mary thought, that there is a solution for what is called the race problem. . . . The others all stared at him. . . . You know old Booker T was all for conciliation; then Du Bois came along and was all for an aggressive policy. Now neither of these methods worked for a very simple reason, because fundamentally, and generally speaking, the white race is not vitally interested in the Negro problem. In the mass they are quite indifferent to it. It doesn't bother *them*, so they just forget it. I learned that much at Harvard. They don't argue about it or even think about it much. Rather, they are inclined to ignore it, until some jig or other annoys them and then they lynch him or start a riot or something.

Then, he continued, still speaking earnestly, there is the policy of the young coloured intellectuals, from whom we have heard so much during the past two years, which is simply to adopt a mental attitude of equality and break the bars down gradually through the work of our artists. That won't be successful either, except for the artists. Of course, Paul Robeson and Roland Hayes and Countee Cullen can go anywhere within reason. They will be invited to white dinner parties, but I don't see how that's going to affect the rest of us.

Why not? Olive demanded.

Because the white people they meet will regard them as geniuses, in other words, exceptions. Yes, they will say to themselves, these are certainly unusually brilliant and delightful individuals; it's a pity all Negroes aren't like them. So they will go on neglecting the plight in which our respectable middle class finds itself.

Well, Mary said, I thought you had a solution.

So I have. It's simple enough to state, not so easy to achieve. It's merely economic. As soon as we, in the mass, become rich enough we will become powerful. You can't keep up the bars when your pocket-book is affected, no matter how violent your prejudice. As soon as we are rich enough, we will go wherever we really want to go, and do what we want to do. White people may sneer at us, but they will receive us. Look at the Jews. A lot of Nordics despise them, but they can't ignore them. They're much too important financially.

But, Counsellor, you're only stating Booker T's old premise, Dick put in. He said all that—not, to be sure, quite so bluntly—and what has happened? Any time one of us saves a little money, the white world becomes green-eyed with jealousy, to say nothing of our own group.

Booker T did say something like that tentatively, Howard admitted, but we've got to work faster than he expected us to. He urged Negroes to acquire land and work it. It's better to acquire land and sell it. And it's true that in the South the poor whites are envious if we get on and in Harlem the shines are jealous. I said it was going to be difficult. All of us have very serious handicaps to overcome. Nevertheless . . .

Bottle it, Howard, Olive cried, yawning. I've heard enough of this lecture for one evening. Let's listen to Clara Smith. She wound up the phonograph and put on a record. Soon the moaning wonder of the Blues singer's voice sounded in the little room:

> Nobody knows duh way Ah feel dis mornin',
> Nobody knows duh way Ah feel dis mornin',
> Ah feel like Ah could scream an' cry,
> But Ah'm too downh'ahted an' Ah'd rather die!
> Nobody knows duh way Ah feel dis mornin'.

The tears were streaming down Mary's cheeks. The others were sitting in solemn, dejected silence.

Oh hell, Ollie, Dick complained, I don't see that you've improved matters much. Try the Funny Blues!

REVIEWS OF *NIGGER HEAVEN*

No other single event divided the black artistic and intellectual community as did the publication of *Nigger Heaven*. Some loved it, praising it as the first honest portrayal of black urban life in fiction; others hated it and accused Van Vechten of taking advantage of the hospitality of his black friends by slandering all honest hardworking Harlemites. Coincidently, the novel reached the bookstores during the time that Du Bois and *The Crisis* were hosting a debate about the role of literature and race in the black community. From the moment of its publication *Nigger Heaven* and its influence on African American literature dominated the conversation. Du Bois and James Weldon Johnson, both prominent officials in the NAACP, took opposing positions on the novel. In the next section, *FIRE!!*, Wallace Thurman provides a more even-handed assessment of the book.

"Romance and Tragedy in Harlem—A Review"
James Weldon Johnson
Opportunity, October 1926

From its intriguing prologue to its tragic end, here is an absorbing story. Whether you like it or dislike it you will read it through, every chapter, every page. Mr. Van Vechten is the first white novelist of note to undertake a portrayal of modern American Negro life under metropolitan conditions. Mr. Van Vechten is also the only white novelist I can now think of who has not viewed the Negro as a type, who has not treated the race as a unit, either good or bad. In *NIGGER HEAVEN* the author has chosen as his scene Harlem, where Negro life is at its highest point of urbanity and sophistication, and there the entire action of the story is played out. The economy of stage Mr. Van Vechten imposes for himself enables him to gain in dramatic intensity but it does not limit him in the scope of the action. The story comprehends nearly every phase of life in the Negro metropolis. It draws on the components of that life from the dregs to the froth.

It was inevitable that the colorful life of Harlem would sooner or later claim the pen of Carl Van Vechten. He has taken the material it offered, him and achieved the most revealing, significant and powerful novel based exclusively on Negro life yet written. A Negro reviewer might pardonably express the wish that a colored novelist had been the first to take this material and write a book of equal significance and power. Mr. Van Vechten is a modernist. In literature he is the child of his age. In *NIGGER HEAVEN* he has written a modern novel in every sense. He has written about the most modern aspects of Negro life, and he has done it in the most modern manner; for he has completely discarded and scrapped the old formula and machinery for a Negro novel. He has no need of a *deus ex machina* from the white world either to involve or evolve the plot. There is, of course, the pressure of the white world, but it is external. The white characters are less than incidental. The story works itself out through the clashes and reactions of Negro character upon Negro character. Its factors are the loves, the hates, the envies, the ambitions, the pride, the shamelessness, the intelligence, the ignorance, the goodness, the wickedness of Negro characters. In this the author pays colored people the rare tribute of writing about them as people rather than as puppets. This representation of Negro characters in a novel as happy or unhappy, successful or unsuccessful, great or mean, not because of the fortuitous attitudes of white characters in the book but because of the way in which they themselves meet and master their environment—a task imposed upon every group—is new, and in close accord with the present psychology of the intelligent element of the race. The only other full length novel following this scheme that I can recall at this moment is Jessie Fauset's *THERE IS CONFUSION*. It is a scheme for the interpretation of Negro life in America that opens up a new world for colored writers.

There are those who will prejudge the book unfavorably on account of the title. This was the attitude taken by many toward Sheldon's *THE NIGGER*, perhaps the finest and fairest play on the race question that has yet been successfully produced in New York. This attitude is natural, but it is probable that the reaction against the title of the novel will not be so strong as it was against the title of the play which was produced sixteen years ago. Indeed, one gauge of the Negro's rise and development may be found in the degrees in which a race epithet loses its power to sting and hurt him. The title of Sheldon's play was purely ironic, and the title of *NIGGER HEAVEN* is taken from the ironic use of the phrase made by the characters in the book. But whatever may be the attitudes and opinions on this point, the book and not the title is the thing. In the book Mr. Van Vechten does not stoop to burlesque or caricature. There are characters and incidents in the book that many will regard as worse than unpleasant, but always the author handles them with sincerity and fidelity. Anatoles and Rubys and Lascas and number kings and cabarets and an underworld there are as well as there are Mary Loves and Byron Kassons and Olive Hamiltons and Howard Allisons and Dr. Lancasters and Underwoods and Sumners and young intellectuals. There are, too, Dick Sills and Buda Greens, living on both sides of the line, and then passing over. It is all life. It is all reality. And Mr. Van Vechten has taken these various manifestations of life and, as a true artist, depicted them as he sees them rather than as he might wish them to be. But the author again as a true artist, deftly maintains the symmetry and proportions of his work. The scenes of gay life, of night life, the glimpses of the underworld, with all their tinsel, their licentiousness, their depravity serve actually to set off in sharper relief the decent, cultured, intellectual life of Negro Harlem. But all these phases of life, good and bad, are merely the background for the story, and the story is the love life of Byron Kasson and Mary Love.

Mary is a beautiful, golden-brown girl who works as an assistant librarian in one of the New York public libraries. She is intelligent, cultured and refined. She is sweet, pure and placid until she meets Byron; she remains sweet and pure, but her placidity is shattered, the emotions which she sometimes feared she did not possess are stirred to the depths. Byron, bronze-colored, handsome, proud, impetuous and headstrong has just been graduated from the University of Pennsylvania. At college he had made a literary reputation in the university periodicals; his professors had encouraged him; so he comes to Harlem to make writing his profession and to conquer New York. He and Mary first meet at a gay week-end house party given by a wealthy woman of the smart set at her country home on Long Island—a house party at which Mary is sadly out of place. They meet again at a dinner given by the Sumners, one of the well-to-do, cultured colored families of Harlem. Byron calls to see Mary at her home, and the beginnings of love burst into a flame. The author makes an idyl of the awakening of love in Mary's heart. Byron starts out buoyant and sanguine. He receives a small monthly allowance from his father, but he must work to supplement that sum while he makes his way as a writer. He smarts under the rebuffs he meets with in trying to find work he considers in keeping with his training. He grows bitter and cynical under failure. He finally takes a job as an elevator boy, but this job he fails to hold. In the meantime he is devoting such time as the distractions of New York leave him to irresolute efforts at his writing. But there is something wrong with his stories, he sends them out and they regularly come back. Byron begins to slip. Mary tries to give him the benefit of her intelligent opinion and her knowledge of literature but his pride will not let her. His pride also keeps him from going for assistance to the Sumners and other influential friends to whom his father had given him letters; he does not want to be "patronized" by them. Byron cannot adapt himself, he cannot bend the bars of his environment to accommodate his own needs and desires. He has already failed, but he is not yet lost. Mary's love is what he needs to keep him steady, but the very fullness of her love raises for him a wall which his rebellious nature will not permit him to get over or through. Mary's love has developed in a two-fold manner, passionately and maternally; she jealously wants her handsome young lover wholly for herself, and she wants to watch over him and guide and protect him as she would a child, which in many respects he is. Byron is irritated by her jealousy and her attitude of guardianship he resents. He realizes that he is a failure compared to the young intellectuals and professional men of Mary's acquaintance and he feels that she, too, is pitying him, is patronizing him; and he will not be patronized. He begins to think of the fascinating, exotic Lasca Sartoris, whom he had met and danced with at a big charity ball. Her wit and beauty had amazed him and the talk about her purple past had stirred his imagination. He compares the tender, solicitous Mary with this superb woman, Lasca, who tramples all conventions under her shapely feet, who recognizes no limitations, who takes what she wants. Why couldn't he know intimately such a woman? That would be life— that would be inspiration.

One day Byron receives a letter from Russett Durwood, the editor of a great magazine, asking him to call regarding a story he had sent in. It is the story that carries all of Byron's hopes, his great story. He forgets all about Lasca. He rushes as fast as his feet can carry him to Mary. It is Mary to whom he wants to break the good news. He is again the buoyant, sanguine and the lovable Byron. He is sure of success now, he has regained his self-confidence and self-respect, Mary's love and solicitude are now grateful to him. The outcome of the interview is a lecture from the great editor on the defects of the story. He has sent for Byron because he is interested in Negro literature and Negro writers. He has seen from parts of Byron's story that he has talent and ability and can write. But "why in hell" doesn't he write about something he knows about? Negro life—Harlem—West Indians, Abyssinian Jews, religious Negroes, pagan Negroes, Negro intellectuals all living together in the same community. Why continue to employ the old clichés that have been worked to death by Nordics? Why not use this fresh material before a new crop of Nordics spring up and exploit it before Negro writers get around to it? Byron is stricken dumb, he can make no answer. He drags himself out of the building and makes his way to Central Park. Through whirling emotions of disappointment and heartbreak there surges a flame of fury. He will go back to the editor and tell him what he thinks of him; he will not stand to be treated as a Nigger. But he does not; instead, he sinks upon a park bench discouraged, disheartened, beaten. He hears a woman's voice calling him, he raises his head to see Lasca beckoning him from her luxurious limousine, Lasca, who takes what she wants. She takes Byron. She showers him with all the fragrance, the beauty, the wild ecstacies, the cruelsweets of love that her perfect body and her lawless soul know. Byron, now, has not only failed, he is lost. And yet his is a fate before which self-righteousness should take no occasion to preen itself. One must, indeed, be much of a prig not to make some allowances for youth caught in the circle of the lure of Lasca, the courtesan supreme. Lasca keeps Byron for a period, then, as she had done others before, she throws him out, banishes him wholly, and takes Randolph Petijohn, the number king. From here on Byron's journey downward is steep and fast. His moral disintegration is complete. He pleads, he raves, he broods. He becomes obsessed with the desire for revenge; and he procures a revolver and haunts the cabarets, lying in wait for the two objects of his hatred. One night in the Black Venus, drunk to the point of irresponsibility, he sees the number king enter. While Byron is trying to bring together his dissolved will for the accomplishment of his purpose a shot rings out and Petijohn falls dead. The shot had been fired by Anatole, the Scarlet Creeper, who also had a grudge against the number king. Byron, playing his futile role in the drama out to the end, springs up, stands over the prostrate form and is emptying his revolver into the dead body when the law lays its hands upon him. An absorbing, a tragic, a disquieting story.

Byron is at many points a symbol of the tragic struggle of the race thrown as it is in an unsympathetic milieu and surrounded by fateful barriers. But Byron's story is especially true as an individual story. It is a true story—and an old story. It is the story of many a gifted and ambitious young colored man who has come up to New York as the field for success, and has been sucked in and down by the gay life and underworld of the great city. It is the story of talent and brilliancy without stamina and patience. The theme has been used before. Paul Dunbar used it in a measure in *THE SPORT OF THE GODS,* and I myself skirted it in a now forgotten novel. But never before has it been so well and fully used.

The book is written with Mr. Van Vechten's innate light touch and brilliancy, but there is a difference; Van Vechten, the satirist, becomes in *NIGGER HEAVEN* Van Vechten, the realist. In every line of the book he shows that he is serious. But however serious Van Vechten may be, he cannot be heavy. He does not moralize, he does not over-emphasize, there are no mock heroics, there are no martyrdoms. And, yet—Mr. Van Vechten would doubtless count this a defect—the book is packed full of propaganda. Every phase of the race question, from Jim Crow discriminations to miscegenation, is frankly discussed. Here the author's inside knowledge and insight are at times astonishing. But it is not the author speaking, he makes his characters do the talking, and makes each one talk in keeping with his character. If the book has a thesis it is: Negroes are people; they have the same emotions, the same passions, the same shortcomings, the same aspirations, the same graduations of social strata as other people. It will be a revelation, perhaps, a shock to those familiar only with the Negro characters of Thomas Nelson Page, Thomas Dixon and Octavius Cohen. It is the best book Mr. Van Vechten has done, and that is saying a good deal when we remember *PETER WHIFFLE.*

NIGGER HEAVEN is a book which is bound to be widely read and one which is bound to arouse much diverse discussion. This reviewer would suggest reading the book before discussing it.

"Books"
W.E.B. Du Bois
The Crisis
December 1926

Carl Van Vechten's "Nigger Heaven" is a blow in the face. It is an affront to the hospitality of black folk and to the intelligence of white. First, as to its title: my objection is based on no provincial dislike of the nickname. "Nigger" is an English word of wide use and definite connotation. As employed by Conrad, Sheldon, Allen and even Firbanks, its use was justifiable. But the phrase, "Nigger Heaven", as applied to Harlem is a misnomer. "Nigger Heaven" does not mean, as Van Vechten once or twice intimates, (pages 15, 199) a haven for Negroes—a city of refuge for dark and tired souls; it means in common parlance, a nasty, sordid corner into which black folk are herded, and yet a place which they in crass ignorance are fools enough to enjoy. Harlem is no such place as that, and no one knows this better than Carl Van Vechten.

But after all, a title is only a title, and a book must be judged eventually by its fidelity to truth and its artistic merit. I find this novel neither truthful nor artistic. It is not a true picture of Harlem life, even allowing for some justifiable impressionistic exaggeration. It is a caricature. It is worse than untruth because it is a mass of half-truths. Probably some time and somewhere in Harlem every incident of the book has happened; and yet the resultant picture built out of these parts is ludicrously out of focus and undeniably misleading.

The author counts among his friends numbers of Negroes of all classes. He is an authority on dives and cabarets. But he masses this knowledge without rule or reason and seeks to express all of Harlem life in its cabarets. To him the black cabaret is Harlem; around it all his characters gravitate. Here is their stage of action. Such a theory of Harlem is nonsense. The overwhelming majority of black folk there never go to cabarets. The average colored man in Harlem is an everyday laborer, attending church, lodge and movie and as conservative and as conventional as ordinary working folk everywhere.

Something they have which is racial, something distinctively Negroid can be found; but it is expressed by subtle, almost delicate nuance, and not by the wildly, barbaric drunken orgy in whose details Van Vechten revels. There is laughter, color and spontaneity at Harlem's core, but in the current cabaret, financed and supported largely by white New York, this core is so overlaid and enwrapped with cheaper stuff that no one but a fool could mistake it for the genuine exhibition of the spirit of the people.

To all this the author has a right to reply that even if the title is an unhappy catch-phrase for penny purposes and his picture of truth untruthful, that his book has a right to be judged primarily as a work of art. Does it please? Does it entertain? Is it a good and human story? In my opinion it is not; and I am one who likes stories and I do not insist that they be written solely for my point of view. "Nigger Heaven" is to me an astonishing and wearisome hodgepodge of laboriously stated facts, quotations and expressions, illuminated here and there with something that comes near to being nothing but cheap melodrama. Real human feelings are laughed at. Love is degraded. The love of Byron and Mary is stark cruelty and that of Lasca and Byron is simply nasty. Compare this slum picture with Porgy. In his degradation, Porgy is human and interesting. But in "Nigger Heaven" there is not a single loveable character. There is scarcely a generous impulse or a beautiful ideal. The characters are singularly wooden and inhuman. Van Vechten is not the great artist who with remorseless scalpel probes the awful depths of life. To him there are no depths. It is the surface mud he slops about in. His women's bodies have no souls; no children palpitate upon his hands; he has never looked upon his dead with bitter tears. Life to him is just one damned orgy after another, with hate, hurt, gin and sadism.

Both Langston Hughes and Carl Van Vechten know Harlem cabarets; but it is Hughes who whispers

> "One said he heard the jazz band sob
> When the little dawn was grey".

Van Vechten never heard a sob in a cabaret. All he hears is noise and brawling. Again and again with singular lack of invention he reverts to the same climax of two creatures tearing and scratching over "mah man"; lost souls who once had women's bodies; and to Van Vechten this spells comedy, not tragedy.

I seem to see that Mr. Van Vechten began a good tale with the promising figure of Anatol, but that he keeps turning aside to write in from his notebook every fact he has heard about Negroes and their problems; singularly irrelevant quotations, Haitian history, Chesnutt's novels, race-poetry, "blues" written by white folk. Into this mass he drops characters which are in most cases thin disguises; and those who know the originals have only to compare their life and this death, to realize the failure in truth and human interest. The final climax is an utterly senseless murder which appears without preparation or reason from the clouds.

I cannot for the life of me see in this work either sincerity or art, deep thought, or truthful industry. It seems to me that Mr. Van Vechten tried to do something bizarre and he certainly succeeded. I read "Nigger Heaven" and read it through because I had to. But I advise others who are impelled by a sense of duty or curiosity to drop the book gently in the grate and to try the *Police Gazette*. W. E. D. B.

FIRE!!
1926

In November 1926 a group of the young writers and artists associated with the Harlem Renaissance attempted to seize control of the movement both from the black and white critics and intellectuals and from the black and white patrons. *FIRE!!*, an in-your-face magazine of the black arts, survived only one issue, but it helped to define the freedom, independence, and vision that the young writers attempted to bring to their art and literature. The selections from *FIRE!!* capture several aspects of this effort. First is the intensity of the vision as reflected in the "Forward." Then there is the diversity of the art and literature of the movement as seen in the range of material in the magazine. The three poems, by Countee Cullen, Helene Johnson, and Langston Hughes, differ in style and content, but each give voice to social, economic, and racial reality faced by blacks. Likewise the two short prose pieces, Wallace Thurman's sketch of "Cordelia" and Zora Neale Hurston's powerful study of gender oppression, differ in tone, style, and setting, but each addresses a fundamental aspect of the African American experience. Aaron Douglas's graphics frame the literary pieces with a hint of African roots. Thurman's closing piece, one of the most incisive and balanced assessments of *Nigger Heaven*, reflects the seriousness and intellectual rigor of the young writers.

FIRE!!
Devoted to Younger Negro Artists
November 1926

Cover for *Fire!!* by *Aaron Douglas*

Forward

. . . flaming, burning, searing, and penetrating far beneath the superficial items of the flesh to boil the sluggish blood.

FIRE . . . a cry of conquest in the night, warning those who sleep and revitalizing those who linger in the quiet places dozing.

FIRE . . . melting steel and iron bars, poking livid tongues between stone apertures and burning wooden opposition with a cackling chuckle of contempt.

FIRE . . . weaving vivid, hot designs upon an ebon bordered loom and satisfying pagan thirst for beauty unadorned . . . the flesh is sweet and real . . . the soul an inward flush of fire. . . . Beauty? . . . flesh on fire—on fire in the furnace of life blazing. . . .

> "Fy-ah,
> Fy-ah, Lawd,
> Fy-ah gonna burn ma soul!"

FIRE!!
DEVOTED TO YOUNGER NEGRO ARTISTS

Cordelia the Crude: A Harlem Sketch
Wallace Thurman

Physically, if not mentally, Cordelia was a potential prostitute, meaning that although she had not yet realized the moral import of her wanton promiscuity nor become mercenary she had, nevertheless, become quite blasé and bountiful in the matter of bestowing sexual favors upon persuasive and likely young men. Yet, despite her seeming lack of discrimination, Cordelia was quite particular about the type of male to whom she submitted, for numbers do not necessarily denote a lack of taste, and Cordelia had discovered after several months of active observation that one could find the qualities one admires or reacts positively to in a varied hodge-podge of outwardly different individuals.

The scene of Cordelia's activities was The Roosevelt Motion Picture Theatre on Seventh Avenue near 149th Street. Thrice weekly the program changed, and thrice weekly Cordelia would plunk down the necessary twenty-five cents evening admission fee, and saunter gaily into the foul-smelling depths of her favorite cinema shrine. The Roosevelt Theatre presented all of the latest pictures, also, twice weekly, treated its audiences to a vaudeville bill, then too, one could always have the most delightful physical contacts . . . hmm. . . .

Cordelia had not consciously chosen this locale nor had there been any conscious effort upon her part to take advantage of the extra opportunities afforded for physical pleasure. It had just happened that the Roosevelt Theatre was more close to her home than any other neighborhood picture palace, and it had also just happened that Cordelia had become almost immediately initiated into the ways of a Harlem theatre chippie soon after her discovery of the theatre itself.

It is the custom of certain men and boys who frequent these places to idle up and down the aisle until some female is seen sitting alone, to slouch down into a seat beside her, to touch her foot or else press her leg in such a way that it can be construed as accidental if necessary, and then, if the female is wise or else shows signs of willingness to become wise, to make more obvious approaches until, if successful, the approached female will soon be chatting with her baiter about the picture being shown, lolling in his arms, and helping to formulate plans for an after-theatre rendezvous. Cordelia had, you see, shown a willingness to become wise upon her second visit to The Roosevelt. In a short while she had even learned how to squelch the bloated, lewd faced Jews and eager middle aged Negroes who might approach as well as how to inveigle the likeable little yellow or brown half men, embryo avenue sweetbacks, with their well modeled heads, stickily plastered hair, flaming cravats, silken or broadcloth shirts, dirty underwear, low cut vests, form fitting coats, bell-bottom trousers and shiny shoes with metal cornered heels clicking with a brave, brazen rhythm upon the bare concrete floor as their owners angled and searched for prey.

Cordelia, sixteen years old, matronly mature, was an undisciplined, half literate product of rustic South Carolina, and had come to Harlem very much against her will with her parents and her six brothers and sisters. Against her will because she had not been at all anxious to leave the lackadaisical life of the little corn pone settlement where she had been born, to go trooping into the unknown vastness of New York, for she had been in love, passionately in love with one John Stokes who raised pigs, and who, like his father before him, found the raising of pigs so profitable that he could not even consider leaving Lintonville. Cordelia had blankly informed her parents that she would not go with them when they decided to be lured to New York by an older son who had remained there after the demobilization of the war time troops. She had even threatened to run away with John until they should be gone, but of course John could not leave his pigs, and John's mother was not very keen on having Cordelia for a daughter-in-law—those Joneses have bad mixed blood in 'em—so Cordelia had had to join the Gotham bound caravan and leave her lover to his succulent porkers.

However, the mere moving to Harlem had not doused the rebellious flame. Upon arriving Cordelia had not only refused to go to school and refused to hold even the most easily held job, but had also victoriously defied her harassed parents so frequently when it came to matters of discipline that she soon found herself with a mesmerizing lack of home restraint, for the stress of trying to maintain themselves and their family in the new environment was far too much of a task for Mr. and Mrs. Jones to attend to facilely and at the same time try to control a recalcitrant child. So, when Cordelia had refused either to work or to attend school, Mrs. Jones herself had gone out for day's work, leaving Cordelia at home to take care of their five room railroad flat, the front room of which was rented out to a couple "living together," and to see that the younger children, all of whom were of school age, made their four trips daily between home and the nearby public school—as well as see that they had their greasy, if slim, food rations and an occasional change of clothing. Thus Cordelia's days were full—and so were her nights. The only difference being that the days belonged to the folks at home while the nights (since the folks were too tired or too sleepy to know or care when she came in or went out) belonged to her and to—well—whosoever will, let them come.

Cordelia had been playing this hectic, entrancing game for six months and was widely known among a certain group of young men and girls on the avenue as a fus' class chippie when she and I happened to enter the theatre simultaneously. She had clumped down the aisle before me, her open galoshes swishing noisily, her two arms busy wriggling themselves free from the torn sleeve lining of a shoddy imitation fur coat that one of her mother's wash clients had sent to her. She was of medium height and build, with overly developed legs and bust, and had a clear, keen light brown complexion. Her too slick, too naturally bobbed hair, mussed by the removing of a tight, black turban was of an undecided nature, i.e., it was undecided whether to be kinky or to be kind, and her body, as she sauntered along in the partial light had such a conscious sway of invitation that unthinkingly I followed, slid into the same row of seats and sat down beside her.

Naturally she had noticed my pursuit, and thinking that I was eager to play the game, let me know immediately that she was wise, and not the least bit averse to spooning with me during the evening's performance. Interested, and, I might as well confess, intrigued physically, I too became wise, and played up to her with all the fervor, or so I thought, of an old timer, but Cordelia soon remarked that I was different from mos' of des' sheiks, and when pressed for an explanation brazenly told me in a slightly scandalized and patronizing tone that I had not even felt her legs . . . !

At one o'clock in the morning we strolled through the snowy bleakness of one hundred and forty-fourth street between Lenox and Fifth Avenues to the walk-up tenement flat in which she lived, and after stamping the snow from our feet, pushed through the double outside doors, and followed the dismal hallway to the rear of the building where we began the tedious climbing of the crooked, creaking, inconveniently narrow stairway. Cordelia had informed me earlier in the evening that she lived on the top floor—four flights up east side rear—and on our way we rested at each floor and at each half way landing, rested long enough to mingle the snowy dampness of our respective coats, and to hug clumsily while our lips met in an animal kiss.

Finally only another half flight remained, and instead of proceeding as was usual after our amorous demonstration I abruptly drew away from her, opened my overcoat, plunged my hand into my pants pocket, and drew out two crumpled one dollar bills which I handed to her, and then, while she stared at me foolishly, I muttered good-night, confusedly pecked her on her cold brown cheek, and darted down into the creaking darkness.

Six months later I was taking two friends of mine, lately from the provinces, to a Saturday night house-rent party in a well known whore house on one hundred and thirty-fourth street near Lenox Avenue. The place as we entered seemed to be a chaotic riot of raucous noise and clashing color all rhythmically merging in the red, smoke filled room. And there I saw Cordelia savagely careening in a drunken abortion of the Charleston and surrounded by a perspiring circle of handclapping enthusiasts. Finally fatigued, she whirled into an abrupt finish, and stopped so that she stared directly into my face, but being dizzy from the calisthenic turns and the cauterizing liquor she doubted that her eyes recognized someone out of the past, and, visibly trying to sober herself, languidly began to dance a slow drag with a lean hipped pimply faced yellow man who had walked between her and me. At last he released her, and seeing that she was about to leave the room I rushed forward calling Cordelia?—as if I was not yet sure who it was. Stopping in the doorway, she turned to see who had called, and finally recognizing me said simply, without the least trace of emotion,—'Lo kid. . . .

And without another word turned her back and walked into the hall to where she joined four girls standing there. Still eager to speak, I followed and heard one of the girls ask: Who's the dicty kid? . . .

And Cordelia answered: The guy who gimme ma' firs' two bucks. . . .

Flame From the Dark Tower
A Selection of Poetry

From the Dark Tower
Countée Cullen

We shall not always plant while others reap
The golden increment of bursting fruit,
Nor always countenance, abject and mute,
That lesser men should hold their brothers cheap;
Not everlastingly while others sleep
Shall we beguile their limbs with mellow flute,
Not always bend to some more subtle brute;
We were not made eternally to weep.

The night whose sable breast relieves the stark,
White stars is no less lovely being dark,
And there are buds that cannot bloom at all
In light, but crumple, piteous, and fall.
So in the dark we hide the heart that bleeds,
And wait, and tend our agonizing seeds.

A Southern Road
Helene Johnson

Yolk-colored tongue
Parched beneath a burning sky,
A lazy little tune
Hummed up the crest of some
Soft sloping hill.

One streaming line of beauty
Flowing by a forest
Pregnant with tears.
A hidden nest for beauty
Idly flung by God
In one lonely lingering hour
Before the Sabbath.
A blue-fruited black gum,
Like a tall predella,
Bears a dangling figure,—
Sacrificial dower to the raff,
Swinging alone,
A solemn, tortured shadow in the air.

Elevator Boy
Langston Hughes

I got a job now
Runnin' an elevator
In the Dennison Hotel in Jersey,
Job aint no good though.
No money around.
Jobs are just chances
Like everything else.
Maybe a little luck now,
Maybe not.
Maybe a good job sometimes:
Step out o' the barrel, boy.
Two new suits an'
A woman to sleep with.
Maybe no luck for a long time.
Only the elevators
Goin' up an' down,
Up an' down,
Or somebody else's shoes
To shine,
Or greasy pots in a dirty kitchen.
I been runnin' this
Elevator too long.
Guess I'll quit now.

Sweat
Zora Neale Hurston

It was eleven o'clock of a Spring night in Florida. It was Sunday. Any other night, Delia Jones would have been in bed for two hours by this time. But she was a washwoman, and Monday morning meant a great deal to her. So she collected the soiled clothes on Saturday when she returned the clean things. Sunday night after church, she sorted them and put the white things to soak. It saved her almost a half day's start. A great hamper in the bedroom held the clothes that she brought home. It was so much neater than a number of bundles lying around.

She squatted in the kitchen floor beside the great pile of clothes, sorting them into small heaps according to color, and humming a song in a mournful key, but wondering through it all where Sykes, her husband, had gone with her horse and buckboard.

Just then something long, round, limp and black fell upon her shoulders and slithered to the floor beside her. A great terror took hold of her. It softened her knees and dried her mouth so that it was a full minute before she could cry out or move. Then she saw that it was the big bull whip her husband liked to carry when he drove.

She lifted her eyes to the door and saw him standing there bent over with laughter at her fright. She screamed at him.

"Sykes, what you throw dat whip on me like dat? You know it would skeer me—looks just like a snake, an' you knows how skeered Ah is of snakes."

"Course Ah knowed it! That's how come Ah done it." He slapped his leg with his hand and almost rolled on the ground in his mirth. "If you such a big fool dat you got to have a fit over a earth worm or a string, Ah don't keer how bad Ah skeer you."

"You aint got no business doing it. Gawd knows it's a sin. Some day Ah'm gointuh drop dead from some of yo' foolishness. 'Nother thing, where you been wid mah rig? Ah feeds dat pony. He aint fuh you to be drivin' wid no bull whip."

"You sho is one aggravatin' nigger woman!" he declared and stepped into the room. She resumed her work and did not answer him at once. "Ah done tole you time and again to keep them white folks' clothes outa dis house."

He picked up the whip and glared down at her. Delia went on with her work. She went out into the yard and returned with a galvanized tub and sit it on the -washbench. She saw that Sykes had kicked all of the clothes together again, and now stood in her way truculently, his whole manner hoping, *praying*, for an argument. But she walked calmly around him and commenced to re-sort the things.

"Next time, Ah'm gointer kick 'em outdoors," he threatened as he struck a match along the leg of his corduroy breeches.

Delia never looked up from her work, and her thin, stooped shoulders sagged further.

"Ah aint for no fuss t'night Sykes. Ah just come from taking sacrament at the church house." He snorted scornfully. "Yeah, you just come from de church house on a Sunday night, but heah you is gone to work on them clothes. You ain't nothing but a hypocrite. One of them amen-corner Christians—sing, whoop, and shout, then come home and wash white folks clothes on the Sabbath."

He stepped roughly upon the whitest pile of things, kicking them helter-skelter as he crossed the room. His wife gave a little scream of dismay, and quickly gathered them together again.

"Sykes, you quit grindin' dirt into these clothes! How can Ah git through by Sat'day if Ah don't start on Sunday?"

"Ah don't keer if you never git through. Anyhow, Ah done promised Gawd and a couple of other men, Ah aint gointer have it in mah house. Don't gimme no lip neither, else Ah'll throw 'em out and put mah fist up side yo' head to boot."

Delia's habitual meekness seemed to slip from her shoulders like a blown scarf. She was on her feet; her poor little body, her bare knuckly hands bravely defying the strapping hulk before her.

"Looka heah, Sykes, you done gone too fur. Ah been married to you fur fifteen years, and Ah been takin' in washin' fur fifteen years. Sweat, sweat, sweat! Work and sweat, cry and sweat, pray and sweat!"

"What's that got to do with me?" he asked brutally.

"What's it got to do with you, Sykes? Mah tub of suds is filled yo' belly with vittles more times than yo' hands is filled it. Mah sweat is done paid for this house and Ah reckon Ah kin keep on sweatin' in it."

She seized the iron skillet from the stove and struck a defensive pose, which act surprised him greatly, coming from her. It cowed him and be did not strike her as he usually did.

"Naw you won't," she panted, "that ole snaggletoothed black woman you runnin' with aint comin' heah to pile up on mah sweat and blood. You aint paid for nothin' on this place, and Ah'm gointer stay right heah till Ah'm toted out foot foremost."

"Well, you better quit gittin' me riled up, else they'll be totin' you out sooner than you expect. Ah'm so tired of you Ah don't know whut to do. Gawd! how Ah hates skinny wimmen!"

A little awed by this new Delia, he sidled out of the door and slammed the back gate after him. He did not say where he had gone, but she knew too well. She knew very well that he would not return until nearly daybreak also. Her work over, she went on to bed but not to sleep at once. Things had come to a pretty pass!

She lay awake, gazing upon the debris that cluttered their matrimonial trail. Not an image left standing along the way. Anything like flowers had long ago been drowned in the salty stream that had been pressed from her heart. Her tears, her sweat, her blood. She had brought love to the union and he had brought a longing after the flesh. Two months after the wedding, he had given her the first brutal beating. She had the memory of his numerous trips to Orlando with all of his wages when he had returned to her penniless, even before the first year had passed. She was young and soft then, but now she thought of her knotty, muscled limbs, her harsh knuckly hands, and drew herself up into an unhappy little ball in the middle of the big feather bed. Too late now to hope for love, even if it were not Bertha it would be someone else. This case differed from the others only in that she was bolder than the others. Too late for everything except her little home. She had built it for her old days, and planted one by one the trees and flowers there. It was lovely to her, lovely.

Somehow, before sleep came, she found herself saying aloud: "Oh well, whatever goes over the Devil's back, is got to come under his belly. Sometime or ruther, Sykes, like everybody else, is gointer reap his sowing." After that she was able to build a spiritual earthworks against her husband. His shells could no longer reach her. *Amen.* She went to sleep and slept until he announced his presence in bed by kicking her feet and rudely snatching the cover away.

"Gimme some kivah heah, an' git yo' damn foots over on yo' own side! Ah oughter mash you in yo' mouf fuh drawing dat skillet on me."

Delia went clear to the rail without answering him. A triumphant indifference to all that he was or did.

The week was as full of work for Delia as all other weeks, and Saturday found her behind her little pony, collecting and delivering clothes.

It was a hot, hot day near the end of July. The village men on Joe Clarke's porch even chewed cane listlessly. They did not hurl the cane-knots as usual. They let them dribble over the edge of the porch. Even conversation had collapsed under the heat.

"Heah come Delia Jones," Jim Merchant said, as the shaggy pony came 'round the bend of the road toward them. The rusty buckboard was heaped with baskets of crisp, clean laundry.

"Yep," Joe Lindsay agreed. "Hot or col', rain or shine, jes ez reg'lar ez de weeks roll roun' Delia carries 'em an' fetches 'em on Sat'day."

"She better if she wanter eat," said Moss. "Syke Jones aint wuth de shot an' powder hit would tek tuh kill 'em. Not to *huh* he aint."

"He sho' aint," Walter Thomas chimed in. "It's too bad, too, cause she wuz a right pritty lil trick when he got huh. Ah'd uh mah'ied huh mahseff if he had-nter beat me to it."

Delia nodded briefly at the men as she drove past.

"Too much knockin' will ruin any 'oman. He done beat huh 'nough tuh kill three women, let 'lone change they looks," said Elijah Mosely. "How Syke kin stommuck dat big black greasy Mogul he's layin' roun' wid, gits me. Ah swear dat eight-rock couldn't kiss a sardine can Ah done thowed out de back do' 'way las' yeah."

"Aw, she's fat, thass how come. He's allus been crazy 'bout fat women," put in Merchant. "He'd a' been tied up wid one long time ago if he could a' found one tuh have him. Did Ah tell yuh 'bout him come sidlin' roun' *mah* wife-bringin' her a basket uh pee-cans outa his yard fuh a present? Yessir, mah wife! She tol' him tuh take 'em right straight back home, cause Delia works so hard ovah dat washtub she reckon everything on de place taste lak sweat an' soapsuds. Ah jus' wisht Ah'd a' caught 'im 'roun' dere! Ah'd a' made his hips ketch on fiah down dat shell road."

"Ah know he done it, too. Ah sees 'im grinnin' at every 'oman dat passes," Walter Thomas said. "But even so, he useter eat some mighty big hunks uh humble pie tuh git dat lil' 'oman he got. She wuz ez pritty ez a speckled pup! Dat wuz fifteen yeahs ago. He useter be so skeered uh losin' huh, she could make him do some parts of a husband's duty. Dey never wuz de same in de mind."

"There oughter be a law about him," said Lindsay. "He aint fit tuh carry guts tuh a bear." Clarke spoke for the first time. "Taint no law on earth dat kin make a man be decent if it aint in 'im. There's plenty men dat takes a wife lak dey do a joint uh sugar-cane. It's round, juicy an' sweet when dey gits it. But dey squeeze an' grind, squeeze an' grind an' wring tell dey wring every drop uh pleasure dat's in 'em out. When dey's satisfied dat dey is wrung dry, dey treats 'em jes lak dey do a cane-chew. Dey thows 'em away. Dey knows whut dey is doin' while dey is at it, an' hates theirselves fuh it but they keeps on hangin' after huh tell she's empty. Den dey hates huh fuh bein' a canechew an' in de way."

"We oughter take Syke an' dat stray 'oman uh his'n down in Lake Howell swamp an' lay on de rawhide till they cain't say 'Lawd a' mussy.' He allus wuz uh ovahbearin' niggah, but since dat white 'oman from up north done teached 'im how to run a automobile, he done got to biggety to live—an' we oughter kill 'im." Old Man Anderson advised.

A grunt of approval went around the porch. But the heat was melting their civic virtue and Elijah Moseley began to bait Joe Clarke.

"Come on, Joe, git a melon outa dere an' slice it up for yo' customers. We'se all sufferin' wid de heat. De bear's done got *me!*"

"Thass right, Joe, a watermelon is jes' whut Ah needs tuh cure de eppizu-dicks," Walter Thomas joined forces with Moseley. "Come on dere, Joe. We all is steady customers an' you aint set us up in a long time. Ah chooses dat long, bow-legged Floridy favorite."

"A god, an' be dough. You all gimme twenty cents and slice away," Clarke retorted. "Ah needs a col' slice m'self. Heah, everybody chip in. Ah'll lend y'll mah meat knife."

The money was quickly subscribed and the huge melon brought forth. At that moment, Sykes and Bertha arrived. A determined silence fell on the porch and the melon was put away again.

Merchant snapped down the blade of his jackknife and moved toward the store door.

"Come on in, Joe, an' gimme a slab uh sow belly an' uh pound uh coffee al-most fuhgot 'twas Sat'day. Got to git on home." Most of the men left also.

Just then Delia drove past on her way home, as Sykes was ordering magnif-icently for Bertha. It pleased him for Delia to see.

"Git whutsoever yo' heart desires, Honey. Wait a minute, Joe. Give huh two botles uh strawberry soda-water, uh quart uh parched ground-peas, an' a block uh chewin' gum."

With all this they left the store, with Sykes reminding Bertha that this was his town and she could have it if she wanted it.

The men returned soon after they left, and held their watermelon feast.

"Where did Syke Jones git dat 'oman from nohow?" Lindsay asked.

"Ovah Apopka. Guess dey musta been cleanin' out de town when she lef'. She don't look lak a thing but a hunk uh liver wid hair on it."

"Well, she sho' kin squall," Dave Carter contributed. "When she gits ready tuh laff, she jes' opens huh mouf an' latches it back tuh de las' notch. No ole grandpa alligator down in Lake Bell ain't got nothin' on huh."

Bertha had been in town three months now. Sykes was still paying her room rent at Della Lewis'—the only house in town that would have taken her in. Sykes took her frequently to Winter Park to "stomps." He still assured her that he was the swellest man in the state.

"Sho' you kin have dat lil' ole house soon's Ah kin git dat 'oman outa dere. Everything b'longs tuh me an' you sho' kin have it. Ah sho' 'bominates uh skinny 'oman. Lawdy, you sho' is got one portly shape on you! You kin git *anything* you wants. Dis is *mah* town an' you sho' kin have it."

Delia's work-worn knees crawled over the earth in Gethsemane and up the rocks of Calvary many, many times during these months. She avoided the villagers and meeting places in her efforts to be blind and deaf. But Bertha nullified this to a degree, by coming to Delia's house to call Sykes out to her at the gate.

Delia and Sykes fought all the time now with no peaceful interludes. They slept and ate in silence. Two or three times Delia had attempted a timid friendliness, but she was repulsed each time. It was plain that the breaches must remain agape.

The sun had burned July to August. The heat streamed down like a million hot arrows, smiting all things living upon the earth. Grass withered, leaves browned, snakes went blind in shedding and men and dogs went mad. Dog days!

Delia came home one day and found Sykes there before her. She wondered, but started to go on into the house without speaking, even though he was standing in the kitchen door and she must either stoop under his arm or ask him to move. He made no room for her. She noticed a soap box beside the steps, but paid no particular attention to it, knowing that he must have brought it there. As she was stooping to pass under his outstretched arm, he suddenly pushed her backward, laughingly.

"Look in de box dere Delia, Ah done brung yuh somethin'!"

She nearly fell upon the box in her stumbling, and when she saw what it held, she all but fainted outright.

"Syke! Syke, mah Gawd! You take dat rattlesnake 'way from heah! You *gottuh*. Oh, Jesus, have mussy!"

"Ah aint gut tuh do nuthin' uh de kin'—fact is Ah aint got tuh do nothin' but die. Taint no use uh you puttin' on airs makin' out lak you skeered uh dat snake— he's gointer stay right heah tell he die. He wouldn't bite me cause Ah knows how tuh handle 'im. Nohow he wouldn't risk breakin' out his fangs 'gin yo' skinny laigs."

"Naw, now Syke, don't keep dat thing 'roun' heah tuh skeer me tuh death. You knows Ah'm even feared uh earth worms. Thass de biggest snake Ah evah did see. Kill 'im Syke, please."

"Doan ast me tuh do nothin' fuh yuh. Goin' 'roun' tryin' tuh be so damn asterperious. Naw, Ah aint gonna kill it. Ah think uh damn sight mo' uh him dan you! Dat's a nice snake an' anybody doan lak 'im kin jes' hit de grit."

The village soon heard that Sykes had the snake, and came to see and ask questions.

"How de hen-fire did you ketch dat six-foot rattler, Syke?" Thomas asked.

"He's full uh frogs so he caint hardly move, thass how Ah eased up on 'm. But Ah'm a snake charmer an' knows how tuh handle 'em. Shux, dat aint nothin'. Ah could ketch one eve'y day if Ah so wanted tuh."

"Whut he needs is a heavy hick'ry club leaned real heavy on his head. Dat's de bes 'way tuh charm a rattlesnake."

"Naw, Walt, y'll jes' don't understand dese diamon' backs lak Ah do," said Sykes in a superior tone of voice.

The village agreed with Walter, but the snake stayed on. His box remained by the kitchen door with its screen wire covering. Two or three days later it had digested its meal of frogs and literally came to life. It rattled at every movement in the kitchen or the yard. One day as Delia came down the kitchen steps she saw his chalky-white fangs curved like scimitars hung in the wire meshes. This time she did not run away with averted eyes as usual. She stood for a long time in the doorway in a red fury that grew bloodier for every second that she regarded the creature that was her torment.

That night she broached the subject as soon as Sykes sat down to the table.

"Syke, Ah wants you tuh take dat snake 'way fum heah. You done starved me an' Ah put up widcher, you done beat me an Ah took dat, but you done kilt all mah insides bringin' dat varmint heah."

Sykes poured out a saucer full of coffee and drank it deliberately before he answered her.

"A whole lot Ah keer 'bout how you feels inside uh out. Dat snake aint goin' no damn wheah till Ah gits ready fuh 'im tuh go. So fur as beatin' is concerned, yuh aint took near all dat you gointer take ef yuh stay 'roun' me."

Delia pushed back her plate and got up from the table. "Ah hates you, Sykes," she said calmly. "Ah hates you tuh de same degree dat Ah useter love yuh. Ah done took an' took till mah belly is full up tuh mah neck. Dat's de reason Ah got mah letter fum de church an' moved mah membership tuh Woodbridge—so Ah don't haftuh take no sacrament wid yuh. Ah don't wantuh see yuh 'roun' me atall. Lay 'roun' wid dat 'oman all yuh wants tuh, but gwan 'way fum me an' mah house. At hates yuh lak uh suck-egg dog."

Sykes almost let the huge wad of corn bread and collard greens he was chewing fall out of his mouth in amazement. He had a hard time whipping himself up to the proper fury to try to answer Delia.

"Well, Ah'm glad you does hate me. Ah'm sho' tiahed uh you hangin' ontuh me. Ah don't want yuh. Look at yuh stringey ole neck! Yo' rawbony laigs an' arms is enough tuh cut uh man tuh death. You looks jes' lak de devvul's doll-baby tuh me. You cain't hate me no worse dan Ah hates you. Ah been hatin' *you* fuh years.

"Yo' ole black hide don't look lak nothin' tuh me, but uh passle uh wrinkled up rubber, wid yo' big ole yeahs flappin' on each side lak up paih uh buzzard wings. Don't think Ah'm gointuh be run 'way fum mah house neither. Ah'm goin' tuh de white folks bout *you*, mah young man, de very nex' time you lay yo' han's on me. Mah cup is done run ovah." Delia said this with no signs of fear and Sykes departed from the house, threatening her, but made not the slightest move to carry out any of them.

That night he did not return at all, and the next day being Sunday, Delia was glad that she did not have to quarrel before she hitched up her pony and drove the four miles to Woodbridge.

She stayed to the night service—"love feast" which was very warm and full of spirit. In the emotional winds her domestic trials were borne far and wide so that she sang as she drove homeward,

> *"Jurden water, black an' col'*
> *Chills de body, not de soul*
> *An' Ah wantah cross Jurden in uh calm time."*

She came from the barn to the kitchen door and stopped. "Whut's de mattah, ol' satan, you aint kickin' up yo' racket?" She addressed the snake's box. Complete silence. She went on into the house with a new hope in its birth struggles.

Perhaps her threat to go to the white folks had frightened Sykes! Perhaps he was sorry! Fifteen years of misery and suppression had brought Delia to the place where she would hope *anything* that looked towards a way over or through her wall of inhibitions.

She felt in the match safe behind the stove at once for a match. There was only one there.

"Dat niggah wouldn't fetch nothin' heah tuh save his rotten neck, but he kin run thew whut Ah brings quick enough. Now he done toted off nigh on tuh haff uh box uh matches. He done had dat 'oman heah in mah house, too."

Nobody but a woman could tell how she knew this even before she struck the match. But she did and it put her into a new fury.

Presently she brought in the tubs to put the white things to soak. This time she decided she need not bring the hamper out of the bedroom; she would go in there and do the sorting. She picked up the pot-bellied lamp and went in. The room was small and the hamper stood hard by the foot of the white iron bed. She could sit and reach through the bedposts—resting as she worked.

"Ah wantah cross Jurden in uh calm time." She was singing again. The mood of the "love feast" had returned. She threw back the lid of the basket almost gaily. Then, moved by both horror and terror, [s]he spring back toward the door. *There lay the snake in the basket!* He moved sluggishly at first, but even as she turned round and round, jumped up and down in an insanity of fear, he began to stir vigorously. She saw him pouring his awful beauty from the basket upon the bed, then she seized the lamp and ran as fast as she could to the kitchen. The wind from the open door blew out the light and the darkness added to her terror. She sped to the darkness of the yard, slamming the door after her before she thought to set down the lamp. She did not feel safe even on the ground, so she climbed up in the hay barn.

There for an hour or more she lay sprawled upon the hay a gibbering wreck.

Finally she grew quiet, and after that, coherent thought. With this, stalked through her a cold, bloody rage. Hours of this. A period of introspection, a space of retrospection, then a mixture of both. Out of this an awful calm.

"Well, Ah done de bes' Ah could. If things aint right, Gawd knows taint mah fault."

She went to sleep—a twitchy sleep—and woke up to a faint gray sky. There was a loud hollow sound below. She peered out. Sykes was at the wood-pile, de-molishing a wire-covered box.

He hurried to the kitchen door, but hung outside there some minutes before he entered, and stood some minutes more inside before he closed it after him.

The gray in the sky was spreading. Delia descended without fear now, and crouched beneath the low bedroom window. The drawn shade shut out the dawn, shut in the night. But the thin walls held back no sound.

"Dat ol' scratch is woke up now!" She mused at the tremendous whirr inside, which every woodsman knows, is one of the sound illusions. The rattler is a ven-triloquist. His whirr sounds to the right, to the left, straight ahead, behind, close under foot—everywhere but where it is. Woe to him who guesses wrong unless he is prepared to hold up his end of the argument! Sometimes he strikes without rat-tling at all.

Inside, Sykes heard nothing until he knocked a pot lid off the stove while try-ing to reach the match safe in the dark. He had emptied his pockets at Bertha's.

The snake seemed to wake up under the stove and Sykes made a quick leap into the bedroom. In spite of the gin he had had, his head was clearing now.

"Mah Gawd !" he chattered, "ef Ah could on'y struck uh light!"

The rattling ceased for a moment as he stood paralyzed. He waited. It seemed that the snake waited also.

"Oh, fuh de light! Ah thought he'd be too sick"—Sykes was muttering to himself when the whirr began again, closer, right underfoot this time. Long before this, Sykes' ability to think had been flattened down to primitive instinct and he leaped— onto the bed.

Outside Delia heard a cry that might have come from a maddened chimpanzee, a stricken gorilla. All the terror, all the horror, all the rage that man possibly could express, without a recognizable human sound.

A tremendous stir inside there, another series of animal screams, the intermittent whirr of the reptile. The shade torn violently down from the window, letting in the red dawn, a huge brown hand seizing the window stick, great dull blows upon the wooden floor punctuating the gibberish of sound long after the rattle of the snake had abruptly subsided. All this Delia could see and hear from her place beneath the window, and it made her ill. She crept over to the four-o'clocks and stretched herself on the cool earth to recover.

She lay there. "Delia, Delia!" She could hear Sykes calling in a most despairing tone as one who expected no answer. The sun crept on up, and he called. Delia could not move—her legs were gone flabby. She never moved, he called, and the sun kept rising.

"Mah Gawd!" She heard him moan, "Mah Gawd fum Heben!" She heard him stumbling about and got up from her flower-bed. The sun was growing warm. As she approached the door she heard him call out hopefully, "Delia, is dat you Ah heah ?"

She saw him on his hands and knees as soon as she reached the door. He crept an inch or two toward her—all that he was able, and she saw his horribly swollen neck and [h]is one open eye shining with hope. A surge of pity too strong to support bore her away from that eye that must, could not, fail to see the tubs. He would see the lamp. Orlando with its doctors was too far. She could scarcely reach the Chinaberry tree, where she waited in the growing heat while inside she knew the cold river was creeping up and up to extinguish that eye which must know by now that she knew.

Fire Burns
A Department of Comment
Wallace Thurman

Some time ago, while reviewing Carl Van Vechten's lava laned Nigger Heaven I made the prophecy that Harlem Negroes, once their aversion to the "nigger" in the title was forgotten, would erect a statue on the corner of 135th Street and Seventh Avenue, and dedicate it to this ultrasophisticated Iowa New Yorker.

So far my prophecy has failed to pan out, and superficially it seems as if it never will, for instead of being enshrined for his pseudo-sophisticated, semi-serious, semi-ludicrous effusion about Harlem, Mr. Van Vechten is about to be lynched, at least in effigy.

Yet I am loathe to retract or to temper my first prophecy. Human nature is too perverse and prophecies do not necessarily have to be fulfilled within a generation. Rather, they can either be fulfilled or else belied with startling two-facedness throughout a series of generations, which, of course, creates the possibility that the fulfillments may outnumber the beliements and thus gain credence for the prophecy with posterity. Witness the Bible.

However, in defending my prophecy I do not wish to endow Mr. Van Vechten's novel (?) with immortality, but there is no real reason why Nigger Heaven should not eventually be as stupidly acclaimed as it is now being stupidly damned by the majority of Harlem's dark inhabitants. Thus I defiantly reiterate that a few years hence Mr. Van Vechten will be spoken of as a kindly gent rather than as a moral leper exploiting people who had believed him to be a sincere friend.

I for one, and strange as it may sound, there are others, who believe that Carl Van Vechten was rendered sincere during his explorations and observations of Negro life in Harlem, even if he remained characteristically superficial. Superficiality does not necessarily denote a lack of sincerity, and even superficiality may occasionally delve into deep pots of raw life. What matter if they be flesh pots?

In writing Nigger Heaven the author wavered between sentimentality and sophistication. That the sentimentality won out is his funeral. That the sophistication stung certain Negroes to the quick is their funeral.

The odds are about even. Harlem cabarets have received another public boost and are wearing out cash register keys, and entertainers' throats and orchestra instruments. The so-called intelligentsia of Harlem has exposed its inherent stupidity. And Nigger Heaven is a best seller.

Group criticism of current writings, morals, life, politics, or religion is always ridiculous, but what could be more ridiculous than the wholesale condemnation of a book which only one-tenth of the condemnators have or will read. And even if the book was as vile, as degrading, and as defamatory to the character of the Harlem Negro as the Harlem Negro now declares, his criticisms would not be considered valid by an intelligent person as long as the critic had had no reading contact with the book.

The objectors to Nigger Heaven claim that the author came to Harlem, ingratiated himself with Harlem folk, and then with a supercilious grin and a salacious smirk, lolled at his desk downtown and dashed off a pornographic document about uptown in which all of the Negro characters are pictured as being debased, lecherous creatures not at all characteristic or true to type, and that, moreover, the author provokes the impression that all of Harlem's inhabitants are cabaret hounds and thirsty neurotics. He did not tell, say his critics, of our well bred, well behaved church-going majorities, nor of our night schools filled with eager elders, nor of our brilliant college youth being trained in the approved contemporary manner, nor of our quiet, home loving thousands who hardly know what the word cabaret connotes. He told only of lurid night life and of uninhibited sybarites. Therefore, since he has done these things and neglected to do these others the white people who read the book will believe that all Harlem Negroes are like the Byrons, the Lascas, the Pettijohns, the Rubys, the Creepers, the Bonifaces, and the other lewd hussies and whoremongers in the book.

It is obvious that these excited folk do not realize that any white person who would believe such poppy-cock probably believes it anyway, without any additional aid from Mr. Van Vechten, and should such a person read a tale anent our non-cabareting, church-going Negroes, presented in all their virtue and glory and with their human traits, their human hypocrisy and their human perversities glossed over, written, say, by Jessie Fauset, said person would laugh derisively and allege that Miss Fauset had not told the truth, the same as Harlem

Negroes are alleging that Carl Van Vechten has not told the truth. It really makes no difference to the race's welfare what such ignoramuses think, and it would seem that any author preparing to write about Negroes in Harlem or anywhere else (for I hear that DuBose Heyward has been roundly denounced by Charlestonian Negroes for his beautiful Porgy) should take whatever phases of their life that seem the most interesting to him, and develop them as he pleases. Why Negroes imagine that any writer is going to write what Negroes think he ought to write about them is too ridiculous to merit consideration. It would seem that they would shy away from being pigeon-holed so long have they been the rather lamentable victims of such a typically American practice, yet Negroes would have all Negroes appearing in contemporary literature made as ridiculous and as false to type as the older school of pseudo-humorous, sentimental white writers made their Uncle Toms, they Topsys, and their Mammies, or as the Octavius Roy Cohen school now make their more modern "cullud" folk.

One young lady, prominent in Harlem collegiate circles, spoke forth in a public forum (oh yes, they even have public forums where they spend their time anouncing that they have not read the book, and that the author is a moral leper who also commits literary sins), that there was only one character in Nigger Heaven who was true to type. This character, the unwitting damsel went on, was Mary Love. It seems as if all the younger Negro women in Harlem are prototypes of this Mary Love, and it is pure, poor, virtuous, vapid Mary, to whom they point as a typical life model.

Again there has been no realization that Mary Love is the least life-life character in the book, or that it is she who suffers most from her creator's newly acquired seriousness and sentimentality, she who suffers most of the whole ensemble because her creator discovered, in his talented trippings around Manhattan, drama at which he could not chuckle the while his cavalier pen sped cleverly on in the same old way yet did not—could not spank.

But—had all the other characters in Nigger Heaven approximated Mary's standard, the statue to Carl Van Vechten would be an actualized instead of a deferred possibility, and my prophecy would be gloriously fulfilled instead of being ignominiously belied.

THE FIRE!! PRESS

V

THE HARLEM RENAISSANCE, 1926–1930

By the end of 1926 the Harlem Renaissance was in full swing. Literary production accelerated. From 1927 through 1930 the major writers of the Harlem Renaissance published an additional twenty-two books of poetry, fiction, or literary anthologies. Lesser-known poets and writers, among them Ann Spencer, Gwendolyn Bennett, Frank Horne, Helene Johnson, Waring Cuney, Georgia Douglas Johnson, and Eric Walrond continued to contribute to the literary scene. Black art and music thrived. Tthe sculptors Augusta Savage and Richmond Barthe, painters Palmer Hayden and Archibald Motley, and the photographer James VanDerZee joined Aaron Douglas to create a vibrant community of visual and plastic artists. Jazz and the blues entered the American mass culture as white fans toured the cabarets and nightclubs of Harlem, and black musicians took their music downtown. African American musical theater and musical reviews remained popular, while small theater groups organized to produce the works of black playwrights and black interpretations of classic theater pieces. The new artistic venues of radio and film attracted talented African American artists, or exploited the fascination with Harlem and black life. The motion picture industry witnessed the emergence of black filmmakers such as Oscar Micheaux and motion picture stars like Paul Robeson and Josephine Baker; in radio the most popular program in America was *Amos 'n Andy*, a comedy set in the black ghetto, but written and acted by whites.

The Harlem Renaissance did not confine itself to a single artistic vision, style, source of inspiration, or philosophy. In poetry it ranged from the classical structures of Countee Cullen to the free-flowing verses of Langston Hughes; its fiction encompassed the middle class, formal style of Jessie Fauset and Nella Larsen, the simple realism of Langston Hughes, and the biting satire of Wallace Thurman, as well as the lusty depiction of lower class black life of Claude McKay. Amidst this diversity were two unifying factors. The artists and writers were determined to give voice or image to the African American experience, in all of its complexity and manifestations. And they demanded the freedom and independence to do this on their own terms, based on their own vision and aesthetic sense.

By the end of the decade there was no dispute that a cultural upheaval was transforming the African American community and that the resulting creativity in art, literature, theater, and music had an impact on both the black and the larger white world. Argument centered on the nature of the movement, the degree to which it was controlled by or pandered to white expectations, the quality of the art and literature it produced, and the impact of the movement on race in America. W.E.B. Dubois and others worried that white publishers and patrons had taken control of the movement, and co-opted black writers and artists to exposing aspects of the African American experience that intensified negative racial stereotypes. These fears certainly were manifest in the distillation of the African American experience into the comic and stereotyped antics of the *Amos 'n Andy* show—and the frustration that this image of blacks was written, produced, and acted by whites and for white audiences, with the revenues from the show filling white pockets. On the other hand, the quality of the work produced African American writers and artists, and the role of black critics and magazines—*The Crisis, Opportunity*, and the short-lived *Fire!!* and *Harlem*—underscore the complexity of the relationship between black artist and audience, and reveals the determination of most to pursue their artistic vision as freely as possible. In the end their work will stand on its merits.

LANGSTON HUGHES
"The Negro Artist And The Racial Mountain"
The Nation
June 23, 1926

As the Harlem Renaissance flourished in the mid 1920s, the black intelligentsia debated the nature of the movement and the nature of the legitimate expression of African American art and literature. A 1926 essay by Langston Hughes in *The Nation*, continuing in the tradition of *Fire!!*, presents his views on this issue. The twenty-four-year-old poet rejects efforts of black or white critics to restrict the artistic freedom of the movement, instead asserting the freedom to explore all aspects of the black experience.

One of the most promising of the young Negro poets said to me once, "I want to be a poet—not a Negro poet," meaning, I believe, "I want to write like a white poet"; meaning subconsciously, "I would like to be a white poet"; meaning behind that, "I would like to be white." And I was sorry the young man said that, for no great poet has ever been afraid of being himself. And I doubted then that, with his desire to run away spiritually from his race, this boy would ever be a great poet. But this is the mountain standing in the way of any true Negro art in America—this urge within the race toward whiteness, the, desire to pour racial individuality into the mold of American standardization, and to be as little Negro and as much American as possible.

But let us look at the immediate background of this young poet. His family is of what I suppose one would call the Negro middle class: people who are by no means rich yet never uncomfortable nor hungry—smug, contented, respectable folk, members of the Baptist church. The father goes to work every morning. He is a chief steward at a large white club. The mother sometimes does fancy sewing or supervises parties for the rich families of the town. The children go to a mixed school. In the home they read white papers and magazines. And the mother often says "Don't be like niggers" when the children are bad. A frequent phrase from the father is, "Look how well a white man does things." And so the word white comes to be unconsciously a symbol of all virtues. It holds for the children beauty, morality, and money. The whisper of "I want to be white" runs silently through their minds. This young poet's home is, I believe, a fairly typical home of the colored middle class. One sees immediately how difficult it would be for an artist born in such a home to interest himself in interpreting the beauty of his own people. He is never taught to see that beauty. He is taught rather not to see it, or if he does, to be ashamed of it when it is not according to Caucasian patterns.

For racial culture the home of a self-styled "high-class" Negro has nothing better to offer. Instead there will perhaps be more aping of things white than in a less cultured or less wealthy home. The father is perhaps a doctor, lawyer, landowner, or politician. The mother may be a social worker, or a teacher, or she may do nothing and have a maid. Father is often dark but he has usually married the lightest woman he could find. The family attend a fashionable church where few really colored faces are to be found. And they themselves draw a color line. In the North they go to white theatres and white movies. And in the South they have at least two cars and house "like white folks." Nordic manners, Nordic faces, Nordic hair, Nordic art (if any), and an Episcopal heaven. A very high mountain indeed for the would-be racial artist to climb in order to discover himself and his people.

But then there are the low-down folks, the so-called common element, and they are the majority—may the Lord be praised! The people who have their hip of gin on Saturday nights and are not too important to themselves or the community, or too well fed, or too learned to watch the lazy world go round. They live on Seventh Street in Washington or State Street in Chicago and they do not particularly care whether they are like white folks or anybody else. Their joy runs, bang! into ecstasy. Their religion soars to a shout. Work maybe a little today, rest a little tomorrow. Play awhile. Sing awhile. O, let's dance! These common people are not afraid of spirituals, as for a long time their more intellectual brethren were, and jazz is their child. They furnish a wealth of colorful, distinctive material for any artist because they still hold their own individuality in the face of American standardizations. And perhaps these common people will give to the world its truly great Negro artist, the one who is not afraid to be himself. Whereas the better-class Negro would tell the artist what to do, the people at least let him alone when he does appear. And they are not ashamed of him—if they know he exists at all. And they accept what beauty is their own without question.

Certainly there is, for the American Negro artist who can escape the restrictions the more advanced among his own group would put upon him, a great field of unused material ready for his art. Without going outside his race, and even among the better classes with their "white" culture and conscious American manners, but still Negro enough to be different, there is sufficient matter to furnish a black artist with a lifetime of creative work. And when he chooses to touch on the relations between Negroes and whites in this country with their innumerable overtones and undertones surely, and especially for literature and the drama, there is an inexhaustible supply of themes at hand. To these the Negro artist can give his racial individuality, his heritage of rhythm and warmth, and his incongruous humor that so often, as in the Blues, becomes ironic laughter mixed with tears. But let us look again at the mountain.

A prominent Negro clubwoman in Philadelphia paid eleven dollars to hear Raquel Meller sing Andalusian popular songs. But she told me a few weeks before she would not think of going to hear "that woman," Clara Smith, a great black artist, sing Negro folksongs. And many an upper-class Negro church, even now, would not dream of employing a spiritual in its services. The drab melodies in white folks' hymnbooks are much to be preferred. "We want to worship the Lord correctly and quietly. We don't believe in 'shouting.' Let's be dull like the Nordics," they say, in effect.

The road for the serious black artist, then, who would produce a racial art is most certainly rocky and the mountain is high. Until recently he received almost no encouragement for his work from either white or colored people. The fine novels of Chesnutt go out of print with neither race noticing their passing. The quaint charm and humor of Dunbar's dialect verse brought to him, in his day, largely the same kind of encouragement one would give a sideshow freak (A colored man writing poetry! How odd!) or a clown (How amusing!).

The present vogue in things Negro, although it may do as much harm as good for the budding colored artist, has at least done this: it has brought him forcibly to the attention of his own people among whom for so long, unless the other race had noticed him beforehand, he was a prophet with little honor. I understand that Charles Gilpin acted for years in Negro theatres without any special acclaim from his own, but when Broadway gave him eight curtain calls, Negroes, too, began to beat a tin pan in his honor. I know a young colored writer, a manual worker by day, who had been writing well for the colored magazines for some years, but it was not until he recently broke into the white publications and his first book was accepted by a prominent New York publisher that the "best" Negroes in his city took the trouble to discover that he lived there. Then almost immediately they decided to give a grand dinner for him. But the society ladies were careful to whisper to his mother that perhaps she'd better not come. They were not sure she would have an evening gown.

The Negro artist works against an undertow of sharp criticism and misunderstanding from his own group and unintentional bribes from the whites. "Oh, be respectable, write about nice people, show how good we are," say the Negroes. "Be stereotyped, don't go too far, don't shatter our illusions about you, don't amuse us too seriously. We will pay you," say the whites. Both would have told Jean Toomer not to write *Cane*. The colored people did not praise it. The white people did not buy it. Most of the colored people who did read *Cane* hate it. They are afraid of it. Although the critics gave it good reviews the public remained indifferent. Yet (excepting the work of Du Bois) *Cane* contains the finest prose written by a Negro in America. And like the singing of Robeson, it is truly racial.

But in spite of the Nordicized Negro intelligentsia and the desires of some white editors we have an honest American Negro literature already with us. Now I await the rise of the Negro theatre. Our folk music, having achieved world-wide fame, offers itself to the genius of the great individual American composer who is to come. And within the next decade I expect to see the work of a growing school of colored artists who paint and model the beauty of dark faces and create with new technique the expressions of their own soul-world. And the Negro dancers who will dance like flame and the singers who will continue to carry our songs to all who listen—they will be with us in even greater numbers tomorrow.

Most of my own poems are racial in theme and treatment, derived from the life I know. In many of them I try to grasp and hold some of the meanings and rhythms of jazz. I am as sincere as I know how to be in these poems and yet after every reading I answer questions like these from my own people: Do you think Negroes should always write about Negroes? I wish you wouldn't read some of your poems to white folks. How do you find anything interesting in a place like a cabaret? Why do you write about black people? You aren't black. What makes you do so many jazz poems?

But jazz to me is one of the inherent expressions of Negro life in America; the eternal tom-tom beating in the Negro soul-the tom-tom of revolt against weariness in a white world, a world of subway trains, and work, work, work; the tom-tom of joy and laughter, and pain swallowed in a smile. Yet the Philadelphia club-woman is ashamed to say that her race created it and she does not like me to write about it. The old subconscious "white is best" runs through her mind. Years of study under white teachers, a lifetime of white books, pictures, and papers, and white manners, morals, and Puritan standards made her dislike the spirituals. And now she turns up her nose at jazz and all its manifestations—likewise almost everything else distinctly racial. She doesn't care for the Winold Reiss portraits of Negroes because they are "too Negro." She does not want a true picture of herself from anybody. She wants the artist to flatter her, to make the white world believe that all Negroes are as smug and as near white in soul as she wants to be. But, to my mind, it is the duty of the younger Negro artist, if he accepts any duties at all from outsiders, to change through the force of his art that old whispering "I want to be white," hidden in the aspirations of his people, to "Why should I want to be white? I am a Negro—and beautiful"?

So I am ashamed for the black poet who says, "I want to be a poet, not a Negro poet," as though his own racial world were not as interesting as any other world. I am ashamed, too, for the colored artist who runs from the painting of Negro faces to the painting of sunsets after the manner of the academicians because he fears the strange un-whiteness of his own features. An artist must be free to choose what he does, certainly, but he must also never be afraid to do what he might choose.

Let the blare of Negro jazz bands and the bellowing voice of Bessie Smith singing Blues penetrate the closed ears of the colored near-intellectual until they listen and perhaps understand. Let Paul Robeson singing "Water Boy," and Rudolph Fisher writing about the streets of Harlem, and Jean Toomer holding the heart of Georgia in his hands, and Aaron Douglas drawing strange black fantasies cause the smug Negro middle class to turn from their white, respectable, ordinary books and papers to catch a glimmer of their own beauty. We younger Negro artists who create now intend to express our individual dark-skinned selves without fear or shame. If white people are pleased we are glad. If they are not, it doesn't matter. We know we are beautiful. And ugly too. The tom-tom cries and the tom-tom laughs. If colored people are pleased we are glad. If they are not, their displeasure doesn't matter either. We build our temples for tomorrow, strong as we know how, and we stand on top of the mountain, free within ourselves.

W. E. B. DU BOIS
ON ARTISTIC FREEDOM AND RESPONSIBILITY

The most influential critic of Langston Hughes's concept of artistic freedom was W.E.B. Du Bois, editor of the NAACP's *The Crisis*, the most respected black intellectual of his generation, and a poet and novelist in his own right. He disagreed with Hughes and other African Americans writers and artists who insisted on the right to depict black life as they saw it, often writing about the colorful but seamy experiences of Harlem's underworld and of the black masses. For Du Bois anything that depicted blacks in a negative manner contributed to white prejudice and therefore was unacceptable. In February 1926 he launched a symposium in *The Crisis* on the appropriate literary depiction of African Americans when he published "A Questionnaire" and invited writers to respond to the questions posed. Between 1926 and November, 1926 twenty-one writers, critics, and publishers, both black and white, had their responses printed in *The Crisis* in a series entitled "The Negro in Art, How Shall He Be Portrayed?" Du Bois responded himself, first in a speech to the NAACP gathering in Chicago, and then in an essay in the October 1926 issue of *The Crisis*.

W.E.B. Du Bois
"A Questionnaire"
The Crisis, February 1926

There has long been controversy within and without the Negro race as to just how the Negro should be treated in art—how he should be pictured by writers and portrayed by artists. Most writers have said naturally that any portrayal of any kind of Negro was permissible so long as the work was pleasing and the artist sincere. But the Negro has objected vehemently—first in general to the conventional Negro in American literature; then in specific cases: to the Negro portrayed in the "Birth of a Nation"; in MacFall's "Wooings of Jezebel Pettyfer" and in Stribling's "Birthright"; in Octavius Roy Cohen's monstrosities. In general they have contended that while the individual portrait may be true and artistic, the net result to American literature to date is to picture twelve million Americans as prostitutes, thieves and fools and that such "freedom" in art is miserably unfair.

This attitude is natural but as Carl Van Vechten writes us: "It is the kind of thing, indeed, which might be effective in preventing many excellent Negro writers from speaking any truth which might be considered unpleasant. There are plenty of unpleasant truths to be spoken about any race. The true artist speaks out fearlessly. The critic judges the artistic result; nor should he be concerned with anything else".

In order to place this matter clearly before the thinking element of Negro Americans and especially before young authors, THE CRISIS is asking several authors to write their opinions on the following matters:

1. When the artist, black or white, portrays Negro characters is he under any obligations or limitations as to the sort of character he will portray ?

2. Can any author be criticized for painting the worst or the best characters of a group?

3. Can publishers be criticized for refusing to handle novels that portray Negroes of education and accomplishment, on the ground that these characters are no different from white folk and therefore not interesting?

4. What are Negroes to do when they are continually painted at their worst and judged by the public as they are painted?

5. Does the situation of the educated Negro in America with its pathos, humiliation and tragedy call for artistic treatment at least as sincere and sympathetic as "Porgy" received?

6. Is not the continual portrayal of the sordid, foolish and criminal among Ne-

groes convincing the world that this and this alone is really and essentially Negroid, and preventing white artists from knowing any other types and preventing black artists from daring to paint them?

7. Is there not a real danger that young colored writers will be tempted to follow the popular trend in portraying Negro character in the underworld rather than seeking to paint the truth about themselves and their own social class?

We have already received comments on these questions from Sinclair Lewis, Carl Van Vechten, Major Haldane MacFall and others. We shall publish these and other letters in a series of articles. *Meantime let our readers remember our contest for $600 in prizes and send in their manuscripts no matter what attitude they take in regard to this controversy. Manuscripts, etc., will be received until May 1, 1926.*

W.E.B. Du Bois
"Criteria of Negro Art"
The Crisis, October 1926

So many persons have asked for the complete text of the address delivered by Dr. Du Bois at the Chicago Conference of the National Association for the Advancement of Colored People that we are publishing the address here.

I do not doubt but there are some in this audience who are a little disturbed at the subject of this meeting, and particularly at the subject I have chosen. Such people are thinking something like this: "How is it that an organization like this, a group of radicals trying to bring new things into the world, a fighting organization which has come up out of the blood and dust of battle, struggling for the right of black men to be ordinary human beings-how is it that an organization of this kind can turn aside to talk about Art? After all, what have we who are slaves and black to do with Art?"

Or perhaps there are others who feel a certain relief and are saying, "After all it is rather satisfactory after all this talk about rights and fighting to sit and dream of something which leaves a nice taste in the mouth".

Let me tell you that neither of these groups is right. The thing we are talking about tonight is part of the great fight we are carrying on and it represents a forward and an upward look-a pushing onward. You and I have been breasting hills; we have been climbing upward; there has been progress and we can see it day by day looking back along blood-filled paths. But as you go through the valleys and over the foothills, so long as you are climbing, the direction,—north, south, east or west,—is of less importance. But when gradually the vista widens and you begin to see the world at your feet and the far horizon, then it is time to know more precisely whither you are going and what you really want.

What do we want? What is the thing we are after? As it was phrased last night it had a certain truth: We want to be Americans, full-fledged Americans, with all the rights of other American citizens. But is that all? Do we want simply to be Americans? Once in a while through all of us there flashes some clairvoyance, some clear idea, of what America really is. We who are dark can see America in a way that white Americans can not. And seeing our country thus, are we satisfied with its present goals and ideals?

In the high school where I studied we learned most of Scott's "Lady of the Lake" by heart. In after life once it was my privilege to see the lake. It was Sunday. It was quiet. You could glimpse the deer wandering in unbroken forests; you could hear the soft ripple of romance on the waters. Around me fell the cadence of that poetry of my youth. I fell asleep full of the enchantment of the Scottish border. A new day broke and with it came a sudden rush of excursionists. They were mostly Americans and they were loud and strident. They poured upon the little pleasure boat,—men with their hats a little on one side and drooping cigars in the wet corners of their mouths; women who shared their conversation with the world. They all tried to get everywhere first. They pushed other people out of the way. They made all sorts of incoherent noises and gestures so that the quiet home folk and the visitors from other lands silently and half-wonderingly gave way before them. They struck a note not evil but wrong. They carried, perhaps, a sense of strength and accomplishment, but their hearts had no conception of the beauty which pervaded this holy place.

If you tonight suddenly should become full-fledged Americans; if your color faded, or the color line here in Chicago was miraculously forgotten; suppose, too, you became at the same time rich and powerful,—what is it that you would want? What would you immediately seek? Would you buy the most powerful of motor cars and outrace Cook County? Would you buy the most elaborate estate on the North Shore? Would you be a Rotarian or a Lion or a What-not of the very last degree? Would you wear the most striking clothes, give the richest dinners and buy the longest press notices?

Even as you visualize such ideals you know in your hearts that these are not the things you really want. You realize this sooner than the average white American because, pushed aside as we have been in America, there has come to us not only a certain distaste for the tawdry and flamboyant but a vision of what the world could be if it were really a beautiful world; if we had the true spirit; if we had the Seeing Eye, the Cunning Hand, the Feeling Heart; if we had, to be sure, not perfect happiness, but plenty of good hard work, the inevitable suffering that always comes with life; sacrifice and waiting, all that—but, nevertheless, lived in a world where men know, where men create, where they realize themselves and where they enjoy life. It is that sort of a world we want to create for ourselves and for all America.

After all, who shall describe Beauty? What is it? I remember tonight four beautiful things: The Cathedral at Cologne, a forest in stone, set in light and changing shadow, echoing with sunlight and solemn song; a village of the Veys in West Africa, a little thing of mauve and purple, quiet, lying content and shining in the sun; a black and velvet room where on a throne rests, in old and yellowing marble, the broken curves of the Venus of Milo; a single phrase of music in the Southern South—utter melody, haunting and appealing, suddenly arising out of night and eternity, beneath the moon.

Such is Beauty. Its variety is infinite, its possibility is endless. In normal life all may have it and have it yet again. The world is full of it; and yet today the mass of human beings are choked away from it, and their lives distorted and made ugly. This is not only wrong, it is silly. Who shall right this well-nigh universal failing? Who shall let this world be beautiful? Who shall restore to men the glory of sunsets and the peace of quiet sleep?

We black folk may help for we have within us as a race new stirrings; stirrings of the beginning of a new appreciation of joy, of a new desire to create, of a new will to be; as though in this morning of group life we had awakened from some sleep that at once dimly mourns the past and dreams a splendid future; and there has come the conviction that the Youth that is here today, the Negro Youth, is a different kind of Youth, because in some new way it bears this mighty prophecy on its breast, with a new realization of itself, with new determination for all mankind.

What has this Beauty to do with the world? What has Beauty to do with Truth and Goodness—with the facts of the world and the right actions of men? "Nothing", the artists rush to answer. They may be right. I am but an humble disciple of art and cannot presume to say. I am one who tells the truth and exposes evil and seeks with Beauty and for Beauty to set the world right. That somehow, somewhere eternal and perfect Beauty sits above Truth and Right I can conceive, but here and now and in the world in which I work they are for me un-separated and inseparable.

This is brought to us peculiarly when as artists we face our own past as a people. There has come to us—and it has come especially through the man we are going to honor tonight [Carter G. Woodson, recipient of the 12th Spingarn Medal]— a realization of that past, of which for long years we have been ashamed, for which we have apologized. We thought nothing could come out of that past which we wanted to remember; which we wanted to hand down to our children. Suddenly, this same past is taking on form, color and reality, and in a half shame-faced way we are beginning to be proud of it. We are remembering that the romance of the world did not die and lie forgotten in the Middle Age; that if you want romance to deal with you must have it here and now and in your own hands.

I once knew a man and woman. They had two children, a daughter who was white and a daughter who was brown; the daughter who was white married a white man; and when her wedding was preparing the daughter who was brown prepared to go and celebrate. But the mother said, "No!" and the brown daughter went into her room and turned on the gas and died. Do you want Greek tragedy swifter than that?

Or again, here is a little Southern town and you are in the public square. On one side of the square is the office of a colored lawyer and on all the other sides are men who do not like colored lawyers. A white woman goes into the black man's office and points to the white-filled square and says, "I want five hundred dollars now and if I do not get it I am going to scream."

Have you heard the story of the conquest of German East Africa? Listen to the untold tale: There were 40,000 black men and 4,000 white men who talked German. There were 20,000 black men and 12,000 white men who talked English. There were 10,000 black men and 400 white men who talked French. In Africa then where the Mountains of the Moon raised their white and snow-capped heads into the mouth of the tropic sun, where Nile and Congo rise and the Great Lakes swim, these men fought; they struggled on mountain, hill and valley, in river, lake and swamp, until in masses they sickened, crawled and died; until the 4,000 white Germans had become mostly bleached bones; until nearly all the 12,000 white Englishmen had returned to South Africa, and the 400 Frenchmen to Belgium and Heaven; all except a mere handful of the white men died; but thousands of black men from East, West and South Africa, from Nigeria and the Valley of the Nile, and from the West Indies still struggled, fought and died. For four years they fought and won and lost German East Africa; and all you hear about it is that England and Belgium conquered German Africa for the allies!

Such is the true and stirring stuff of which Romance is born and from this stuff come the stirrings of men who are beginning to remember that this kind of material is theirs; and this vital life of their own kind is beckoning them on.

The question comes next as to the interpretation of these new stirrings, of this new spirit: Of what is the colored artist capable? We have had on the part of both colored and white people singular unanimity of judgment in the past. Colored people have said: "This work must be inferior because it comes from colored people." White people have said: "It is inferior because it is done by colored people." But today there is coming to both the realization that the work of the black man is not always inferior. Interesting stories come to us. A professor in the University of Chicago read to a class that had studied literature a passage of poetry and asked them to guess the author. They guessed a goodly company from Shelley and Robert Browning down to Tennyson and Masefield. The author was Countée Cullen. Or again the English critic John Drinkwater went down to a Southern seminary, one of the sort which "finishes" young white women of the South. The students sat with their wooden faces while he tried to get some response out of them. Finally he said, "Name me some of your Southern poets". They hesitated. He said finally, "I'll start out with your best: Paul Laurence Dunbar"!

With the growing recognition of Negro artists in spite of the severe handicaps, one comforting thing is occurring to both white and black. They are whispering, "Here is a way out. Here is the real solution of the color problem. The recognition accorded Cullen, Hughes, Fauset, White and others shows there is no real color line. "Keep quiet! Don't complain! Work! All will be well!"

I will not say that already this chorus amounts to a conspiracy. Perhaps I am naturally too suspicious. But I will say that there are today a surprising number of white people who are getting great satisfaction out of these younger Negro writers because they think it is going to stop agitation of the Negro question. They say, "What is the use of your fighting and complaining, do the great thing and the reward is there." And many colored people are all too eager to follow this advice; especially those who weary of the eternal struggle along the color line, who are afraid to fight and to whom the money of philanthropists and the alluring publicity are subtle and deadly bribes. They say, "What is the use of fighting? Why not show simply what we deserve and let the reward come to us?"

And it is right here that the National Association for the Advancement of Colored People comes upon the field, comes with its great call to a new battle, a new fight and new things to fight before the old things are wholly won; and to say that the beauty of truth and freedom which shall some day be our heritage and the heritage of all civilized men is not in our hands yet and that we ourselves must not fail to realize.

Here there is in New York tonight a black woman molding clay by herself in a little bare room, because there is not a single school of sculpture in New York where she is welcome. Surely there are doors she might burst through, but when God makes a sculptor He does not always make the pushing sort of person who beats his way through doors thrust in his face. This girl is working her hands off to get out of this country so that she can get some sort of training.

There was Richard Brown. If he had been white he would have been alive today instead of dead of neglect. Many helped him when he asked but he was not the kind of boy that always asks. He was simply one who made colors sing.

There is a colored woman in Chicago who is a great musician. She thought she would like to study at Fontainebleau this summer where Walter Damrosch and a score of leaders of art have an American school of music. But the application blank of this school says: "I am a white American and I apply for admission to the school."

We can go on the stage; we can be just as funny as white Americans wish us to be; we can play all the sordid parts that America likes to assign to Negroes; but for anything else there is still small place for us.

And so I might go on. But let me sum up with this: Suppose the only Negro who survived some centuries hence was the Negro painted by white Americans in the novels and essays they have written. What would people in a hundred years say of black Americans? Now turn it around. Suppose you were to write a story and put in it the kind of people you know and like and imagine. You might get it published and you might not. And the "might not" is still far bigger than the "might." The white publishers catering to white folk would say, "It is not interesting"—to white folk, naturally not. They want Uncle Toms, Topsies, good "darkies" and clowns. I have in my office a story with all the earmarks of truth. A young man says that he started out to write and had his stories accepted. Then he began to write about the things he knew best about, that is, about his own people. He submitted a story to a magazine which said, "We are sorry, but we cannot take it." "I sat down and revised my story, changing the color of the characters and the locale and sent it under an assumed name with a change of address and it was accepted by the same magazine that had refused it, the editor promising to take anything else I might send in providing it was good enough."

We have, to be sure, a few recognized and successful Negro artists; but they are not all those fit to survive or even a good minority. They are but the remnants of that ability and genius among us whom the accidents of education and opportunity have raised on the tidal waves of chance. We black folk are not altogether peculiar in this. After all, in the world at large, it is only the accident, the remnant, that gets the chance to make the most of itself, but if this is true of the white world it is infinitely more true of the colored world. It is not simply the great clear tenor of Roland Hayes that opened the ears of America. We have had many voices of all kinds as fine as his and America was as deaf as she was for years to him. Then a foreign land heard Hayes and put its imprint on him and immediately America with all its imitative snobbery woke up. We approved Hayes because London, Paris, and Berlin approved him and not simply because he was a great singer.

Thus it is the bounden duty of black America to begin this great work of the creation of beauty, of the preservation of beauty, of the realization of beauty, and we must use in this work all the methods that men have used before. And what have been the tools of the artist in times gone by? First of all, he has used the truth-not for the sake of truth, not as a scientist seeking truth, but as one upon whom truth eternally thrust itself as the highest handmaid of imagination, as the one great vehicle of universal understanding. Again artists have used goodness—goodness in all its aspects of justice, honor, and right not for sake of an ethical sanction but as the one true method of gaining sympathy and human interest.

The apostle of beauty thus becomes the apostle of truth and right not by choice but by inner and outer compulsion. Free he is but his freedom is ever bounded by truth and justice; and slavery only dogs him when he is denied the right to tell the truth or recognize an ideal of justice.

Thus all art is propaganda and ever must be, despite the wailing of the purists. I stand in utter shamelessness and say that whatever art I have for writing has been used always for propaganda for gaining the right of black folk to love and enjoy. I do not care a damn for any art that is not used for propaganda. But I do care when propaganda is confined to one side while the other is stripped and silent.

In New York we have two plays: "White Cargo" and "Congo." In "White Cargo" there is a fallen woman. She is black. In "Congo" the fallen woman is white. In "White Cargo" the black woman goes down further and further and in "Congo" the white woman begins with degradation but in the end is one of the angels of the Lord.

You know the current magazine story: a young white man goes down to Central America and the most beautiful colored woman there falls in love with him. She crawls across the whole isthmus to get to him. The white man says nobly, "No." He goes back to his white sweetheart in New York.

In such cases, it is not the positive propaganda of people who believe white blood divine, infallible, and holy to which I object. It is the denial of a similar right of propaganda to those who believe black blood human, lovable, and inspired with new ideals for the world. White artists themselves suffer from this narrowing of their field. They cry for freedom in dealing with Negroes because they have so little freedom in dealing with whites. DuBose Heywood writes "Porgy" and writes beautifully of the black Charleston underworld. But why does he do this? Because he cannot do a similar thing for the white people of Charleston, or they would drum him out of town. The only chance he had to tell the truth of pitiful human degradation was to tell it of colored people. I should not be surprised if Octavius Roy Cohen had approached the *Saturday Evening Post* and asked permission to write about a different kind of colored folk than the monstrosities he has created; but if he has, the *Post* has replied, "No. You are getting paid to write about the kind of colored people you are writing about."

In other words, the white public today demands from its artists, literary and pictorial, racial prejudgment which deliberately distorts truth and justice, as far as colored races are concerned, and it will pay for no other.

On the other hand, the young and slowly growing black public still wants its prophets almost equally unfree. We are bound by all sorts of customs that have come down as second-hand soul clothes of white patrons. We are ashamed of sex and we lower our eyes when people will talk of it. Our religion holds us in superstition. Our worst side has been so shamelessly emphasized that we are denying we have or ever had a worst side. In all sorts of ways we are hemmed in and our new young artists have got to fight their way to freedom.

The ultimate judge has got to be you and you have got to build yourselves up into that wide judgment, that catholicity of temper which is going to enable the artist to have his widest chance for freedom. We can afford the truth. White folk today cannot. As it is now we are handing everything over to a white jury. If a colored man wants to publish a book, he has got to get a white publisher and a white newspaper to say it is great; and then you and I say so. We must come to the place where the work of art when it appears is reviewed and acclaimed by our own free and unfettered judgment. And we are going to have a real and valuable and eternal judgment only as we make ourselves free of mind, proud of body and just of soul to all men.

And then do you know what will be said? It is already saying. Just as soon as true art emerges; just as soon as the black artist appears, someone touches the race on the shoulder and says, "He did that because he was an American, not because he was a Negro; he was born here; he was trained here; he is not a Negro—what is a Negro anyhow? He is just human; it is the kind of thing you ought to expect."

I do not doubt that the ultimate art coming from black folk is going to be just as beautiful, and beautiful largely in the same ways, as the art that comes from white folk, or yellow, or red; but the point today is that until the art of the black folk compels recognition they will not be rated as human. And when through art they compel recognition then let the world discover if it will that their art is as new as it is old and as old as new.

I had a classmate once who did three beautiful things and died. One of them was a story of a folk who found fire and then went wandering in the gloom of night seeking again the stars they had once known and lost; suddenly out of blackness they looked up and there loomed the heavens; and what was it that they said? They raised a might cry: "it is the stars, it is the ancient stars, it is the young everlasting stars!"

LANGSTON HUGHES
Poems
1922–1930

Langston Hughes was one of the most gifted and successful poets to emerge during the Harlem Renaissance. His poetry attracted attention in the early 1920s when several pieces appeared in *The Crisis*, and his work, celebrated at the 1924 Civic Club Dinner, won first place in the first *Opportunity* literary contest, and was featured in the Harlem edition of *Survey Graphic*, and again in *The New Negro*. In the second half of the 1920s Hughes published two volumes of poetry, *The Weary Blues* in 1926 and the next year *Fine Clothes to the Jew*. During the 1920s Hughes employed an experimental poetic style characterized by the use of African American musical forms, especially the blues and jazz, to shape the structure and the rhythm of his verse. He also brought into his verse African American themes, from the life of Harlem's streets and cabarets to issues of black identity and racial injustice. Hughes's poetry was controversial, praised for its innovative style and its ability to evoke the black experience through simple language and images, and criticized for pandering to the black masses and the less desirable aspects of the ghetto experience.

The poems presented here illustrate the range of Hughes's work during this period. Verses like "Mother to Son" and "Brass Spittoons" evoke the tension between dreams and the drudgery of poverty and menial work; "Cross," which later provided Hughes the basis for his play "Mulatto," addresses the complexities of racial identity; other poems explore African American and African roots, and expose the horror of racism.

"Mother to Son"
(1922)

Well, son, I'll tell you:
Life for me ain't been no crystal stair.
It's had tacks in it,
And splinters,
And boards torn up,
And places with no carpet on the floor—
Bare.
But all the time
I'se been a-climbin' on,
And reachin' landin's,
And turnin' corners,
And sometimes goin' in the dark
Where there ain't been no light.
So boy, don't you turn back.
Don't you set down on the steps
'Cause you finds it's kinder hard.
Don't you fall now—
For I'se still goin', honey,
I'se still climbin',
And life for me ain't been no crystal stair.

"When Sue Wears Red"
(1922)

When Susanna Jones wears red
Her face is like an ancient cameo
Turned brown by the ages.

Come with a blast of trumpets,
    Jesus!

When Susanna Jones wears red
A queen from some time-dead Egyptian night
Walks once again.

Blow trumpets, Jesus!

And the beauty of Susanna Jones in red
Burns in my heart a love-fire sharp like pain.

Sweet silver trumpets,
    Jesus!

"Cross"
(1925)

My old man's a white old man
And my old mother's black.
If ever I cursed my white old man
I take my curses back.

If ever I cursed my black old mother
And wished she were in hell,
I'm sorry for that evil wish
And now I wish her well.

My old man died in a fine big house.
My ma died in a shack.
I wonder where I'm gonna die,
Being neither white nor black?

"Brass Spittoons"
(1926)

Clean the spittoons, boy.
    Detroit,
    Chicago,
    Atlantic City,
    Palm Beach.
Clean the spittoons.
The steam in hotel kitchens,
And the smoke in hotel lobbies,
And the slime in hotel spittoons:
Part of my life.
    Hey, boy!
    A nickel,
    A dime,
    A dollar,
Two dollars a day.
    Hey, boy!
    A nickel,
    A dime,
    A dollar,
    Two dollars
Buys shoes for the baby.
House rent to pay.
Gin on Saturday,
Church on Sunday.
    My God!
Babies and gin and church
and women and Sunday

all mixed up with dimes and
dollars and clean spittoons
and house rent to pay.
    Hey, boy!
A bright bowl of brass is beautiful to the Lord
Bright polished brass like the cymbals
Of King David's dancers,
Like the wine cups of Solomon.
    Hey, boy!
A clean spittoon on the altar of the Lord.
A clean bright spittoon all newly polished,—
At least I can offer that.
    Come 'ere, boy!

"Song for a Dark Girl"
(1927)

Way Down South in Dixie
    (Break the heart of me)
They hung my black young lover
    To a cross roads tree.

Way Down South in Dixie
    (Bruised body high in air)
I asked the white Lord Jesus
    What was the use of prayer.

Way Down South in Dixie
    (Break the heart of me)
Love is a naked shadow
    On a gnarled and naked tree.

"Aesthete in Harlem"
(1930)

Strange,
That in this nigger place,
I should meet Life face to face
When for years, I had been seeking
Life in places gentler speaking
Until I came to this near street
And found Life—stepping on my feet!

"Afro-American Fragment"
(1930)

So long,
So far away
Is Africa.

Not even memories alive
Save those that history books create,
Save those that songs
Beat back into the blood—
Beat out of blood with words sad-sung
In strange un-Negro tongue—
So long,
So far away
Is Africa.

Subdued and time-lost
Are the drums—and yet
Through some vast mist of race
There comes this song
I do not understand
This song of atavistic land,
Of bitter yearnings lost
Without a place—
So long,
So far away
Is Africa's
Dark face.

COUNTEE CULLEN
Poems from *Color*
1925

Countee Cullen shared honors with Langston Hughes as the most talented of the young African American poets. Like Hughes, he published his first work in magazines like *The Crisis* and *Opportunity*, was a presence at the Civic Club Dinner, and won two prizes in the first *Opportunity* literary contest. Also like Hughes, Cullen assumed a role as an interpreter of the Harlem Renaissance. In October 1926 he guest edited a "Harlem" issue of *Palms: A Magazine of Poetry*, an avant-garde literary magazine published in Guadalajara, Mexico. He published in 1927 an anthology of poetry, *Caroling Dusk*, and between November 1926 and September 1928, he expressed his views on African American art, literature, and culture in "The Dark Tower," a monthly column in *Opportunity*. There were also significant differences between the two poets. In poetic style, Cullen was more traditional and conservative. In his language he emphasized literary and classical allusions rather than the sounds of the streets and cabarets. And in his personal life and literary philosophy, he was more aligned with the conservative and academic figures like Du Bois and Alain Locke, than with the bohemian or politically radical artists. But Cullen addressed many of the same themes in his poetry as did Hughes—the complexity of racial identity, the question of African roots, poverty, and racism.

The poems here from Cullen's first book of poetry, *Color*, published in 1925, speak to these themes, as well as acknowledging his debt to the poet Paul Laurence Dunbar. Cullen published three additional books of poetry during the late 1920s—in 1927 *Copper Sun* and *Ballad of the Brown Girl,* and two years later *The Black Christ, and Other Poems.*

"Yet Do I Marvel"

I doubt not God is good, well-meaning,
    kind,
And did He stoop to quibble could tell
    why
The little buried mole continues blind,
Why flesh that mirrors Him must some day
    die,
Make plain the reason tortured Tantalus
Is baited by the fickle fruit, declare
If merely brute caprice dooms Sisyphus
To struggle up a never-ending stair.
Inscrutable His ways are, and immune
To catechism by a mind too strewn
With petty cares to slightly understand
What awful brain compels His awful hand.
Yet do I marvel at this curious thing:
To make a poet black, and bid him sing!

"For Paul Laurence Dunbar"

Born of the sorrowful of heart,
    Mirth was a crown upon his head;
Pride kept his twisted lips apart
    In jest, to hide a heart that bled.

"Incident"
(For Eric Walrond)

Once riding in old Baltimore,
    Heart-filled, head-filled with glee,
I saw a Baltimorean
    Keep looking straight at me.

Now I was eight and very small,
    And he was no whit bigger,
And so I smiled, but he poked out
    His tongue, and called me, "Nigger."

I saw the whole of Baltimore
    From May until December;

Of all the things that happened there
That's all that I remember.

"Saturday's Child"

Some are teethed on a silver spoon,
   With the stars strung for a rattle;
I cut my teeth as the black raccoon—
   For implements of battle.

Some are swaddled in silk and down,
   And heralded by a star;
They swathed my limbs in a sackcloth gown
   On a night that was black as tar.

For some, godfather and goddame
   The opulent fairies be;
Dame Poverty gave me my name,
   And Pain godfathered me.

For I was born on Saturday—
   "Bad time for planting a seed,"
Was all my father had to say,
   And, "One mouth more to feed."

Death cut the strings that gave me life,
   And handed me to Sorrow,
The only kind of middle wife
   My folks could beg or borrow.

"Two Who Crossed A Line"
(She Crosses)

From where she stood the air she craved
   Smote with the smell of pine;
It was too much to bear; she braved
   Her gods and crossed the line.

And we were hurt to see her go,
   With her fair face and hair,
And veins too thin and blue to show
   What mingled blood flowed there.

We envied her a while, who still
   Pursued the hated track;
Then we forgot her name, until
   One day her shade came back.

Calm as a wave without a crest,
    Sorrow-proud and sorrow-wise,
With trouble sucking at her breast,
    With tear-disdainful eyes,
She slipped into her ancient place,
    And, no word asked, gave none;
Only the silence in her face
    Said seats were dear in the sun.

"Heritage"

What is Africa to me:
Copper sun or scarlet sea,
Jungle star or jungle track,
Strong bronzed men, or regal black
Women from whose loins I sprang
When the birds of Eden sang?
One three centuries removed
From the scenes his fathers loved,
Spicy grove, cinnamon tree,
What is Africa to me?

So I lie, who all day long
Want no sound except the song
Sung by wild barbaric birds
Goading massive jungle herds,
Juggernauts of flesh that pass
Trampling tall defiant grass
Where young forest lovers lie,
Plighting troth beneath the sky.
So I lie, who always hear,
Though I cram against my ear
Both my thumbs, and keep them there,
Great drums throbbing through the air.
So I lie, whose fount of pride,
Dear distress, and joy allied,
Is my somber flesh and skin,
With the dark blood dammed within
Like great pulsing tides of wine
That, I fear, must burst the fine
Channels of the chafing net
Where they surge and foam and fret.

Africa? A book one thumbs
Listlessly, till slumber comes.
Unremembered are her bats
Circling through the night, her cats
Crouching in the river reeds,

Stalking gentle flesh that feeds
By the river brink; no more
Does the bugle-throated roar
Cry that monarch claws have leapt
From the scabbards where they slept.
Silver snakes that once a year
Doff the lovely coats you wear,
Seek no covert in your fear
Lest a mortal eye should see;
What's your nakedness to me?
Here no leprous flowers rear
Fierce corollas in the air;
Here no bodies sleek and wet,
Dripping mingled rain and sweat,
Tread the savage measures of
Jungle boys and girls in love.
What is last year's snow to me,
Last year's anything? The tree
Budding yearly must forget
How its past arose or set—
Bough and blossom, flower, fruit
Even what shy bird with mute
Wonder at her travail there,
Meekly labored in its hair.
One three centuries removed
From the scenes his fathers loved,
Spice grove, cinnamon tree,
What is Africa to me?

So I lie, who find no peace
Night or day, no slight release
From the unremittant beat
Made by cruel padded feet
Walking through my body's street.
Up and down they go, and back,
Treading out a jungle track.
So I lie, who never quite
Safely sleep from rain at night—
I can never rest at all
When the rain begins to fall;
Like a soul gone mad with pain
I must match its weird refrain;
Ever must I twist and squirm,
Writhing like a baited worm,
While its primal measures drip
Through my body, crying, "Strip!
Doff this new exuberance.
Come and dance the Lover's Dance!"

In an old remembered way
Rain works on me night and day.

Quaint, outlandish heathen gods
Black men fashion out of rods,
Clay, and brittle bits of stone,
In a likeness like their own,
My conversion came high-priced;
I belong to Jesus Christ,
Preacher of humility;
Heathen gods are naught to me.

Father, Son, and Holy Ghost,
So I make an idle boast;
Jesus of the twice-turned cheek,
Lamb of God, although I speak
With my mouth thus, in my heart
Do I play a double part.
Ever at Thy glowing altar
Must my heart grow sick and falter,
Wishing He I served were black,
Thinking then it would not lack
Precedent of pain to guide it,
Let who would or might deride it;
Surely then this flesh would know
Yours had borne a kindred woe.
Lord, I fashion dark gods, too,
Daring even to give You
Dark despairing features where,
Crowned with dark rebellious hair,
Patience wavers just so much as
Mortal grief compels, while touches
Quick and hot, of anger, rise
To smitten cheek and weary eyes.
Lord, forgive me if my need
Sometimes shapes a human creed.

All day long and all night through,
One thing only must I do:
Quench my pride and cool my blood,
Lest I perish in the flood.
Lest a hidden ember set
Timber that I thought was wet
Burning like the dryest flax,
Melting like the merest wax,
Lest the grave restore its dead.
Not yet has my heart or head
In the least way realized
They and I are civilized.

JAMES WELDON JOHNSON
God's Trombones
1927

Much of James Weldon Johnson's time was occupied during the 1920s with his work for the NAACP and his efforts to promote the Harlem Renaissance and provide a liaison between black writers and the white literary establishment. Still he remained active as a poet, essayist and anthologist. In 1927 he published a collection of poems, *God's Trombones*, that used as inspiration the language and drama of black preachers. Using this component of African American folk culture, Johnson produced eight poetic sermons. The strength of these pieces is the simple but powerful language and the message that captures the depth of black religious feeling. Others, notably Zora Neale Hurston, would use black religion and black preachers as inspirations for their art. None captured this aspect of black life as effectively as Johnson.

God's Trombones was illustrated by Aaron Douglas. The image reproduced here accompanied the poem "Go Down Death."

Illustration by Aaron Douglsa for James Weldon Johnson's Poem, "Go Down Death"

"Go Down Death"

Weep not, weep not,
She is not dead;
She's resting in the bosom of Jesus.
Heart-broken husband—weep no more;
Grief-stricken son—weep no more;
Left-lonesome daughter—weep no more;
She's only just gone home.

Day before yesterday morning,
God was looking down from his great, high heaven,
Looking down on all his children,
And his eye fell on Sister Caroline,
Tossing on her bed of pain.
And God's big heart was touched with pity,
With the everlasting pity.

And God sat back on his throne,
And he commanded that tall, bright angel standing at his right hand:
Call me Death!
And that tall, bright angel cried in a voice
That broke like a clap of thunder:
Call Death!—Call Death!
And the echo sounded down the streets of heaven
Till it reached away back to that shadowy place,
Where Death waits with his pale, white horses.

And Death heard the summons,
And he leaped on his fastest horse,
Pale as a sheet in the moonlight.
Up the golden street Death galloped,
And the hoofs of his horse struck fire from the gold,
But they didn't make no sound.
Up Death rode to the Great White Throne,
And waited for God's command.

And God said: Go down, Death, go down,
Go down to Savannah, Georgia,
Down in Yamacraw,
And find Sister Caroline.
She's borne the burden and heat of the day,
She's labored long in my vineyard,
And she's tired—
She's weary—
Go down, Death, and bring her to me.

And Death didn't say a word,
But he loosed the reins on his pale, white horse,
And he clamped the spurs to his bloodless sides,

And out and down he rode,
Through heaven's pearly gates,
Past suns and moons and stars;
On Death rode,
And the foam from his horse was like a comet in the sky;
On Death rode,
Leaving the lightning's flash behind;
Straight on down he came.

While we were watching round her bed,
She turned her eyes and looked away,
She saw what we couldn't see;
She saw Old Death. She saw Old Death
Coming like a falling star.
But Death didn't frighten Sister Caroline;
He looked to her like a welcome friend.
And she whispered to us: I'm going home.
And she smiled and closed her eyes.

And Death took her up like a baby,
And she lay in his icy arms,
But she didn't feel no chill.
And Death began to ride again—
Up beyond the evening star,
Out beyond the morning star,
Into the glittering light of glory,
On to the Great White Throne.
And there he laid Sister Caroline
On the loving breast of Jesus.

And Jesus took his own hand and wiped away her tears,
And he smoothed the furrows from her face,
And the angels sang a little song,
And Jesus rocked her in his arms,
And kept a-saying: Take your rest,
Take your rest, take your rest.

Weep not—weep not,
She is not dead;
She's resting in the bosom of Jesus.

CLAUDE McKAY
Home to Harlem
1928

Jamaican-born poet Claude McKay turned to fiction in 1928, at least partly to cash in on the market for Harlem local color created by Carl Van Vechten's *Nigger Heaven*. *Home to Harlem* is the first of McKay's four novels, and the only one set in Harlem. McKay wrote it after he had left Harlem for a decade-long sojourn in the Soviet Union, France, and North Africa. For the most part it centers in the adventures of Jake, a sometimes railroad dining-car worker and vagabond, who is at home in the dives, jazz-joints, and house-rent parties that characterized working-class Harlem in the early 1920s. McKay's strength is in his descriptions of Harlem and the lives and experiences its people. The novel is filled with sex and sin, joy and sorrow, alcohol and drugs, and the poverty of a marginalized world with a smattering of crime and violence. McKay had a feel for African American urban life, and he depicted it vividly. While the novel enjoyed some commercial success, critical reaction was mixed. To Du Bois it epitimized everything that was wrong with Harlem Renaissance: it was exploitive, and it revealed a side of black life that no white needed to see.

The chapter included here is typical in its depiction of Jake's experiences, and demonstrates McKay's talent in describing the urban mileau. Du Bois's review, comparing the work unfavorably with Nella Larsen's first novel, reiterates his disenchantment with the Van Vechten school of black writers and condemns the *Home to Harlem* in strong terms. A.B. Doggett, Jr., writing for the *Southern Workman*, presents a positive assessment of McKay's book.

Chapter 6
Myrtle Avenue

Zeddy was excited over Jake's success in love. He thought how often he had tried to make up to Rose, without succeeding. He was crazy about finding a woman to love him for himself.

He had been married when he was quite a lad to a crust-yellow girl in Petersburg. Zeddy's wife, after deceiving him with white men, had run away from him to live an easier life. That was before Zeddy came North. Since then he had had many other alliances. But none had been successful.

It was true that no Black Belt beauty would ever call Zeddy "mah han'some brown." But there were sweetmen of the Belt more repulsive than he, that women would fight and murder each other for. Zeddy did not seem to possess any of that magic that charms and holds women for a long time. All his attempts at homemaking had failed. The women left him when he could not furnish the cash to meet the bills. They never saw his wages. For it was gobbled up by his voracious passion for poker and crap games. Zeddy gambled in Harlem. He gambled with white men down by the piers. And he was always losing.

"If only I could get those kinda gals that falls foh Jake," Zeddy mused. "And Jake is such a fool spade. Don't know how to handle the womens."

Zeddy's chance came at last. One Saturday a yellow-skinned youth, whose days and nights were wholly spent between pool-rooms and Negro speakeasies, invited Zeddy to a sociable at a grass-widow's who lived in Brooklyn and worked as a cook downtown in New York. She was called Gin-head Susy. She had a little apartment in Myrtle Avenue near Prince Street.

Susy was wonderfully created. She was of the complexion known among Negroes as spade or chocolate-to-the-bone. Her eyes shone like big white stars. Her chest was majestic and the general effect like a mountain. And that mountain was overgrand because Susy never wore any other but extremely French-heeled shoes. Even over the range she always stood poised in them and blazing in bright-hued clothes.

The burning passion of Susy's life was the yellow youth of her race. Susy came from South Carolina. A yellow youngster married her when she was fifteen and left her before she was eighteen. Since then she had lived with a yellow complex at the core of her heart.

Civilization had brought strikingly exotic types into Susy's race. And like many, many Negroes, she was a victim to that. . . . Ancient black life rooted upon its base with all its fascinating new layers of brown, low-brown, high-brown, nut-brown, lemon, maroon, olive, mauve gold. Yellow balancing between black and white. Black reaching out beyond yellow. Almost-white on the brink of a change. Sucked back down into the current of black by the terribly sweet rhythm of black blood. . . .

Susy's life of yellow complexity was surcharged with gin. There were whisky and beer also at her sociable evenings, but gin was the drink of drinks. Except for herself, her parties were all-male. Like so many of her sex, she had a congenital contempt for women. All-male were her parties and as yellow as she could make them. A lemon-colored or paper-brown pool-room youngster from Harlem's Fifth Avenue or from Prince Street. A bell-boy or railroad waiter or porter. Sometimes a chocolate who was a quick, nondiscriminating lover and not remote of attitude like the pampered high-browns. But chocolates were always a rarity among Susy's front-roomful of gin-lovers.

Yet for all of her wages drowned in gin, Susy carried a hive of discontents in her majestic breast. She desired a lover, something like her undutiful husband, but she desired in vain. Her guests consumed her gin and listened to the phonograph, exchanged rakish stories, and when they felt fruit-ripe to dropping, left her place in pursuit of pleasures elsewhere.

Sometimes Susy managed to lay hold of a yellow one for some time. Something all a piece of dirty rags and stench picked up in the street. Cleansed, clothed, and booted it. But so soon as he got his curly hair straightened by the process of Harlem's Ambrozine Palace of Beauty, and started in strutting the pavement of Lenox Avenue, feeling smart as a moving-picture dandy, he would leave Susy.

Apart from Susy's repellent person, no youthful sweetman attempting to love her could hold out under the ridicule of his pals. Over their games of pool and craps the boys had their cracks at Susy.

"What about Gin-head Susy tonight?"

"Sure, let's go and look the crazy old broad over."

"I'll go anywheres foh swilling of good booze."

"She's sho one ugly spade, but she's right there with her Gordon Dry."

"She ain't got 'em from creeps to crown and her trotters is B flat, but her gin is regal."

But now, after all the years of gin sociables and unsatisfactory lemons, Susy was changing just a little. She was changing under the influence of her newly acquired friend, Lavinia Curdy, the only woman whom she tolerated at her parties. That was not so difficult, as Miss Curdy was less attractive than Susy. Miss Curdy was a putty-skinned mulattress with purple streaks on her face. Two of her upper front teeth had been knocked out and her lower lip slanted pathetically leftward. She was skinny and when she laughed she resembled an old braying jenny.

When Susy came to know Miss Curdy, she unloaded a quantity of the stuff of her breast upon her. Her drab childhood in a South Carolina town. Her early marriage.

No girlhood. Her husband leaving her. And all the yellow men that had beaten her, stolen from her, and pawned her things.

Miss Curdy had been very emphatic to Susy about "yaller men." "I know them from long experience. They never want to work. They're a lazy and shiftless lot. Want to be kept like women. I found that out a long, long time ago. And that's why when I wanted a man foh keeps I took me a black plug-ugly one, mah dear."

It wouldn't have supported the plausibility of Miss Curdy's advice if she had mentioned that more than one black plug-ugly had ruthlessly cut loose from her. As the black woman had had her entanglements in yellow, so had the mulattress hers of black. But, perhaps, Miss Curdy did not realize that she could not help desiring black. In her salad days as a business girl her purse was controlled by many a black man. Now, however, her old problems did not arise in exactly the same way—her purse was old and worn and flat and attracted no attention.

"A black man is as good to me as a yaller when I finds a real one." Susy lied a little to Miss Curdy from a feeling that she ought to show some pride in her own complexion.

"But all these sociables—and you spend so much coin on gin," Miss Curdy had said.

"Well, that's the trute, but we all of us drinks it. And I loves to have company in mah house, plenty of company."

But when Susy came home from work one evening and found that her latest "yaller" sweetie had stolen her suitcase and best dresses and pawned even her gas range, she resolved never to keep another of his kind as a "steady." At least she made that resolve to Miss Curdy. But the sociables went on and the same types came to drink the Saturday evenings away, leaving the two women at the finish to their empty bottles and glasses. Once Susy did make a show of a black lover. He was the house man at the boarding-house where she cooked. But the arrangement did not hold any time, for Susy demanded of the chocolate extremely more than she ever got from her yellows.

"Well, boh, we's Brooklyn bound tonight," said Zeddy to Jake.

"You got to show me that Brooklyn's got any life to it," replied Jake.

"Theah's life anywheres theah's booze and jazz, and theah's cases o' gin and a gramophone whar we's going."

"Has we got to pay foh it, buddy?"

"No, boh, eve'ything is f. o. c. ef the lady likes you."

"Blimey!" A cockney phrase stole Jake's tongue. "Don't bull me."

"I ain't. Honest-to-Gawd Gordon Dry, and moh—ef you're the goods, all f.o.c."

"Well, I'll be browned!" exclaimed Jake.

Zeddy also took along Strawberry Lips, a new pal, burnt-cork black, who was thus nicknamed from the peculiar stage-red color of his mouth. Strawberry Lips was typically the stage Negro. He was proof that a generalization has some foundation in truth. . . . You might live your life in many black belts and arrive at the conclusion that there is no such thing as a typical Negro—no minstrel coon off the stage, no Thomas Nelson Page's nigger, no Octavus Roy Cohen's porter, no lineal descendant of Uncle Tom. Then one day your theory may be upset through meeting with a type by far more perfect than any created counterpart.

"Myrtle Avenue used to be a be-be itching of a place," said Strawberry Lips, "when Doc Giles had his gambling house on there and Elijah Bowers was running his cabaret. H'm. But Bowers was some big guy. He knew swell white folks in politics, and had a grand automobile and a high-yaller wife that hadn't no need of painting to pass. His cabaret was running neck and neck with Marshall's in Fifty-third Street. Then one night he killed a man in his cabaret, and that finished him. The lawyers got him off. But they cleaned him out dry. Done broke him, that case did. And today he's plumb down and out."

Jake, Zeddy, and Strawberry Lips had left the subway train at Borough Hall and were walking down Myrtle Avenue.

"Bowers' cabaret was some place for the teasing-brown pick-me-up then, brother—and the snow. The stuff cheap then. You sniff, boh?" Strawberry Lips asked and Zeddy.

"I wouldn't know befoh I sees it," Jake laughed.

"I ain't no habitual prisoner," said Zeddy, "but I does any little thing for a change. Keep going and active anything, says I."

The phonograph was discharging its brassy jazz notes when they entered the apartment. Susy was jerking herself from one side to the other with a potato-skinned boy. Miss Curdy was half-hopping up and down with the only chocolate that was there. Five lads, ranging from brown to yellow in complexion, sat drinking with jaded sneering expressions on their faces. The one that had invited Zeddy was among them. He waved to him to come over with his friends.

"Sit down and try some gin," he said. . . .

Zeddy dipped his hand in his pocket and sent two bones rolling on the table.

"Ise with you, chappie," his yellow friend said. The others crowded around. The gramophone stopped and Susy, hugging a bottle, came jerking on her French heels over to the group. She filled the glasses and everybody guzzled gin.

Miss Curdy looked the newcomers over, paying particular attention to Jake. A sure-enough eye-filling chocolate, she thought. I would like to make a steady thing of him.

Over by the door two light-brown lads began arguing about an actress of the leading theater of the Black Belt.

"I tell you I knows Gertie Kendall. I know her more'n I know you."

"Know her mah granny. You knows her just like I do, from the balcony of the Lafayette. Don't hand me none o' that fairy stuff, for I ain't gwine to swallow it."

"Youse an aching pain. I knows her, I tell you. I even danced with her at Madame Mulberry's apartment. You thinks I only hangs out with low-down trash becassin Ise in a place like this, eh? I done met mos'n all our big niggers: Jack Johnson, James Reese Europe, Adah Walker, Buddy, who used to play that theah drum for them Castle Walkers, and Madame Walker."

"Yaller, it 'pears to me that youse jest a nacherally-born story-teller. You really spec's me to believe youse been associating with the mucty-mucks of the race? Gwan with you. You'll be telling me next you done speaks with Charlie Chaplin and John D. Rockefeller—"

Miss Curdy had tuned her ears to the conversation and broke in: "Why, what is that to make so much fuss about? Sure he can dance with Gertie Kendall and know the dickty niggers. In my sporting days I knew Bert Williams and Walker and Adah Overton and Editor Tukslack and all that upstage race gang that would-n't touch Jack Johnson with a ten-foot pole. I lived in Washington and had Congressmen for my friends—foop! Why you can get in with the top-crust crowd at any swell ball in Harlem. All you need is clothes and the coin. I know them all, yet I don't feel a bit haughty mixing here with Susy and you all."

"I guess you don't now," somebody said.

Gin went round . . . and round . . . and round. . . . Desultory dancing. . . . Dice. . . . Blackjack. . . . Poker. . . . The room became a close, live, intense place. Tight-faced, the men seemed interested only in drinking and gaming, while Susy and Miss Curdy, guzzling hard, grew uglier. A jungle atmosphere pervaded the room, and, like shameless wild animals hungry for raw meat, the females savagely searched the eyes of the males. Susy's eyes always came back to settle upon the lad that had invited Zeddy. He was her real object. And Miss Curdy was ginned up with high hopes of Jake.

Jake threw up the dice and Miss Curdy seized her chance to get him alone for a little while.

"The cards do get so tiresome," she said. "I wonder how you men can go on and on all night long poking around with poker."

"Better than worser things," retorted Jake. Disgusted by the purple streaks, he averted his eyes from the face of the mulattress.

"I don't know about that," Miss Curdy bridled. "There's many nice ways of spending a sociable evening between ladies and gentlemen."

"Got to show me," said Jake, simply because the popular phrase intrigued his tongue.

"And that I can."

Irritated, Jake turned to move away.

"Where you going? Scared of a lady?"

Jake recoiled from the challenge, and shuffled away from the hideous mulattress. From experience in seaport towns in America, in France, in England, he had concluded that a woman could always go farther than a man in coarseness, depravity, and sheer cupidity. Men were ugly and brutal. But beside women they were merely vicious children. Ignorant about the aim and meaning and fulfillment of life; uncertain and indeterminate; weak. Rude children who loved excelling in spectacular acts to win the applause of women.

But women were so realistic and straight-going. *They* were the real controlling force of life. Jake remembered the Bal Musette fights between colored and white soldiers in France. Black, browns, yellows, whites. . . . He remembered the interracial sex skirmishes in England. Men fought, hurt, wounded, killed each other. Women, like blazing torches, egged them on or denounced them. Victims of sex, the men seemed foolish, ape-like blunderers in their pools of blood. Didn't know what they were fighting for, except it was to gratify some vague feeling about women. . . .

Jake's thoughts went roaming after his little lost brown of the Baltimore. The difference! She, in one night, had revealed a fine different world to him. Mystery again. A little stray girl. Finer than the finest!

Some of the fellows were going. In a vexed spirit, Susy had turned away from her unresponsive mulatto toward Zeddy. Relieved, the mulatto yawned, threw his hands backwards and said: "I guess mah broad is home from Broadway by now. Got to final on home to her. Harlem, lemme see you."

Miss Curdy was sitting against the mantelpiece, charming Strawberry Lips. Marvellous lips. Salmon-pink and planky. She had hoisted herself upon his knees, her arm around his thick neck.

Jake went over to the mantelpiece to pour a large chaser of beer and Miss Curdy leered at him. She disgusted him. His life was a free coarse thing, but he detested nastiness and ugliness. Guess I'll haul bottom to Harlem, he thought. Congo Rose was a rearing wild animal, all right, but these women, these boys. . . . Skunks, tame skunks, all of them!

He was just going out when a chocolate lad pointed at a light-brown and said: "The pot calls foh four bits, chappie. Come across or stay out."

"Lemme a quarter!"

"Ain't got it. Staying out?"

Biff! Square on the mouth. The chocolate leaped up like a tiger-cat at his assailant, carrying over card table, little pile of money, and half-filled gin glasses with a crash. Like an enraged ram goat, he held and butted the light-brown boy twice, straight on the forehead. The victim crumpled with a thud to the floor. Susy jerked over to the felled boy and hauled him, his body leaving liquid trail, to the door. She flung him out in the corridor and slammed the door.

"Sarves him right, pulling off that crap in mah place And you, Mis'er Jack Johnson," she said to the chocolate youth, "lemme miss you quick."

"He done hits me first," the chocolate said.

"I knows it, but I ain't gwina stand foh no rough-house in mah place. Ise got a dawg heah wif me all ready foh bawking."

"K-hhhh, K-hhhhh," laughed Strawberry Lips. "Oh boh, I know it's the trute, but—"

The chocolate lad slunk out of the flat.

"Lavinia," said Susy to Miss Curdy, "put on that theah 'Tickling Blues' on the victroly."

The phonograph began its scraping and Miss Curdy started jig-jagging with Strawberry Lips. Jake gloomed with disgust against the door.

"Getting outa this, buddy?" he asked Zeddy.

"Nobody's chasing *us,* boh." Zeddy commenced stepping with Susy to the "Tickling Blues."

Outside, Jake found the light-brown boy still half stunned against the wall.

"Ain't you gwine at home?" Jake asked him.

"I can't find a nickel foh car fare," said the boy.

Jake took him into a saloon and bought him a lemon squash. Drink that to clear you' haid," he said. "And heah's car fare." He gave the boy a dollar. "Whar you living at?"

"San Juan Hill."

"Come on, le's git the subway, then."

The Myrtle Avenue Elevated train passed with a high raucous rumble over their heads.

"Myrtle Avenue," murmured Jake. "Pretty name, all right, but it stinks like a sewer. Legs and feets! Come take me outa it back home to Harlem."

W.E.B. Du Bois
"The Browsing Reader"
The Crisis, June 1928

TWO NOVELS

Nella Larsen "Quicksand" (Knopf) Claude McKay "Home to Harlem" (Harper and Brothers)

I have just read the last two novels of Negro America. The one I liked; the other I distinctly did not. I think that Mrs. Imes, writing under the pen name of Nella Larsen, has done a fine, thoughtful and courageous piece of work in her novel. It is, on the whole, the best piece of fiction that Negro America has produced since the heyday of Chesnutt, and stands easily with Jessie Fauset's "There is Confusion", in its subtle comprehension of the curious cross currents that swirl about the black American.

Claude McKay's "Home to Harlem", on the other hand, for the most part nauseates me, and after the dirtier parts of its filth I feel distinctly like taking a bath. This does not mean that the book is wholly bad. McKay is too great a poet to make any complete failure in writing. There are bits of "Home to Harlem", beautiful and fascinating: the continued changes upon the theme of the beauty of colored skins; the portrayal of the fascination of their new yearnings for each other which Negroes are developing. The chief character, Jake, has something appealing, and the glimpses of the Haitian, Ray, have all the materials of a great piece of fiction.

But it looks as though, despite this, McKay has set out to cater for that prurient demand on the part of white folk for a portrayal in Negroes of that utter licentiousness which conventional civilization holds white folk back from enjoying—if enjoyment it can be called. That which a certain decadent section of the white American world, centered particularly in New York, longs for with fierce and unrestrained passions, it wants to see written out in black and white, and saddled on black Harlem. This demand, as voiced by a number of New York publishers, McKay has certainly satisfied, and added much for good measure. He has used every art and emphasis to paint drunkenness, fighting, lascivious sexual promiscuity and utter absence of restraint in as bold and as bright colors as he can.

If this had been done in the course of a well-conceived plot or with any artistic unity, it might have been understood if not excused. But "Home to Harlem" is padded. Whole chapters here and there are inserted with no connection to the main plot, except that they are on the same dirty subject. As a picture of Harlem life or of Negro life anywhere, it is, of course, nonsense. Untrue, not so much as on account of its facts, but on account of its emphasis and glaring colors. I am sorry that the author of "Harlem Shadows" stooped to this. I sincerely hope that he will some day rise above it and give us in fiction the strong, well-knit as well as beautiful theme, that it seems to me he might do.

Nella Larsen on the other hand has seized an interesting character and fitted her into a close yet delicately woven plot. There is no "happy ending" and yet the theme is not defeatist like the work of Peterkin and Green. Helga Crane sinks at last still master of her whimsical, unsatisfied soul. In the end she will be beaten down even to death but she never will utterly surrender to hypocricy and convention. Helga is typical of the new, honest, young fighting Negro woman—the one on whom "race" sits negligibly and Life is always first and its wandering path is but darkened, not obliterated by the shadow of the Veil. White folk will not like this book. It is not near nasty enough for New York columnists. It is too sincere for the South and middle West. Therefore, buy it and make Mrs. Imes write many more novels.

A.B. Doggett, Jr.
Review of *Home to Harlem*
Southern Workman, May 1928

The over-civilized or supersensitive will not enjoy reading all of Claude McKay's "Home to Harlem." It carves into a raw, red bit of Harlem life on the level of the longshoreman. The none too closely related incidents of the story are bound together by the happy, fearless, virile Jake, and all his companions are pictured with a sincerity and trueness to their environment that takes away sordidness. McKay is no outsider searching for dregs in Harlem. He gives us a series of authentic pictures, interesting and fascinating to anyone interested in human life with capacity to get outside a circumscribed area of life and enter into another at least as genuine.

Jake takes a turn in the dining car and we are taken behind the scenes there, and into the hell-hole provided by the Pennsylvania Railroad for its Negro employees in Pittsburgh. Most of the time we are with him in Harlem where his incidental and unsought conquests enrich the life he knows. In contrast to Jake, who is unhampered by any but self-education in his manner of living, comes Ray, brilliant, sensitive, and saturated with the pre-war European dramatists, but a tragic figure in his inability to relate his knowledge and philosophy to the environment in which he found himself.

Passages in the book are poetry, many are rich; all are sincere. As a picture of phases of Harlem life it has a sociological interest apart from that of style and incident value. Those who like people for their human qualities, even though they be crude and unmoral, will like "Home to Harlem."

NELLA LARSEN
Passing
1929

Passing was the second of Nella Larsen's two Harlem Renaissance novels. In this work Larsen picks up the theme that James Weldon Johnson had explored in *The Autobiography of an Ex-Colored Man* and Cullen examined in "Two Who Crossed a Line"—the decision of light-skinned African Americans to cross over the color line and, hiding their identity, assimilate into the white world. Larsen was particularly adept at exploring the psychological cost to black women of race and racism. In the selection here Irene Redfield, herself a light-skinned black woman is defying tradition by enjoying tea at the roof garden of a posh Chicago hotel, where black patrons are not welcome. She notices to her discomfort that she has attracted the attention of another woman patron. Initially she is afraid that her charade has been exposed and that she will be asked to leave the restaurant; then she realizes that the other woman is a childhood friend, Clara, whom she has not seen for twelve years. She then discovers that Clara has passed over and was living the life of a white woman.

Again she looked up, and for a moment her brown eyes politely returned the stare of the other's black ones, which never for an instant fell or wavered. Irene made a little mental shrug. Oh well, let her look! She tried to treat the woman and her watching with indifference, but she couldn't. All her efforts to ignore her, it, were futile. She stole another glance. Still looking. What strange languorous eyes she had!

And gradually there rose in Irene a small inner disturbance, odious and hatefully familiar. She laughed softly, but her eyes flashed.

Did that woman, could that woman, somehow know that here before her very eyes on the roof of the Drayton sat a Negro?

Absurd! Impossible! White people were so stupid about such things for all that they usually asserted that they were able to tell; and by the most ridiculous means, finger-nails, palms of hands, shapes of ears, teeth, and other equally silly rot. They always took her for an Italian, a Spaniard, a Mexican, or a gipsy. Never, when she was alone, had they even remotely seemed to suspect that she was a Negro. No, the woman sitting there staring at her couldn't possibly know.

Nevertheless, Irene felt, in turn, anger, scorn, and fear slide over her. It wasn't that she was ashamed of being a Negro, or even of having it declared. It was the idea of being ejected from any place, even in the polite and tactful way in which the Drayton would probably do it, that disturbed her. . . .

Suddenly her small fright increased. Her neighbour had risen and was coming towards her. What was going to happen now?

"Pardon me," the woman said pleasantly, "but I think I know you." Her slightly husky voice held a dubious note.

Looking up at her, Irene's suspicions and fears vanished. There was no mistaking the friendliness of that smile or resisting its charm. Instantly she surrendered to it and smiled too, as she said: "I'm afraid you're mistaken."

"Why, of course, I know you!" the other exclaimed. "Don't tell me you're not Irene Westover. Or do they still call you 'Rene? . . ."

"Yes, I'm Irene Westover. And though nobody calls me 'Rene any more, it's good to hear the name again. And you—" She hesitated, ashamed that she could not remember, and hoping that the sentence would be finished for her.

"Don't you know me? Not really, 'Rene?"

"I'm sorry, but just at the minute I can't seem to place you. . . ."

"Perhaps," Irene began, "you—"

The woman laughed, a lovely laugh, a small sequence of notes that was like a trill and also like the ringing of a delicate bell fashioned of a precious metal, a tinkling.

Irene drew a quick sharp breath. "Clare!" she exclaimed, "not really Clare Kendry?"

So great was her astonishment that she had started to rise.

"No, no, don't get up," Clare Kendry commanded, and sat down herself. "You've simply got to stay and talk. We'll have something more. Tea? Fancy meeting you here! It's simply too, too lucky!"

"Perhaps," Clare replied. "Oh, just a second."

She gave her attention to the waiter at her side. "M-mm, let's see. Two teas. And bring some cigarettes. Y-es, they'll be all right. Thanks. . . ."

While Clare had been giving the order, Irene made a rapid mental calculation. It must be, she figured, all of twelve years since she, or anybody that she knew, had laid eyes on Clare Kendry.

After her father's death she'd gone to live with some relatives, aunts or cousins two or three times removed, over on the west side relatives that nobody had known the Kendry's possessed until they had turned up at the funeral and taken Clare away with them.

For about a year or more afterwards she would appear occasionally among her old friends and acquaintances on the south side for short little visits that were, they understood, always stolen from the endless domestic tasks in her new home. With each succeeding one she was taller, shabbier, and more belligerently sensitive. And each time the look on her face was more resentful and brooding. "I'm worried about Clare, she seems so unhappy," Irene remembered her mother saying. The visits dwindled, becoming shorter, fewer, and further apart until at last they ceased.

Irene's father, who had been fond of Bob Kendry, made a special trip over to the west side about two months after the last time Clare had been to see them and returned with the bare information that he had seen the relatives and that Clare had disappeared. What else he had confided to her mother, in the privacy of their own room, Irene didn't know.

But she had had something more than a vague suspicion of its nature. For there had been rumours. Rumours that were, to girls of eighteen and nineteen years, interesting and exciting.

There was the one about Clare Kendry's having been seen at the dinner hour in a fashionable hotel in company with another woman and two men, all of them white. And *dressed!* And there was another which told of her driving in Lincoln Park with a man, unmistakably white, and evidently rich. Packard limousine, chauffeur in livery, and all that. There had been others whose context Irene could no longer recollect, but all pointing in the same glamorous direction.

And she could remember quite vividly how, when they used to repeat and discuss these tantalizing stories about Clare, the girls would always look knowingly at one another and then, with little excited giggles, drag away their eager shining eyes and say with lurking undertones of regret or disbelief some such thing as "Oh, well, maybe she's got a job or something," or "After all, it mayn't have been Clare," or "You can't believe all you hear."

And always some girl, more matter-of-fact or more frankly malicious than the rest, would declare: "Of course it was Clare! Ruth said it was and so did Frank, and they certainly know her when they see her as well as we do." And someone else would say: "Yes, you can bet it was Clare all right." And then they would all join in asserting that there could be no mistake about it's having been Clare, and that such circumstances could mean only one thing. Working indeed! People didn't take their servants to the Shelby for dinner. Certainly not all dressed up like that. There would follow insincere regrets, and somebody would say: "Poor girl, I suppose it's true enough, but what can you expect. Look at her father. And her mother, they say, would have run away if she hadn't died. Besides, Clare always had a—a—having way with her."

Precisely that! The words came to Irene as she sat there on the Drayton roof, facing Clare Kendry. "A having way." Well, Irene acknowledged, judging from her appearance and manner, Clare seemed certainly to have succeeded in having a few of the things that she wanted.

It was, Irene repeated, after the interval of the waiter, a great surprise and a very pleasant one to see Clare again after all those years, twelve at least.

"Why, Clare, you're the last person in the world I'd have expected to run into. I guess that's why I didn't know you."

Clare answered gravely: "Yes. It is twelve years. But I'm not surprised to see you, 'Rene. That is, not so very. In fact, ever since I've been here, I've more or less hoped that I should, or someone. Preferably you, though. Still, I imagine that's because I've thought of you often and often, while you—I'll wager you've never given me a thought. . . ."

No, Irene hadn't thought of Clare Kendry. Her own life had been too crowded. So, she supposed, had the lives of other people. She defended her—their—forget-fulness. "You know how it is. Everybody's so busy. People leave, drop out, maybe for a little while there's talk about them, or questions; then, gradually they're for-gotten."

"Yes, that's natural," Clare agreed. And what, she inquired, had they said of her for that little while at the beginning before they'd forgotten her altogether?

Irene looked away. She felt the telltale colour rising in her cheeks. "You can't," she evaded, "expect me to remember trifles like that over twelve years of mar-riages, births, deaths, and the war."

There followed that trill of notes that was Clare Kendry's laugh, small and clear and the very essence of mockery.

"Oh, 'Rene !" she cried, "of course you remember! But I won't make you tell me, because I know just as well as if I'd been there and heard every unkind word. Oh, I know, I know. Frank Danton saw me in the Shelby: one night. Don't tell me he didn't broadcast that, and with embroidery. Others may have seen me at other times. I don't know. But once I met Margaret Hammer in Marshall Field's. I'd have spoken, was on the very point of doing it, but she cut me dead. . . .

"And now 'Rene, I want to hear all about you and everybody and everything. You're married, I s'pose?"

Irene nodded.

"Yes," Clare said knowingly, "you would be. Tell me about it."

And so for an hour or more they had sat there smoking and drinking tea and filling in the gap of twelve years with talk. That is, Irene did. She told Clare about her marriage and removal to New York, about her husband, and about her two sons, who were having their first experience of being separated from their parents at a summer camp, about her mother's death, about the marriages of her two broth-ers. She told of the marriages, births and deaths in other families that Clare had known, opening up, for her, new vistas on the lives of old friends and acquain-tances. . .

Somewhere outside, a clock struck. Brought back to the present, Irene looked down at her watch and exclaimed: "Oh, I must go, Clare! . . ."

The waiter came with Clare's change. Irene reminded herself that she ought immediately to go. But she didn't move.

The truth was, she was curious. There were things that she wanted to ask Clare Kendry. She wished to find out about this hazardous business of "passing," this breaking away from all that was familiar and friendly to take one's chance in another environment, not entirely strange, perhaps, but certainly not entirely friendly. What, for example, one did about background, how one accounted for oneself. And how one felt when one came into contact with other Negroes. But she couldn't. She was unable to think of a single question that in its context or its phrasing was not too frankly curious, if not actually impertinent.

As if aware of her desire and her hesitation, Clare remarked, thoughtfully: "You know, 'Rene, I've often wondered why more coloured girls, girls like you and Margaret Hammer and Esther Dawson and—oh, lots of others—never 'passed' over. It's such a frightfully easy thing to do. If one's the type, all that's needed is a little nerve."

"What about background? Family, I mean. Surely you can't just drop down on people from nowhere and expect them to receive you with open arms, can you?"

"Almost," Clare asserted. "You'd be surprised, 'Rene, how much easier that is with white people than with us. Maybe because there are so many more of them, or maybe because they are secure and so don't have to bother. I've never quite decided."

Irene was inclined to be incredulous. "You mean that you didn't have to explain where you came from? It seems impossible."

Clare cast a glance of repressed amusement across the table at her. "As a matter of fact, I didn't. Though I suppose under any other circumstances I might have had to provide some plausible tale to account for myself. I've a good imagination, so I'm sure I could have done it quite creditably, and credibly. But it wasn't necessary. There were my aunts, you see, respectable and authentic enough for anything or anybody."

"I see. They were 'passing' too."

"No. They weren't. They were white."

"Oh!" And in the next instant it came back to Irene that she had heard this mentioned before; by her father, or, more likely, her mother. They were Bob Kendry's aunts. He had been a son of their brother's, on the left hand. A wild oat.

"They were nice old ladies," Clare explained, "very religious and as poor as church mice. That adored brother of theirs, my grandfather, got through every penny they had after he'd finished his own little bit."

Clare paused in her narrative to light another cigarette. Her smile, her expression, Irene noticed, was faintly resentful.

"Being good Christians," she continued, "when dad came to his tipsy end, they did their duty and gave me a home of sorts. I was, it was true, expected to earn my keep by doing all the housework and most of the washing. But do you realize, 'Rene, that if it hadn't been for them, I shouldn't have had a home in the world?"

Irene's nod and little murmur were comprehensive, understanding.

Clare made a small mischievous grimace and proceeded. "Besides, to their notion, hard labour was good for me. I had Negro blood and they belonged to the generation that had written and read long articles headed: 'Will the Blacks Work?' Too, they weren't quite sure that the good God hadn't intended the sons and daughters of Ham to sweat because he had poked fun at old man Noah once when he had taken a drop too much. I remember the aunts telling me that that old drunkard had cursed Ham and his sons for all time."

Irene laughed. But Clare remained quite serious.

"It was more than a joke, I assure you, 'Rene. It was a hard life for a girl of sixteen. Still, I had a roof over my head, and food, and clothes—such as they were. And there were the Scriptures, and talks on morals and thrift and industry and the loving-kindness of the good Lord."

"Have you ever stopped to think, Clare," Irene demanded, "how much unhappiness and downright cruelty are laid to the loving-kindness of the Lord? And always by His most ardent followers, it seems."

"Have I?" Clare exclaimed. "It, they, made me what I am today. For, of course, I was determined to get away, to be a person and not a charity or a problem, or even a daughter of the indiscreet Ham. Then, too, I wanted things. I knew I wasn't bad-looking and that I could 'pass.' You can't know, 'Rene, how, when I used to go over to the south side, I used almost to hate all of you. You had all the things I wanted and never had had. It made me all the more determined to get them, and others. Do you, can you understand what I felt?"

She looked up with a pointed and appealing effect, and, evidently finding the sympathetic expression on Irene's face sufficient answer, went on. "The aunts were queer. For all their Bibles and praying and ranting about honesty, they didn't want anyone to know that their darling brother had seduced—ruined, they called it—a Negro girl. They could excuse the ruin, but they couldn't forgive the tar-brush. They forbade me to mention Negroes to the neighbours, or even to mention the south side. You may be sure that I didn't. I'll bet they were good and sorry afterwards."

She laughed and the ringing bells in her laugh had a hard metallic sound.

"When the chance to get away came, that omission was of great value to me. When Jack, a schoolboy acquaintance of some people in the neighbourhood, turned up from South America with untold gold, there was no one to tell him that I was coloured, and many to tell him about the severity and the religiousness of Aunt Grace and Aunt Edna. You can guess the rest. After he came, I stopped slipping off to the south side and slipped off to meet him instead. I couldn't manage both. In the end I had no great difficulty in convincing him that it was useless to talk marriage to the aunts. So on the day that I was eighteen, we went off and were married. So that's that. Nothing could have been easier."

"Yes, I do see that for you it was easy enough. By the way! I wonder why they didn't tell father that you were married. He went over to find out about you when you stopped coming over to see us. I'm sure they didn't tell him. Not that you were married."

Clare Kendry's eyes were bright with tears that didn't fall. "Oh, how lovely! To have cared enough about me to do that. The dear sweet man! Well, they couldn't tell him because they didn't know it. I took care of that, for I couldn't be sure that those consciences of theirs wouldn't begin to work on them afterwards and make them let the cat out of the bag. The old things probably thought I was living in sin, wherever I was. And it would be about what they expected."

An amused smile lit the lovely face for the smallest fraction of a second. After a little silence she said soberly: "But I'm sorry if they told your father so. That was something I hadn't counted on."

"I'm not sure that they did," Irene told her. "He didn't say so, anyway."

"He wouldn't, 'Rene dear. Not your father."

"Thanks. I'm sure he wouldn't."

"But you've never answered my question. Tell me, honestly, haven't you ever thought of 'passing'?"

Irene answered promptly: "No. Why should I?" And so disdainful was her voice and manner that Clare's face flushed and her eyes glinted. Irene hastened to add: "You see, Clare, I've everything I want. Except, perhaps, a little more money."

At that Clare laughed, her spark of anger vanished as quickly as it had appeared. "Of course," she declared, "that's what everybody wants, just a little more money, even the people who have it. And I must say I don't blame them. Money's awfully nice to have. In fact, all things considered, I think, 'Rene, that it's even worth the price."

Irene could only shrug her shoulders. Her reason partly agreed, her instinct wholly rebelled. And she could not say why. And though conscious that if she didn't hurry away, she was going to be late to dinner, she still lingered. It was as if the woman sitting on the other side of the table, a girl that she had known, who had done this rather dangerous and, to Irene Redfield, abhorrent thing successfully and had announced herself well satisfied, had for her a fascination, strange and compelling.

Clare Kendry was still leaning back in the tall chair, her sloping shoulders against the carved top. She sat with an air of indifferent assurance, as if arranged for, desired. About her clung that dim suggestion of polite insolence with which a few women are born and which some acquire with the coming of riches or importance.

Clare, it gave Irene a little prick of satisfaction to recall, hadn't got that by passing herself off as white. She herself had always had it.

Just as she'd always had that pale gold hair, which, unsheared still, was drawn loosely back from a broad brow, partly hidden by the small close hat. Her lips, painted a brilliant geranium-red, were sweet and sensitive and a little obstinate. A tempting mouth. The face across the forehead and cheeks was a trifle too wide, but the ivory skin had a peculiar soft lustre. And the eyes were magnificent! dark, sometimes absolutely black, always luminous, and set in long, black lashes. Arresting eyes, slow and mesmeric, and with, for all their warmth, something withdrawn and secret about them.

Ah! Surely! They were Negro eyes! mysterious and concealing. And set in that ivory face under that bright hair, there was about them something exotic.

Yes, Clare Kendry's loveliness was absolute, beyond challenge, thanks to those eyes which her grandmother and later her mother and father had given her.

Into those eyes there came a smile and over Irene the sense of being petted and caressed. She smiled back.

"Maybe," Clare suggested, "you can come Monday, if you're back. Or, if you're not, then Tuesday."

With a small regretful sigh, Irene informed Clare that she was afraid she wouldn't be back by Monday and that she was sure she had dozens of things for Tuesday, and that she was leaving Wednesday. It might be, however, that she could get out of something Tuesday.

"Oh, do try. Do put somebody else off. The others can see you any time, while I—Why, I may never see you again! Think of that, 'Rene! You'll have to come. You'll simply have to! I'll never forgive you if you don't."

At that moment it seemed a dreadful thing to think of never seeing Clare Kendry again. Standing there under the appeal, the caress, of her eyes, Irene had the desire, the hope, that this parting wouldn't be the last.

WALLACE THURMAN
The Blacker The Berry

Wallace Thurman was one of the most talented writers of the Harlem Renaissance, but his work never matched his potential. He was also one of its primary organizers, especially among the younger, bohemian group. His apartment at 237 West 136th Street was a gathering place and a haven for Harlem's young literati, and he was the principal mover behind two failed literary journals, *Fire!!* in 1926 and then *Harlem* three years later. He wrote essays for several literary journals, served on the staff of *The Messenger* and *World Tomorrow*; he was the only Harlem Renaissance writer to win a job on the editorial staff of a major New York publishing house.

Thurman published two major novels, *The Blacker the Berry* in 1929 and, in 1932, *Infants of the Spring*. The latter is noted for its ironic analysis of the declining Harlem Renaissance. *The Blacker the Berry* addresses the subject of color prejudice within the black community, but it also satirizes many aspects of black urban and intellectual life, including the Harlem literary set. The selection here involves a gathering of young black writers and intellectuals and a field-trip to a working class house-rent party. The house-rent party was a common event in working-class Harlem, initiated by tenants who made their rent money by hosting parties and charging admission. The concept evolved into a regular feature of Harlem social life, with food, drink, and entertainment, as described by Thurman and other Harlem Renaissance writers. The people in this chapter are thinly disguised caricatures of Thurman's literary cadre, including Langston Hughes, Zora Neale Hurston, Carl Van Vechten, and Thurman himself (Truman Walter). Aaron Douglas provided the cover art for the book.

Aaron Douglas's Promotional Illustration for Wallace Thurman's *The Blacker the Berry*

The Blacker the Berry . . .
A Novel of Negro Life
1929

Part 4
Rent Party

Saturday evening. Alva had urged her to hurry uptown from work. He was going to take her on a party with some friends of his. This was the first time he had ever asked her to go to any sort of social affair with him. She had never met any of his friends save Braxton, who scarcely spoke to her, and never before had Alva suggested taking her to any sort of social gathering either public or semi-public. He often took her to various motion picture theaters, both downtown and in Harlem, and at least three nights a week he would call for her at the theater and escort her to Harlem. On these occasions they often went to Chinese restaurants or to ice cream parlors before going home. But usually they would go to City College Park, find an empty bench in a dark corner where they could sit and spoon before retiring either to her room or to Alva's.

Emma Lou had, long before this, suggested going to a dance or to a party, but Alva had always countered that he never attended such affairs during the summer months, that he stayed away from them for precisely the same reason that he stayed away from work, namely, because it was too hot. Dancing, said he, was a matter of calisthenics, and calisthenics were work. Therefore it, like any sort of physical exercise, was taboo during hot weather.

Alva sensed that sooner or later Emma Lou would become aware of his real reason for not taking her out among his friends. He realized that one as color-conscious as she appeared to be would, at some not so distant date, jump to what for him would be uncomfortable conclusions. He did not wish to risk losing her before the end of summer, out neither could he risk taking her out among his friends, for he knew too well that he would be derided for his unseemly preference for "dark meat," and told publicly without regard for her feelings, that "black cats must go."

Furthermore he always took Geraldine to parties and dances. Geraldine with her olive colored skin and straight black hair. Geraldine, who of all the people he pretended to love, really inspired him emotionally as well as physically, the one person he conquested without thought of monetary gain. Yet he had to do something with Emma Lou, and release from the quandary presented itself from most unexpected quarters.

Quite accidentally, as things of the sort happen in Harlem with its complex but interdependable social structure, he had become acquainted with a young Negro writer, who had asked him to escort a group of young writers and artists to a house-rent party. Though they had heard much of this phenomenon, none had been on the inside of one, and because of their rather polished manners and exteriors, were afraid that they might not be admitted. Proletarian Negroes are as suspicious of their more sophisticated brethren as they are of white men, and resent as keenly their intrusions into their social world. Alva had consented to act as cicerone, and, realizing that these people would be more or less free from the color prejudice exhibited by his other friends, had decided to take Emma Lou along too. He was also aware of her intellectual pretensions, and felt that she would be especially pleased to meet recognized talents and outstanding personalities. She did not have to know that these were not his regular companions, and from then on she would have no reason to feel that he was ashamed to have her meet his friends.

Emma Lou could hardly attend to Arline's change of complexion and clothes between acts and scenes, so anxious was she to get to Alva's house and to the promised party. Her happiness was complete. She was certain now that Alva loved her, certain that he was not ashamed or even aware of her dusky complexion. She had felt from the first that he was superior to such inane truck, now she knew it. Alva loved her for herself alone, and loved her so much that he didn't mind her being a coal scuttle blond.

Sensing something unusual, Arline told Emma that she would remove her own make-up after the performance, and let her have time to get dressed for the party. This she proceeded to do all through the evening, spending much time in front of the mirror at Arline's dressing table, manicuring her nails, marcelling her hair, and applying various creams and cosmetics to her face in order to make her despised darkness less obvious. Finally, she put on one of Arline's less pretentious afternoon frocks, and set out for Alva's house.

As she approached his room door, she heard much talk and laughter, moving her to halt and speculate whether or not she should go in. Even her unusual and high-tensioned jubilance was not powerful enough to overcome immediately her shyness and fears. Suppose these friends of Alva's would not take kindly to her? Suppose they were like Braxton, who invariably curled his lip when he saw her, and seldom spoke even as much as a word of greeting? Suppose they were like the people who used to attend her mother's and grandmother's teas, club meetings and receptions, dismissing her with— "It beats me how this child of yours looks so unlike the rest of you . . . Are you sure it isn't adopted." Or suppose they were like the college youth she had known in Southern California? No, that couldn't be. Alva would never invite her where she would not be welcome. These were his friends. And so was Braxton, but Alva said he was peculiar. There was no danger. Alva had invited her. She was here. Anyway she wasn't so black. Hadn't she artificially lightened her skin about four or five shades until she was almost brown? Certainly it was all right. She needn't be a foolish ninny all her life. Thus, reassured, she knocked on the door, and felt herself trembling with excitement and internal uncertainty as Alva let her in, took her hat and coat, and proceeded to introduce her to the people in the room.

"Miss Morgan, meet Mr. Tony Crews. You've probably seen his book of poems. He's the little jazz boy, you know."

Emma Lou bashfully touched the extended hand of the curly-headed poet. She had not seen or read his book, but she bad often noticed his name in the newspapers and magazines. He was all that she had expected him to be except that he had pimples on his face. These didn't fit in with her mental picture.

"Miss Morgan, this is Cora Thurston. Maybe I should'a introduced you ladies first."

"I'm no lady, and I hope you're not either, Miss Morgan." She smiled, shook Emma Lou's hand, then turned away to continue her interrupted conversation with Tony Crews.

"Miss Morgan, meet . . . ," he paused, and addressed a tall, dark yellow youth stretched out on the floor, "What name you going by now?"

The boy looked up and smiled.

"Why, Paul, of course."

"All right then, Miss Morgan, this is Mr. Paul, he changes his name every season."

Emma Lou sought to observe this person more closely, and was shocked to see that his shirt was open at the neck and that he was sadly in need of a haircut and shave. "Miss Morgan, meet Mr. Walter." A small slender dark youth with an infectious smile and small features. His face was familiar. Where had she seen him before?

"Now that you've met every one, sit down on the bed there beside Truman and have a drink. Go on with your talk folks," he urged as he went over to the dresser to fill a glass with a milk colored liquid. Cora Thurston spoke up in answer to Alva's adjuration:

"Guess there ain't much more to say. Makes me mad to discuss it anyhow."

"No need of getting mad at people like that," said Tony Crews simply and softly. "I think one should laugh at such stupidity."

"And ridicule it, too," came from the luxurious person sprawled over the floor, for he did impress Emma Lou as being luxurious, despite the fact that his suit was unpressed, and that he wore neither socks nor necktie. She noticed the many graceful gestures he made with his hands, but wondered why he kept twisting his lips to one side when he talked. Perhaps he was trying to mask the size of his mouth.

Truman was speaking now, "Ridicule will do no good, nor mere laughing at them. I admit those weapons are about the only ones an intelligent person would use, but one must also admit that they are rather futile."

"Why futile?" Paul queried indolently.

"They are futile," Truman continued, "because, well, those people cannot help being like they are—their environment has made them that way."

Miss Thurston muttered something. It sounded like "hooey," then held out an empty glass. "Give me some more firewater, Alva." Alva hastened across the room and refilled her glass. Emma Lou wondered what they were talking about. Again Cora broke the silence, "You can't tell me they can't help it. They kick about white people, then commit the same crime."

There was a knock on the door, interrupting something Tony Crews was about to say. Alva went to the door.

"Hello, Ray." A tall, blond, fair-skinned youth entered. Emma Lou gasped, and was more bewildered than ever. All of this silly talk and drinking, and now—here was a white man!

"Hy, everybody. Jusas Chraust, I hope you saved me some liquor." Tony Crews held out his empty glass and said quietly, "We've had about umpteen already, so I doubt if there's any more left."

"You can't kid me, bo. I know Alva would save me a dram or two." Having taken off his hat and coat he squatted down on the floor beside Paul.

Truman turned to Emma Lou. "Oh, Ray, meet Miss Morgan. Mr. Jorgenson, Miss Morgan."

"Glad to know you; pardon my not getting up, won't you?" Emma Lou didn't know what to say, and couldn't think of anything appropriate, but since he was smiling, she tried to smile too, and nodded her head.

"What's the big powwow?" he asked. "All of you look so serious. Haven't you had enough liquor, or are you just trying of settle the ills of the universe?"

"Neither," said Paul. "They're just damning our 'pink niggers'."

Emma Lou was aghast. Such extraordinary people—saying "nigger" in front of a white man! Didn't they have any race pride or proper bringing up? Didn't they have any common sense?

"What've they done now?" Ray asked, reaching out to accept the glass Alva was handing him.

"No more than they've always done," Tony Crews answered. "Cora here just felt like being indignant, because she heard of a forthcoming wedding in Brooklyn to which the prospective bride and groom have announced they will *not* invite any dark people."

"Seriously now," Truman began. Ray interrupted him.

"Who in the hell wants to be serious?"

"As I was saying," Truman continued, "you can't blame light Negroes for being prejudiced against dark ones. All of you know that white is the symbol of everything pure and good, whether that everything be concrete or abstract. Ivory Soap is advertised as being ninety-nine and some fraction per cent pure, and Ivory Soap is white. Moreover, virtue and virginity are always represented as being clothed in white garments. Then, too, the God we, or rather most Negroes worship is a patriarchal white man, seated on a white throne, in a spotless white Heaven, radiant with white streets and white-apparelled angels eating white honey and drinking white milk

"Listen to the boy rave. Give him another drink," Ray shouted, but Truman ignored him and went on, becoming more and more animated.

"We are all living in a totally white world, where all standards are the standards of the white man, and where almost invariably what the white man does is right, and what the black man does is wrong, unless it is precedented by something a white man has done."

"Which," Cora added scornfully, "makes it all right for light Negroes to discriminate against dark ones?"

"Not at all," Truman objected. "It merely explains, not justifies, the evil—or rather, the fact of intraracial segregation. Mulattoes have always been accorded more consideration by white people than their darker brethren. They were made to feel superior even during slave days . . . made to feel proud, as Bud Fisher would say, that they were bastards. It was for the mulatto offspring of white masters and Negro slaves that the first schools for Negroes were organized, and say what you will, it is generally the Negro with a quantity of mixed blood in his veins who finds adaptation to a Nordic environment more easy than one of pure blood, which, of course, you will admit, is, to an American Negro, convenient if not virtuous."

"Does that justify their snobbishness and self-evaluated superiority?"

"No, Cora, it doesn't," returned Truman. "I'm not trying to excuse them. I'm merely trying to give what I believe to be an explanation of this thing. I have never been to Washington and only know what Paul and you have told me about conditions there, but they seem to be just about the same as conditions in Los Angeles,

Omaha, Chicago, and other cities in which I have lived or visited. You see, people have to feel superior to something, and there is scant satisfaction in feeling superior to domestic animals or steel machines that one can train or utilize. It is much more pleasing to pick out some individual or some group of individuals on the same plane to feel superior to. This is almost necessary when one is a member of a supposedly despised, mistreated minority group. Then consider that the mulatto is much nearer white than he is black, and is therefore more liable to act like a white man than like a black one, although I cannot say that I see a great deal of difference in any of their actions. They are human beings first and only white or black incidentally."

Ray pursed his lips and whistled.

"But you seem to forget," Tony Crews insisted, "that because a man is dark, it doesn't necessarily mean he is not of mixed blood. Now look at. . . ."

"Yeah, let him look at you or at himself or at Cora," Paul interrupted. "There ain't no unmixed Negroes."

"But I haven't forgotten that," Truman said, ignoring the note of finality in Paul's voice. "I merely took it for granted that we were talking only about those Negroes who were light-skinned."

"But all light-skinned Negroes aren't color struck or color prejudiced," interjected Alva, who, up to this time, like Emma Lou, had remained silent. This was, he thought, a strategic moment for him to say something. He hoped Emma Lou would get the full significance of this statement.

"True enough," Truman began again. "But I also took it for granted that we were only talking about those who were. As I said before, Negroes are, after all, human beings, and they are subject to be influenced and controlled by the same forces and factors that influence and control other human beings. In an environment where there are so many color-prejudiced whites, there a bound to be a number of color-prejudiced blacks Color prejudice and religion are akin in one respect. Some folks have it and some don't, and the kernel that is responsible for it is present in us all, which is to say, that potentially we are all color-prejudiced as long as we remain in this environment. For, as you know, prejudices are always caused by differences, and the majority group sets the standard. Then, too, since black is the favorite color of vaudeville comedians and jokesters, and conversely, as intimately associated with tragedy, it is no wonder that even the blackest individual will seek out some one more black than himself to laugh at."

"So saith the Lord," Tony answered soberly.

"And the Holy Ghost saith, let's have another drink."

"Happy thought, Ray," returned Cora. "Give us some more ice cream and gin, Alva."

Alva went into the alcove to prepare another concoction. Tony started the victrola. Truman turned to Emma Lou, who, all this while, had been sitting there with Alva's arm around her, every muscle in her body feeling as if it wanted to twitch, not knowing whether to be sad or to be angry. She couldn't comprehend all of this talk. She couldn't see how these people could sit down and so dispassionately discuss something that seemed particularly tragic to her. This fellow Truman, whom she was certain she knew, with all his hi-faluting talk, disgusted her immeasurably. She wasn't sure that they weren't all poking fun at her. Truman was speaking:

"Miss Morgan, didn't you attend school in Southern California?" Emma Lou

at last realized where she had seen him before. So *this* was Truman Walter, the little "cock o' the walk," as they had called him on the campus. She answered him
with difficulty, for there was a sob in her throat. "Yes, I did." Before Truman could
say more to her, Ray called to him:

> "Say, Bozo, what time are we going to the party? It's almost one
> o'clock now."

"Is it?" Alva seemed surprised. "But Aaron and Alta aren't here yet."
"They've been married just long enough to be late to everything."
"What do you say we go by and ring their bell?" Tony suggested, ignoring
Paul's Greenwich Village wit.
"'Sall right with me." Truman lifted his glass to his lips. "Then on to the
house-rent party . . . on to the bawdy bowels of Beale Street!"
They drained their glasses and prepared to leave.

"Ahhhh, sock it." . . . "Ummmm" . . . Piano playing-slow, loud, and discor-
dant, accompanied by the rhythmic sound of shuffling feet. Down a long, dark
hallway to an inside room, lit by a solitary red bulb. "Oh, play it you dirty no-
gooder." . . . A room full of dancing couples, scarcely moving their feet, arms
completely encircling one another's bodies . . . cheeks being warmed by one another's breath . . . eyes closed . . . animal ecstasy agitating their perspiring faces.
There was much panting, much hip movement, much shaking of the buttocks. . . .
"Do it twice in the same place." . . . "Git off that dime." Now somebody was
singing, "I ask you very confidentially. . . ." "Sing it man, sing it." . . . Piano tre-
ble moaning, bass rumbling like thunder. A swarm of people, motivating their bodies to express in suggestive movements the ultimate consummation of desire.

The music stopped, the room was suffocatingly hot, and Emma Lou was dis-
turbingly dizzy. She clung fast to Alva, and let the room and its occupants whirl
around her. Bodies and faces glided by. Leering faces and lewd bodies. Anxious
faces and angular bodies. Sad faces and obese bodies. All mixed up together. She
began to wonder how such a small room could hold so many people. "Oh, play it
again . . ." She saw the pianist now, silhouetted against the dark mahogany piano,
saw him bend his long, slick-haired head, until it hung low on his chest, then lift
his hands high in the air, and as quickly let them descend upon the keyboard. There
was one moment of cacophony, then the long supple fingers evolved a slow, tantalizing melody out of the deafening chaos.

Every one began to dance again. Body called to body, and cemented themselves together, limbs lewdly intertwined. A couple there kissing, another couple
dipping to the floor, and slowly shimmying, belly to belly, as they came back to
an upright position. A slender dark girl with wild eyes and wilder hair stood in
the center of the room, supported by the strong, lithe arms of a longshoreman. She
bent her trunk backward, until her head hung below her waistline, and all the while
she kept the lower portion of her body quivering like jello.

"She whips it to a jelly," the piano player was singing now, and banging on
the keys with such might that an empty gin bottle on top of the piano seemed to
be seized with the ague. "Oh, play it Mr. Charlie." Emma Lou grew limp in Alva's
arms.

"What's the matter, honey, drunk?" She couldn't answer. The music augmented by the general atmosphere of the room and the liquor she had drunk had presumably created another person in her stead. She felt like flying into an emotional frenzy—felt like flinging her arms and legs in insane unison. She had become very fluid, very elastic, and all the while she was giving in more and more to the music and to the liquor and to the physical madness of the moment.

When the music finally stopped, Alva led Emma Lou to a settee by the window which his crowd had appropriated. Every one was exceedingly animated, but they all talked in hushed, almost reverential tones.

"Isn't this marvelous?" Truman's eyes were ablaze with interest and excitement. Even Tony Crews seemed unusually alert.

"It's the greatest I've seen yet," he exclaimed.

Alva seemed the most unemotional one in the crowd. Paul the most detached. "Look at 'em all watching Ray."

"Remember, Bo," Truman counselled him. "Tonight you're 'passing.' Here's a new wrinkle, white man 'passes' for Negro."

"Why not? Enough of you pass for white." They all laughed, then transferred their interest back to the party. Cora was speaking:

"Didya see that little girl in pink—the one with the scar on her face—dancing with that tall, lanky, one-armed man? Wasn't she throwing it up to him?"

"Yeah," Tony admitted, "but she didn't have anything on that little Mexican-looking girl. She musta been born in Cairo."

"Saay, but isn't that one bad looking darkey over there, two chairs to the left; is he gonna smother that woman?" Truman asked excitedly.

"I'd say she kinda liked it," Paul answered, then lit another cigarette.

"Do you know they have corn liquor in the kitchen? They serve it from a coffee pot." Aaron seemed proud of his discovery.

"Yes," said Alva, "and they got hoppin'-john out there too."

"What the hell is hoppin'-john?"

"Ray, I'm ashamed of you. Here you are passing for colored and don't know what hoppin'-john is!"

"Tell him, Cora, I don't know either."

"Another one of these foreigners." Cora looked at Truman disdainfully. "Hoppin'-john is blackeyed peas and rice. Didn't they ever have any out in Salt Lake City?"

"Have they any chitterlings?" Alta asked eagerly.

"No, Alta," Alva replied, dryly. "This isn't Kansas. They have got pig's feet though."

"Lead me to 'em," Aaron and Alta shouted in unison, and led the way to the kitchen. Emma Lou clung to Alva's arm and tried to remain behind. "Alva, I'm afraid."

"Afraid of what? Come on, snap out of it! You need another drink." He pulled her up from the settee and led her through the crowded room down the long narrow dark hallway to the more crowded kitchen.

When they returned to the room, the pianist was just preparing to play again. He was tall and slender, with extra long legs and arms, giving him the appearance of a scarecrow. His pants were tight in the waist and full in the legs. He wore no coat, and a blue silk shirt hung damply to his body. He acted as if he were king of the occasion, ruling all from his piano stool throne. He talked familiarly to every one in the room, called women from other men's arms, demanded drinks from any bottle he happened to see being passed around, laughed uproariously, and made many grotesque and ofttimes obscene gestures.

There were sounds of a scuffle in an adjoining room, and an excited voice exclaimed, "You goddam son-of-a-bitch, don't you catch my dice no more." The piano player banged on the keys and drowned out the reply, if there was one.

Emma Lou could not keep her eyes off the piano player. He was acing like a maniac, occasionally turning completely around on his stool, grimacing like a witch doctor, and letting his hands dawdle over the keyboard of the piano with an agonizing indolence, when compared to the extreme exertion to which he put the rest of his body. He was improvising. The melody of the piece he had started to play was merely a base for more bawdy variations. His left foot thumped on the floor in time with the music, while his right punished the piano's loud-pedal. Beads of perspiration gathered grease from his slicked-down hair, and rolled oleagenously down his face and neck, spotting the already damp baby-blue shirt, and streaking his already greasy black face with more shiny lanes.

A sailor lad suddenly ceased his impassioned hip movement and strode out of the room, pulling his partner behind him, pushing people out of the way as he went. The spontaneous moans and slangy ejaculations of the piano player and of the more articulate dancers became more regular, more like a chanted obligato to the music. This lasted for a couple of hours interrupted only by hectic intermissions. Then the dancers grew less violent in their movements, and though the piano player seemed never to tire there were fewer couples on the floor, and those left seemed less loathe to move their legs.

Eventually, the music stopped for a long interval, and there was a more concerted drive on the kitchen's corn liquor supply. Most of the private flasks and bottles were empty. There were more calls for food, too, and the crap game in the side room annexed more players and more kibitzers. Various men and women had disappeared altogether. Those who remained seemed worn and tired. There was much petty person to person badinage and many whispered consultations in corners. There was an argument in the hallway between the landlord and two couples, who wished to share one room without paying him more than the regulation three dollars required of one couple. Finally, Alva suggested that they leave. Emma Lou had drifted off into a state of semi-consciousness and was too near asleep or drunk to distinguish people or voices. All she knew was that she was being led out of that dreadful place, that the perturbing "pilgrimage to the proletariat's parlor social," as Truman had called it, was ended, and that she was in a taxicab, cuddled up in Alva's arms.

LANGSTON HUGHES
Not Without Laughter
1930

After establishing himself as a poet, Langston Hughes turned somewhat reluctantly to prose in the last year of the 1920s. He took this course at the urging of his mentor and patron Charlotte Osgood Mason, "Godmother," who provided financial support and guided the careers of several Harlem Renaissance figures in the late 1920s and early 1930s. Hughes took Mason's advice and wrote the novel, but it was a project he did not really enjoy. The result, *Not Without Laughter*, was successful. It is the story of the coming of age of Sandy, a black youth living in Lawrence, Kansas during the second decade of the twentieth century. Part autobiographical, part fiction, it examines family, youth, and race in small town mid-America.

Not Without Laughter marked a turning point in Hughes's life and career. The novel was written as he ended his studies at Lincoln University, and it was published as his relationship with Mason was coming to a traumatic end. It also appeared as the Harlem Renaissance phase of Hughes's career was coming to an end. Hughes would enjoy three more decades as a writer and a poet, but during the rest of the 1930s, he spent much of his time away from Harlem, and his writing, especially his poetry, became much more concerned with class and economic issues as his politics moved to the left.

The episode of *Not Without Laughter* below presents Sandy's family intact, but reveals the stresses and tensions that soon begins to unravel Sandy's secure, close-knit world.

Work

The sunflowers in Willie-Mae's back yard were taller than Tom Johnson's head, and the hollyhocks, in the fence corners were almost as high. The nasturtiums, blood-orange and gold, tumbled over themselves all around Madam de Carter's house. Aunt Hager's sweet-william, her pinks, and her tiger-lilies were abloom and the apples on her single tree would soon be ripe. The adjoining yards of the three neighbors were gay with flowers. "Watch out for them dogs!" his grandmother told Sandy hourly, for the days had come when the bright heat made gentle animals go mad. Bees were heavy with honey, great green flies hummed through the air, yellow-black butterflies suckled at the rambling roses . . . and watermelons were on the market.

The Royal African Knights and Ladies of King Solomon's Scepter were preparing a drill for the September Emancipation celebration, a "Drill of All Nations," in which Annjee was to represent Sweden. It was not to be given for a month or more, but the first rehearsal would take place tonight.

"Sandy," his mother said, shaking him early in the morning as he lay on his pallet at the foot of Aunt Hager's bed, "listen here! I want you to come out to Mis' Rice's this evening and help me get through the dishes so's I can start home early, in time to wash and dress myself to go to the lodge hall. You hears me?"

"Yes'm," said Sandy, keeping his eyes closed to the bright stream of morning sunlight entering the window. But half an hour later, when Jimboy kicked him and said: "Hey, bo! You wanta go fishin'?" he got up at once, slid into his pants; and together they went out in the garden to dig worms. It was seldom that his father took him anywhere, and, of course, he wanted to go. Sandy adored Jimboy, but Jimboy, amiable and indulgent though he was, did not often care to be bothered with his ten-year-old son on his fishing expeditions.

Harriett had gone to her job, and Hager had long been at the tubs under the apple-tree when the two males emerged from the kitchen-door. "Huh! You ain't workin' this mawnin', is you?" the old woman grunted, bending steadily down, then up, over the wash-board.

"Nope," her tall son-in-law answered. "Donahoe laid me off yesterday on account o' the white bricklayers said they couldn't lay bricks with a nigger."

"Always something to keep you from workin'," panted Hager.

"Sure is," agreed Jimboy pleasantly. "But don't worry, me and Sandy's gonna catch you a mess o' fish for supper today. How's that, ma?"

"Don't need no fish," the old woman answered. "An' don't come ma-in' me! Layin' round here fishin' when you ought to be out makin' money to take care o' this house an' that chile o' your'n." The suds rose foamy white about her black arms as the clothes plushed up and down on the zinc washboard. "Lawd deliver me from a lazy darky!"

But Jimboy and Sandy were already behind the tall corn, digging for bait near the back fence.

"Don't never let no one woman worry you," said the boy's father softly, picking the moist wriggling worms from the upturned loam. "Treat 'em like chickens, son. Throw 'em a little corn and they'll run after you, but don't give 'em too much. If you do, they'll stop layin' and expect you to wait on 'em."

"Will they?" asked Sandy.

The warm afternoon sun made the river a languid sheet of muddy gold, glittering away towards the bridge and the flour-mills a mile and a half off. Here in the quiet, on the end of a rotting jetty among the reeds, Jimboy and his son sat silently. A long string of small silver fish hung down into the water, keeping fresh, and the fishing-lines were flung far out in the stream, waiting for more bites. Not a breeze on the flat brown-gold river, not a ripple, not a sound. But once the train came by behind them, pouring out a great cloud of smoke and cinders and shaking the jetty.

"That's Number Five," said Jimboy. "Sure is flyin'," as the train disappeared between rows of empty box-cars far down the track, sending back a hollow clatter as it shot past the flour-mills, whose stacks could be dimly seen through the heat haze. Once the engine's whistle moaned shrilly.

"She's gone now," said Jimboy, as the last click of the wheels died away. And, except for the drone of a green fly about the can of bait, there was again no sound to disturb the two fishermen.

Jimboy gazed at his lines. Across the river Sandy could make out, in the brilliant sunlight, the gold of wheat-fields and the green of trees on the hills. He wondered if it would be nice to live over there in the country.

"Man alive!" his father cried suddenly, hauling vigorously at one of the lines. "Sure got a real bite now. . . . Look at this catfish." From the water he pulled a large flopping lead-colored creature, with a fierce white mouth bleeding and gaping over the hook.

"He's on my line!" yelled Sandy. "I caught him!"

"Pshaw!" laughed Jimboy. "You was setting there dreaming."

"No, I wasn't!"

But just then, at the mills, the five-o'clock whistles blew. "Oh, gee, dad!" cried the boy, frightened. "I was s'posed to go to Mis' Rice's to help mama, and I come near forgetting it. She wants to get through early this evenin' to go to lodge meeting. I gotta hurry and go help her."

"Well, you better beat it then, and I'll look out for your line like I been doing and bring the fishes home."

So the little fellow balanced himself across the jetty, scrambled up the bank, and ran down the railroad track towards town. He was quite out of breath when he reached the foot of Penrose Street, with Mrs. Rice's house still ten blocks away, so he walked awhile, then ran again, down the long residential street, with its large houses sitting in green shady lawns far back from the sidewalk. Sometimes a sprinkler, attached to a long rubber hose, sprayed fountain-like jets of cold water on the thirsty grass. In one yard three golden-haired little girls were playing under an elm-tree, and in another a man and some children were having a leisurely game of croquet.

Finally Sandy turned into a big yard. The delicious scent of frying beefsteak greeted the sweating youngster as he reached the screen of the white lady's kitchen-door. Inside, Annjee was standing over the hot stove seasoning something in a saucepan, beads of perspiration on her dark face, and large damp spots under the arms of her dress.

"You better get here!" she said. "And me waiting for you for the last hour. Here, take this pick and break some ice for the tea." Sandy climbed up on a stool and raised the ice-box lid while his mother opened the oven and pulled out a pan of golden-brown biscuits. "Made these for your father," she remarked. "The white folks ain't asked for 'em, but they like 'em, too, so they can serve for both. . . . Jimboy's crazy about biscuits. . . .Did he work today?"

"No'm," said Sandy, jabbing at the ice. "We went fishing."

At that moment Mrs. Rice came into the kitchen, tall and blond, in a thin flowered gown. She was a middle-aged white woman with a sharp nasal voice.

"Annjee, I'd like the potatoes served just as they are in the casserole. And make several slices of very thin toast for my father. Now, be sure they *are* thin!"

"Yes, m'am," said Annjee stirring a spoonful of flour into the frying-pan, making a thick brown gravy.

"Old thin toast," muttered Annjee when Mrs. Rice had gone back to the front. "Always bothering round the kitchen! Here 'tis lodge-meeting night—dinner late anyhow—and she coming telling me to stop and make toast for the old man! He ain't too indigestible to eat biscuits like the rest of 'em. . . . White folks sure is a case!" She laid three slices of bread on top of the stove. "So spoiled with colored folks waiting on 'em all their days! Don't know what they'll do in heaven, 'cause I'm gonna sit down up there myself."

Annjee took the biscuits, light and brown, and placed some on a pink plate she had warmed. She carried them, with the butter and jelly, into the dining-room. Then she took the steak from the warmer, dished up the vegetables into gold rimmed serving-dishes, and poured the gravy, which smelled deliciously onion-flavored.

"Gee, I'm hungry," said the child, with his eyes on the big steak ready to go in to the white people.

"Well, just wait," replied his mother. "You come to work, not to eat. . . . Whee! but it's hot today!" She wiped her wet face and put on a large white bungalow apron that had been hanging behind the door. Then she went with the iced tea and a pitcher of water into the dining-room, struck a Chinese gong, and came back to the kitchen to get the dishes of steaming food, which she carried in to the table.

It was some time before she returned from waiting on the table; so Sandy, to help her, began to scrape out the empty pans and put them to soak in the sink. He ate the stewed corn that had stuck in the bottom of one, and rubbed a piece of bread in the frying-pan where the gravy had been. His mother came out with the water-pitcher, broke some ice for it, and returned to the dining-room where Sandy could hear laughter, and the clinking of spoons in tea-glasses, and women talking. When Annjee came back into the kitchen, she took four custards from the ice-box and placed them on gold-rimmed plates.

"They're about through," she said to her son. "Sit down and I'll fix you up."

Sandy was very hungry and he hoped Mrs. Rice's family hadn't eaten all the steak, which had looked so good with its brown gravy and onions.

Shortly, his mother returned carrying the dishes, that had been filled with hot food. She placed them on the kitchen-table in front of Sandy, but they were no longer full and no longer hot. The corn had thickened to a paste, and the potatoes were about gone; but there was still a ragged piece of steak left on the platter.

"Don't eat it all," said Annjee warningly. "I want to take some home to your father."

The bell rang in the dining-room. Annjee went through the swinging door and returned bearing a custard that had been but little touched.

"Here, sonny—the old man says it's too sweet for his stomach, so you can have this." She set the yellow cornstarch before Sandy. "He's seen these ripe peaches out here today and he wants some, that's all. More trouble than he's worth, po' old soul, and me in a hurry!" She began to peel the fruit. "Just like a chile, 'deed he is!" she added, carrying the sliced peaches into the dining-room and leaving Sandy with a plate of food before him, eating slowly. "When you rushing to get out, seems like white folks tries theirselves."

In a moment she returned, ill-tempered, and began to scold Sandy for taking so long with his meal.

"I asked you to help me so's I can get to the lodge on time, and you just set and chew and eat! . . . Here, wipe these dishes, boy!" Annjee began hurriedly to lay plates in a steaming row on the shelf of the sink; so Sandy got up and, between mouthfuls of pudding, wiped them with a large dish-towel.

Soon Mrs. Rice came into the kitchen again, briskly, through the swinging door and glanced about her. Sandy felt ashamed for the white woman to see him eating a left-over pudding from her table, so he put the spoon down.

"Annjee," the mistress said sharply. "I wish you wouldn't put quite so much onion in your sauce for the steak. I've mentioned it to you several times before, and you know very well we don't like it."

"Yes, m'am," said Annjee.

"And do *please* be careful that our drinking water is cold before meals are served. . . . You were certainly careless tonight. You must think more about what you are doing, Annjee."

Mrs. Rice went out again through the swinging door, but Sandy stood near the sink with a burning face and eyes that had suddenly filled with angry tears. He couldn't help it—hearing his sweating mother reprimanded by this tall white woman in the flowered dress. Black, hard-working Annjee answered: "Yes, m'am," and that was all—but Sandy cried.

"Dry up," his mother said crossly when she saw him, thinking he was crying because she had asked him to work. "What's come over you, anyway—can't even wipe a few plates for me and act nice about it!"

He didn't answer. When the dining-room had been cleared and the kitchen put in order, Annjee told him to empty the garbage while she wrapped in newspapers several little bundles of food to carry to Jimboy. Then they went out the back door, around the big house to the street, and trudged the fourteen blocks to Aunt Hager's, taking short cuts through alleys, passing under arc-lights that sputtered whitely in the deepening twilight, and greeting with an occasional "Howdy" other poor colored folks also coming home from work.

"How are you, Sister Jones?"

"Right smart, I thank yuh!" as they passed.

Once Annjee spoke to her son. "Evening's the only time we niggers have to ourselves!" she said. "Thank God for night . . . 'cause all day you gives to white folks."

VI

SLOW FADE TO BLACK: THE 1930s

Contrary to popular myth as well as the theories of some writers and critics, the Harlem Renaissance did not end with the 1929 stock market crash or the Great Depression that followed. Measured by the production of literature, the Harlem Renaissance thrived in the early 1930s. Fifteen major books were published between 1931 and 1935. Among the authors were Countee Cullen who continued to write poetry and published his first novel in 1932. Langston Hughes wrote throughout the decade, and published a collection of short stories and three plays, as well as several volumes of poetry. Claude McKay, Jessie Fauset, and Wallace Thurman each produced new novels. It was during the 1930s that Zora Neale Hurston was most creative, publishing three novels and two books of folklore. Several new writers and artists enjoyed their most productive period during the decade. Sterling Brown published his book of poems, Arna Bontemps published three novels, and Jacob Lawrence emerged as a major African American painter. African Americans also continued their creativity in theater and music. And yet in spite of this record of literary and artistic productivity, the Harlem Renaissance was changing, and year by year becoming less important as the driving force in African American literary and artistic creativity.

Among a number of factors that led to the steady decline of the Harlem Renaissance in the early and mid-1930s was the departure from Harlem of a number of figures central to the movement. In 1927 Charles S. Johnson of the Urban League left Harlem for Fisk University and four years later James Weldon Johnson of the NAACP followed. Du Bois became increasingly disillusioned with the movement in the late 1920s and left New York and the NAACP in 1934. In that year also came the untimely death of two Renaissance novelists, Wallace Thurman and Rudolph Fisher. After the publication of *Not Without Laughter* in 1930, Langston Hughes effectively severed his relationship with the movement and began a lengthy hiatus from Harlem. These events did not occur at one time, and no one of them alone would have had much of an impact on the movement. But the cumulative effect was to shift emphasis away from Harlem and the Harlem Renaissance.

The Renaissance suffered as well when several intellectuals, including some like Alain Locke who had been enthusiastic supporters of the Renaissance, joined the movement's critics. To a large degree they became dissatisfied with the "art for arts sake" philosophy and absence of an overlying social or political ideology. As economic times worsened the bohemianism of the Renaissance seemed an extravagant and irresponsible luxury; in the 1930s even a champion of artistic freedom like Langston Hughes became committed to political poetry. Both the NAACP and the Urban League shifted their focus from literature to economic and social issues. Finally, the Harlem Renaissance no longer attracted talented young writers and artists. Richard Wright, the greatest literary talent to emerge in the 1930s criticized the movement largely for its emphasis on individualism and for failure to develop a social or class consciousness.

The Harlem Renaissance did not end abruptly. It extended well into the 1930s and then faded as its participants and proponents shifted their interests and activities.

ALAIN LOCKE
"This Year of Grace"

Beginning in January 1929 Alain Locke launched a series of annual reviews of African American literature for *Opportunity*. These essays, which appeared yearly through the 1930s, provided Locke with the opportunity to chronicle the declining years of the Harlem Renaissance. In 1931, he began his review essay with a death announcement for the Renaissance. While this obituary was premature, it made public the disenchantment with the Harlem Renaissance that had engulfed one of the most ardent supporters of the movement.

"This Year Of Grace:
Outstanding Books Of The Year In Negro Literature"
Opportunity
February, 1931

Since it is 1930 that is under retrospective review, there is no need for that superstitious unction which made every year of our Lord a year of grace. The much exploited Negro renaissance was after all a product of the expansive period we are now willing to call the period of inflation and overproduction ; perhaps there was much in it that was unsound, and perhaps our aesthetic gods are turning their backs only a little more gracefully than the gods of the market-place. Are we then, in a period of cultural depression, verging on spiritual bankruptcy? Has the afflatus of Negro self-expression died down? Are we outliving the Negro fad? Has the Negro creative artist wandered into the ambush of the professional exploiters? By some signs and symptoms. Yes. But to anticipate my conclusion,—'Let us rejoice and be exceedingly glad.' The second and truly sound phase of the cultural development of the Negro in American literature and art cannot begin without a collapse of the boom, a change to more responsible and devoted leadership, a revision of basic values, and along with a penitential purgation of spirit, a wholesale expulsion of the moneychangers from the temple of art.

I think the main fault of the movement thus far has been the lack of any deep realization of what was truly Negro, and what was merely superficially characteristic. It has been assumed that to be a Negro automatically put one in a position to know; and that any deviation on the part of a white writer from the trite stereotypes was a deeply revealing insight. Few indeed they are who know the folk-spirit whose claims they herald and proclaim. And with all the improvement of fact and attitude, the true Negro is yet to be discovered and the purest values of the Negro spirit yet to be refined out from the alloys of our present cultural currency. It is, therefore, significant that this year has witnessed a waning of creative expression and an increasing trend toward documentation of the Negro subject and objective analysis of the facts. But even after this has been done, there will remain the more difficult problem of spiritual interpretation, so that at last we shall know what we mean when we talk of the Negro folk-spirit, the true Negro character, the typical Negro spirit. At present we do not know, and at last 'it can be told.'

One of the symptoms of progress in the field of fiction is the complete eclipse of the propaganda novel, and the absence of formula and problem even in the novels of white Southern writers. A review of Gilmore Millen's *Sweet Man* says: "The book might have been written by a Negro, so accurate it seems in its details, so eager it seems in sympathy and understanding of the black people." Marie Stanley's *Gulf Stream,* the frank study of the cross-fires of the caste in an Alabama village, may lack the maturity of the best Southern fiction of its subject, but it outdoes them all in sensitive delineation. "You ask those poor blacks," says Berzelia to the Catholic priest, "to worship a simpering white woman with a rosy child in her arms; No, Father, its against reason, and they've got the right idea! We are done with your white God, they say, give us a God of our own who will understand us, who is black like ourselves! But all the same, they hadn't the courage or the pride or what not to go the whole way. For she's a Madonna with No-Kink on her hair. That's where they failed themselves, Father. They've made her hallowed hair straight; they lacked the courage for the kink. What a pity." When a sensitive mulatto heroines's daughter, near-white herself, swings deliberately back to a black marriage in "poignant opposition" to her mother's ambition for white recognition, you may be sure that the Negro sphinx has come nearer to our literary Thebes. May some real young genius, black or white, go blithely out of the walls to question her.

That almost has happened with the first novel of Langston Hughes, *Not Without Laughter.* If this book were a trilogy, and carried its young hero, Sandy, through a typical black boy's journey from the cradle to the grave we might perhaps have the all-too-longprayed for Negro novel. As it is despite immaturity of narrative technique, this novel is one of the high-water marks of the Negro's self-depiction in prose. *Not Without Laughter* owes its inspiration to a force far different from the flippant exhibitionism by which some of our younger writers aimed to out-Herod *Nigger Heaven.* Indeed it was born in Mr. Hughes poetry, which aims to evoke the folk temperament truly and reverently; and in its best chapters, *Storm, Guitar* and *Dance,* its style palpitates with the real spiritual essences of Negro life. Should its promise be fulfilled, we shall have a Negro novelist to bracket with Julia Peterkin and Du Bose Heyward. . . .

Except for a slender volume by James Weldon Johnson, and some significant magazine verse of Sterling Brown and Langston Hughes, there has been a noticeable lull in the output of the Negro poets. Of course, a good deal of poetizing upon the race question, both by white and Negro sentimentalists, still persists; but that is far from making Negro poetry,—the obsessions of these dilettantes notwithstanding. Indeed, Mr. Johnson's poem, *St. Peter Narrates an Incident of Resurrection Day,* comes itself somewhat under the same criticism, as a half-ironical, half-sentimental bit of propaganda in couplet stanzas.

It is in *Black Manhattan* that James Weldon Johnson makes the literary year his happy debtor. This chronicle of the life of the Negro, knit ingeniously into the general history of New York, decade by decade, is a fine and permanently valuable bit of documentation of the Negro's social and cultural history. No one can read it without surprising enlightenment, or without a subtle appreciation of the forces which have prevented the Negro from being spiritually segregated in the life of America. One gets the same impression from those chapters of *Tin Pan Alley,* by Dr. Goldberg, that traces the ragtime and jazz elements as they have carried the Negro's contribution through the stream of popular music into the very lifeblood of the national life. The climax of the year on the musical side, however, is the publication of the *Green Pastures Spirituals,* arranged by one of the most gifted and genuine of Negro musicians, Hall Johnson. Indeed this publication but makes available a small fraction of the extensive repertory of folk music of the Hall Johnson Negro Choir, which I consider to be the greatest and most typical Negro choral organization we possess. . . .

So, to conclude, the constructive gains of the year have been in the literature of criticism and interpretation rather than in the literature of creative expression. Likewise self-expression has, on the whole, encountered what we hope is only a temporary lag. However, greater objectivity and a soberer viewpoint are good gift-horses to stable, and lest they flee overnight, let us lock the stable-doors. The sober Reformation reenforces and clinches the bouyant Renaissance; at least, so it went once upon a time. I am all for history repeating herself on this point. Certainly we shall not have to wait many years to see; meanwhile, in penance for many who have boasted, let some of us pray.

ARNA BONTEMPS
God Sends Sunday
1931

Arna Bontemps came to Harlem in the mid-1920s and quickly joined Langston Hughes and his circle of friends. Bontemps had some early success as a poet, but it was not until the 1930s that he made his mark as a black writer. *God Sends Sunday,* the first of his three novels is set in the 1890s and traces the rise and fall of Augie, an African American jockey. Its strength lies in its descriptions of black life in southern and western cities such as New Orleans and St. Louis. Like Hughes and McKay, Bonetemps was criticized for his concentration on lower class black life and for his descriptions of sin and violence. Nevertheless the novel enjoyed some success and then became the basis for a musical comedy, *St. Louis Woman,* which Bontemps wrote in partnership with Countee Cullen in 1945.

This selection from *God Sends Sunday* tracks Augie's decline from a successful jockey to a life of dissipation.

God Sends Sunday

It was near Christmas when Augie reached New Orleans again, and things were sparkling for the Negroes. The eating-places and hang-outs were crowded with country folks who had come to town following the harvests. That portion of the city blacks who worked in sugar refineries or cotton fields during the warm months in order to loaf throughout the winter had returned. Everybody had money; everybody was nigger-rich. A poker game was not respectable that had less than a hundred dollars in it. Stevedores risked twenty-dollar gold pieces on a single throw of the bones. Certain of the country folks tossed all their nickels and pennies into the gutter in order to keep their pockets from becoming cluttered.

But despite the general affluence, Augie could buy and sell the other blacks by the dozen. His earnings had gone into the thousands. More important than that, his name had risen like a young star; he had become famous.

He and Bad-foot went directly to the barber shop. There they described the St. Louis fancy women to the home-staying fellows. They talked about the Cotton Flower Ball and boasted of Augie's success in taking the cake. Some of the drifters wanted to get tips on horses. Augie assumed an indifference to such questions, but he warned his followers to keep an eye on a young colt named Silver Heels, a recent addition to the Woodbine stables, and a great favorite of Augie's.

The talk switched to other things, and when, a bit later, Mississippi entered the shop, Augie promptly drew him into a corner and asked about Florence.

"I don't know much," Mississippi said. "I ain't got de job no mo'."

"How come dat, Mis'sippi?"

The old frock-tailed Negro seemed embarrassed. "Mistah Woody ain't got Florence now; he done quits."

"Oh! I on'erstand."

"Seems lak his people got wind about it; so he had to duck."

"Lissen, Mis'sippi. You reckon I could ease in *now?*"

"I don't know, Lil Augie. Anuther white man been makin' up to her, but he ain't as fine as Mistah Woody."

"Who he?"

"Gummy, de saloon man."

Augie's lip turned. "Where's yo' rig, Mis'sippi?"

"Down de street a lil piece."

"Come on. Us gonna drive over there."

Half an hour later Augie knocked boldly at Florence's door. Mississippi remained in the high seat. Autumn had touched the leaves of the trees. They kept falling on the old rig, falling like flakes of gold through the transparent golden light. In these fading surroundings, Augie seemed as brilliant as a spring flower. He was dressed in bottle-green with a canary vest and canary spats over pearl-buttoned shoes.

"I jes' come back," he told Florence.

"How you lak St. Louis?"

"There ain't nuthin' there, for me. No peace."

"So you come back on account o' dat?"

"De season is done finish," he said. "I'm gonna be heah a long time, an' I wants yo' company, yella gal."

"How you know I don't b'long to somebody else, Lil Augie?"

"If it ain't Mistah Woody, it don't matter," he said.

Florence stood erect between the dark plush curtains of her front room. She was much taller than Little Augie. She was slim and proud-like, and her crimson painted mouth was beautiful against buff-colored skin. Augie's heart leapt as he watched her. His dream seemed so near he could almost put his hands on it.

"You ain't ask me do I love you, Lil Augie."

His diamonds shook nervously. "I ain't askin' a heap, yella gal."

"You is got enough money to ask for de moon. They tells me you got mo' spikes than Carter is got oats, Lil Augie."

"An' I'm fixin' to spend 'em all on you. I'm gonna make you lucky too."

"Is dat truf?"

"Sho, I was borned wid a veil. I'm lucky, an' everybody whut takes up wid me gets lucky."

"We might could be sweet," she said.

When Augie came out of the house a little later he was swollen like a pouter pigeon.

"This heah is gonna be ma house," he told Mississippi. "I done made maself a home. Come back in de mawnin' an' you can have yo' old job back again."

For the next few days Augie and Florence were always together. Florence, the insolent well-kept girl whom young Horace Church-Woodbine had been smitten on, was pointed out all over town with Little Augie, the sparkling nigger-rich jockey. There was something insulting in the match, something humiliating to the friends of the wealthy sportsman. But Augie was unconscious of it. All he knew was that Florence was the yellowest and best-looking gal he had ever seen and that he loved her worse than a horse loves corn.

In the evening she made him sweetened water and kept filling his glass while he pumped the accordion and sang. Florence did not sing. Augie thought that that was just as well; a girl as fine as Florence needed no other talents. Besides, he felt able to supply enough music for both of them. So he sang for her the new tunes he had learned on Targee Street, sang them over and over again, and his heart was so big and swollen with pleasure he thought it would surely burst.

Wind was coming in from the Gulf with increasing strength, and all through the cool evening crisp gold leaves fell with a tiny clang and rattle against the windows and the door. Augie and Florence spent the hours examining new winter velvets that he had bought her. Recently, money had been short in her house; she had bought no new clothes in months. It gave Augie pleasure to supply these; he outdid himself for lavishness. Nothing was too expensive.

Finally, it was arranged for him to move into Florence's house—the house Mr. Woody had given her. Two full trunks were sent ahead. His remaining possessions he packed in a new wicker suitcase. This with the accordion he proposed to carry himself in the carriage. While Mississippi waited at the door, Augie took leave of Bad-foot.

"Us ain't gonna bus' up, Bad-foot. Us is always gonna be lak dis." He held up his first two fingers.

"I gonna miss you jes' de same," Bad-foot said. "You is ma luck stone, son."

"You is good luck yo' black self," Augie smiled.

"I donno." Bad-foot rubbed his slick head with a hard stubby hand. "I donno 'bout me."

"I do. An' us gonna stay lak dis—no matter whut!"

Augie moved into Florence's house about midday. About midnight she moved out. The white neighbors, along with Gummy and other hostile persons, hastily formed a charge of immorality against the girl as soon as they understood. Florence had been too frankly a white man's girl. There was nothing to do but go.

So together she and Augie took a simple shack on the far fringes of the city, a shack behind a thicket on a yellow golden road near a railroad track. It was too far away from the heart of town for convenience, but there were trees on the road-side, and the air was full of birds. In the thickets there were turkeys the color of gun metal with red enameled heads, and in the road grouse dusting their wings nervously.

Mississippi had come with them. Each day he drove Augie in to the city. Often he returned again with both of them in the evening. Most of their time, it seemed, was spent in the carriage. And Florence did not enjoy it.

All of a sudden bad days came upon Little Augie. An accumulation of bad luck, reserved from many, many days past, fell at once upon his head. For years a successful gambler, he was now unable to draw a single pair from a deck of cards. All the dice that had been so responsive to his cajoling now seemed loaded against him.

In the races his horses stumbled, wrenched their legs, or otherwise failed. Mr. Woody turned spiteful and assigned him to all the impossible mounts. Even Bad-foot, now a trainer and a person of some authority in the stables, seemed distant.

Augie began drinking more than usual. He could not bear to confront his wretched fortunes with a clear mind. He could not bear to look Florence in the face. She had expected so much of him; he had promised so much.

In his misery he returned again and again to the stables; the horses reassured him. As long as he had their mute sympathy, the comfort of their presence, he would never lose hope. Somehow his love of Florence seemed fleeting and unessential, a mere frill on his life, when he was near the horses. As much as he desired to make a fine impression on her, he knew that he would be utterly cast down if he failed. He was no simpering pie-backed nigger who lived by women. He was a race-horse man. A woman was like a fine suit of clothes to him, something to please his vanity, to show him off well in the eyes of his friends.

"Damn 'em all, all de womens! I b'lieve Florence is bad luck to me anyhow."

But that was just mouth-talk. He had hardly spoken the words when he wondered if he were not actually losing his mind about her. How otherwise could he have imagined such an outlandish lie! He sought his accordion.

> Oh, de boat's gone up de river
> An' de tide's gone down. . . .

Augie sat on the edge of his cot, tossing shoes, old shirts, and underclothes into the badly used wicker traveling-bag. It was leaving-time again.

"I thought I was fixed for life," he said. "But I ain't stayed heah no longer'n I stayed anywhere else."

He finished packing and put on the little greasy dirt-colored vest that once had been milk-white with red roses. But he decided not to wear the coat; so he folded it carefully and laid it across the other rags in his bag. A moment later he gathered up his luggage, the bag in one hand, the accordion in the other, and slipped beneath the trees of the yard.

Night had fallen, and the moon was up, glimmering remote and sadlike. The garden corn had been shocked and stood near the fence in little abandoned wig-wams. Augie's heart was full of misery.

"I done carved ole Lissus wid de beet knife," he said. "I done carved him good an' I'm glad I done it. He over yonder now strugglin' in his blood. An' he might be dead. So it's leavin'-time for Lil Augie. Leavin'-time, an' I ain't comin' back."

He paused a moment, leaning on the gate post, chewing the stem of his pipe with toothless gums. The dusty road was white in the moonlight and seemed to curve upward at the end where it went out of sight. Augie crossed it slowly and began climbing the railroad embankment. Standing between the tracks, he gazed first in one direction and then in the other. Both seemed alike from where he stood. At each end there was a dim shining point. One way was familiar to Augie—it was the way by which he had come to Mudtown only a few short weeks earlier. The other way was new and strange. That was the way he chose to go.

He began walking slowly. Beyond the high weeds, nesting in a clump of red castor-bean trees, he saw the Clow shack. Farther away, across the white sandy pasture, was the hut of Lissus and Tisha. Beulah was in one of those houses. But Augie kept on walking. Behind him on the other side of the road Leah and Terry were sitting in their tiny kitchen with no idea of what had happened, no idea that Augie was leaving.

"I done lef' 'em lak a dream," he said. "I'm goin' to Tia Juana, an' I ain't gonna write no letter."

Suddenly Augie heard footsteps under the low fruit trees on the Clows' place. He paused a moment and heard his heart thumping. He saw no one. Still the footsteps kept coming. They were coming toward him.

A moment later Tisha stepped out from the shadows, climbed the barbed-wire fence, and started up the embankment a distance behind Augie. Her head was tied in a handkerchief, her skirts were tucked above her knees, and she was wearing a pair of heavy man's shoes. She had in her hand the blacksnake with which she drove the mules, and her cheeks were swollen with chewing-tobacco.

Augie had time to wonder what she was doing on the railroad tracks at that hour—considering the condition of Lissus. But he promptly realized that she was following him. He began to speed his steps. Tisha was after him with the mule whip. She was after him for hitting Lissus with the beet knife. Her steps were steady and deliberate. Yet she seemed to Augie to be drawing closer and closer to him. He was now walking as fast as his legs would carry him. But it wasn't fast enough. He began to run.

Suddenly the wicker bag went off the handle, fell open and tumbled down the side of the embankment. Augie saw at a glance that his rags were scattered among the dry stalks of wild mustard, his Prince Albert was hung on a briar.

"Tha's de las' button on Gabriel's coat," he muttered sadly. "Tha's eve'thing I got."

Tisha was still following, still threatening him with the whip; so he could not stop to regain his possessions. Instead he added speed to his steps.

A moment later, however, a wave of shame passed over him, and he stopped dead still in his tracks.

"Whut done got in me?" he said. "Heah I is breakin' ma neck runnin' from a woman—dat stinkin' black cat Tisha. Dis ain't lak Lil Augie. Dis ain't me."

Tisha had turned back. Augie could see her between the rails. She now seemed tiny and far away in the moonlight.

Augie rubbed his head. His hat too was gone. The night air felt cool on his bald spot. He chewed the stem of his cob pipe and realized that it was dry. The pipe was lost; it had fallen from the stem.

"I ain't nobody. I ain't nuthin'," he said. "I's jes' a po' picked sparrow. I ain't big as a dime, an' I don't worth a nickel."

But there was no need to turn back. He had carved Lissus with the beet knife, and it was leaving-time. He wasn't tired, and he still had his accordion. Tia Juana was somewhere ahead. He had learned that much from the postman. And there, he had been told, there was horse racing and plenty of liquor.

A few moments later a big locomotive headlight rose above the dim horizon and flashed in Augie's face. He left the embankment and got in the middle of the road. As the train drew nearer he could tell by its labored pulling that it was heavily loaded. The whole countryside, a tiny dark world with its near-by horizon, trembled at its approach. The trees rocked; fences swayed.

At a crossroads Augie stopped and waited for the long freighter to pass. While he stood there a large motor truck drove up and stopped beside him.

Some one shouted from the seat, "Where you goin', governor?"

"'Way down de line,". Augie said. "To Tia Juana."

"Hop on if you wanna."

"Yes, *suh!*"

When the train finished passing, the truck pulled across the tracks and opened up on the smooth gravel road of the opposite side. Augie stretched out on the floor, resting his head on a pile of sacks, and began limbering up his accordion.

> Oh de boat's gone up de river
> An' de tide's gone down.

The night air whizzed about his head. Trees and houses and hills were flying past him like leaves in a hurricane. A little democrat wagon went by like a mere pasteboard toy. A strangely familiar feeling of exhilaration came to Augie, an illusion that came with speed. When had he felt that thrill before? He recalled Mr. Woody and his fast horses. It had been a good many years. So many indeed that Augie could not remember.

STRERLING BROWN
Poems from *Southern Road*
1932

Sterling Brown was among the newer poets who showed the greatest promise as the 1930s began. He was one of the few Harlem Renaissance poets based at a university—he joined the faculty of Howard's English Department in 1929. Like a number of other writers of this period, he was a promoter and critic of black literature as well as a poet. In the early 1930s he served as literary editor of *Opportunity*, and from January 1931 until September 1935 wrote a column on the African American literary scene. Like Langston Hughes, Brown used the music of the African American masses as an inspiration for his poetry, especially folk songs and work songs, and he focused his writing on the southern black working class. In 1932 he published his only book of Harlem Renaissance poetry, *Southern Road.*

The poems that follow illustrate the southern, lower class content that characterized Brown's poetry, as well as his rather grim assessment of the racial situation; they also demonstrate his use of black musical forms—the work song for "Southern Road," folk songs for the middle section of "Memphis Blues." "Frankie and Johnnie," of course, reinterpreted a familiar folk-ballad of the same name.

"Southern Road"

Swing dat hammer—hunh—
Steady, bo';
Swing dat hammer—hunh—
Steady, bo';
Ain't no rush, bebby,
Long ways to go.

Burner tore his—hunh—
Black heart away;
Burner tore his—hunh—
Black heart away;
Got me life, bebby,
An' a day.

Gal's on Fifth Street—hunh—
Son done gone;
Gal's on Fifth Street—hunh—
Son done gone;
Wife's in de ward, bebby,
Babe's not bo'n.

My ole man died—hunh—
Cussin' me;
My ole man died—hunh—
Cussin' me;
Ole lady rocks, bebby,
Huh misery.

Doubleshackled—hunh—
Guard behin';
Doubleshackled—hunh—
Guard behin';
Ball an' chain, bebby,
On my min'.

White man tells me—hunh—
Damn yo' soul;
White man tells me—hunh—

Damn yo' soul;
Got no need, bebby,
To be tole.

Chain gang nevah—hunh—
Let me go;
Chain gang nevah—hunh—
Let me go;
Po' los' boy,
bebby,
Evahmo'. . . .

Reprinted with permission.

"Georgie Grimes"

Georgie Grimes, with a red suitcase,
   Sloshes onward through the rain,
Georgie Grimes, with a fear behind him,
   Will not come back again.

Georgie remembers hot words, lies,
   The knife, and a pool of blood,
And suddenly her staring eyes,
   With their light gone out for good.

Georgie mutters over and over,
   Stumbling through the soggy clay,
"No livin' woman got de right
   To do no man dat way."

Reprinted with permission.

"Memphis Blues"

1

Nineveh, Tyre
Babylon,
Not much lef'
Of either one.
All dese cities
Ashes and rust,
De win' sing sperrichals
Through deir dus'. . . .
Was another Memphis
Mongst de olden days,
Done been destroyed

In many ways. . . .
Dis here Memphis
It may go
Floods may drown it;
Tornado blow;
Mississippi wash it
Down to sea
Like de other Memphis in
History.

2

Watcha gonna do when Memphis on fire,
    Memphis on fire, Mistah Preachin' Man?
Gonna pray to Jesus and nebber tire,
    Gonna pray to Jesus, loud as I can,
        Gonna pray to my Jesus, oh, my Lawd!

Watcha gonna do when de tall flames roar,
    Tall flames roar, Mistah Lovin' Man?
Gonna love my brownskin better'n before—
    Gonna love my baby lak a do right man,
        Gonna love my brown baby, oh, my Lawd!

Watcha gonna do when Memphis falls down,
    Memphis falls down, Mistah Music Man?
Gonna plunk on dat box as long as it soun',
    Gonna plunk dat box fo' to beat de ban',
        Gonna tickle dem ivories, oh, my Lawd!

Watcha gonna do in de hurricane,
    In de hurricane, Mistah Workin' Man?
Gonna put dem buildings up again,
    Gonna put em up dis time to stan',
        Gonna push a wicked wheelbarrow, oh, my Lawd!

Watcha gonna do when Memphis near gone,
    Memphis near gone, Mistah Drinkin' Man?
Gonna grab a pint bottle of Mountain Corn,
    Gonna keep de stopper in my han',
        Gonna get a mean jag on, oh, my Lawd!

Watcha gonna do when de flood roll fas',
    Flood roll fas', Mistah Gamblin' Man?
Gonna pick up my dice fo' one las' pass—
    Gonna fade my way to de lucky lan',
        Gonna throw my las' seven-oh, my Lawd!

3

Memphis go
By Flood or Flame;
Nigger won't worry
All de same—
Memphis go
Memphis come back,
Ain' no skin
Off de nigger's back.
All dese cities
Ashes, rust. . . .
De win' sing sperrichals
Through deir dus'.

"Frankie And Johnny"

Oh Frankie and Johnny were lovers
Oh Lordy how they did love!
Old Ballad

Frankie was a halfwit, Johnny was a nigger,
    Frankie liked to pain poor creatures as a little 'un,
Kept a crazy love of torment when she got bigger,
    Johnny had to slave it and never had much fun.

Frankie liked to pull wings off of living butterflies,
    Frankie liked to cut long angleworms in half,
Frankie liked to whip curs and listen to their drawn out cries,
    Frankie liked to shy stones at the brindle calf.

Frankie took her pappy's lunch week-days to the sawmill,
    Her pappy, red-faced cracker, with a cracker's thirst,
Beat her skinny body and reviled the hateful imbecile,
    She screamed at every blow he struck, but tittered when he curst.

Frankie had to cut through Johnny's field of sugar corn
    Used to wave at Johnny, who didn't *pay no min'*—
Had had to work like fifty from the day that he was born,
    And wan't no cracker hussy gonna put his work behind—.

But everyday Frankie swung along the cornfield lane,
And one day Johnny helped her partly through the wood,
    Once he had dropped his plow lines, he dropped them many times again—
Though his mother didn't know it, else she'd have whipped him good.

Frankie and Johnny were lovers; oh Lordy how they did love!
    But one day Frankie's pappy by a big log laid him low,
To find out what his crazy Frankie had been speaking of;
    He found that what his gal had muttered was exactly so.

Frankie, she was spindly limbed with corn silk on her crazy head,
    Johnny was a nigger, who never had much fun
They swung up Johnny on a tree, and filled his swinging hide with lead,
    And Frankie yowled hilariously when the thing was done.

Reprinted with permission.

LANGSTON HUGHES
A "Social Poet"

After completing his 1930 novel *Not Without Laughter*, Langston Hughes spent much of the decade away from Harlem. He remained active in literature, writing three plays, a book of short stories, and five volumes of poetry. His poetry shifted significantly in the 1930s. He moved away from the rhythms of jazz and the blues, and the intimate pictures of black urban life, toward a more strident and overtly political verse. The Great Depression moved him towards a Marxist-Leninist worldview. Continued racial strife, such as the 1931 Scottsboro case in which nine African American youth were arrested and brought to trial in Alabama for allegedly raping two white prostitutes, hardened his political and racial views, and put him in alliance with the Communists, who led the campaign in defense of the Scottsboro boys. Hughes later wrote about himself as a "social poet," whose political and racial verses during this period resulted in brushes with censorship, political and racial intimidation, and police harassment:

> So goes the life of a social poet. I am sure that none of these things would ever have happened to me had I limited the subject matter of my poems to roses and moonlight. But, unfortunately, I was born poor—and colored—and almost all the prettiest roses I have seen have been in rich white people's yards—not in mine. That is why I cannot write exclusively about roses and moonlight—for sometimes in the moonlight my brothers see a fiery cross and a circle of Klansmen's hoods. Sometimes in the moonlight a dark body swings from a lynching tree—but for his funeral there are no roses. (Langston Hughes, "My Career as a Social Poet," *Phylon* 8, 1947: 212)

The poetry presented here is illustrative of Hughes's work in the 1930s. Much of it is political; some of it is stilted. But in most Hughes demonstrates his ability to write simply and powerfully about highly emotional issues.

"Christ in Alabama"
Contempo, December, 1931
(A comment on the Scottsboro incident)

> Christ is a nigger,
> Beaten and black:
> Oh, bare your back!

Mary is His mother:
Mammy of the South,
Silence your mouth.

God is His father:
White Master above
Grant Him your love.

Most holy bastard
Of the bleeding mouth,
   Nigger Christ
   On the cross
   Of the South.

"Goodbye Christ"
Negro Worker
November-December, 1933

Listen, Christ,
You did alright in your day, I reckon—
But that day's gone now.
They ghosted you up a swell story, too,
Called it Bible—
But it's dead now,
The popes and the preachers've
Made too much money from it.
They've sold you to too many

Kings, generals, robbers, and killers—
Even to the Tzar and the Cossacks,
Even to Rockefeller's Church,
Even to THE SATURDAY EVENING POST,
You ain't no good no more.
They've pawned you
Till you've done wore out.

Goodbye,
Christ Jesus Lord God Jehova,
Beat it on away from here now.
Make way for a new guy with no religion at all—
A real guy named
Marx Communist Lenin Peasant Stalin Worker ME—

I said, ME!
Go ahead on now,
You're getting in the way of things, Lord.
And please take Saint Ghandi with you when you go,

And Saint Pope Pius,
And Saint Aimee McPherson,
And big black Saint Becton
Of the Consecrated Dime.
And step on the gas, Christ!
Move!

Don't be so slow about movin'!
The world is mine from now on—
And nobody's gonna sell ME
To a king, or a general,
Or a millionaire.

Reprinted with permission.

"Park Bench"
New Masses
March 6, 1934

I live on a park bench.
You, Park Avenue.
Hell of a distance
Between us two.

I beg a dime for dinner—
You got a butler and maid.
But I'm wakin' up!
Say, ain't you afraid

That I might, just maybe,
In a year or two,
Move on over
To Park Avenue?

Reprinted with permission.

Three Songs About Lynching
Opportunity
June 1936

"Silhouette"
(With Violins)

Southern gentle lady,
Do not swoon.
They've just hung a nigger

In the dark of the moon.
They've hung a black nigger

To a roadside tree
In the dark of the moon
For the world to see
How Dixie protects
Its white womanhood.

Southern gentle lady,
Be good! Be good!

"Flight"
(With Oboe and Drums)

Plant your toes in the cool swamp mud.
Step and leave no track.
Hurry, sweating runner!
The hounds are at your back.

No, I didn't touch her.
White flesh ain't for me.

Hurry, black boy, hurry!
Or they'll swing you to a tree.

Lynching Song
(With Trumpets)

Pull at the rope! O!
Pull it high!
Let the white folks live
And the nigger die.

Pull it, boys,
With a bloody cry
As the nigger spins
And the white folks die.

The white folks die?
What do you mean—
The white folks die?

The nigger's
Still body
Says

NOT I.

"Genius Child"
Opportunity
August, 1937

This is a song for the genius child.
Sing it softly, for the song is wild.
Sing it softly as ever you can—
Lest the song get out of hand.

Nobody loves a genius child.

Can you love an eagle, tame or wild?
Can you love an eagle, wild though tame?
Can you love a monster of frightening name?
  Nobody loves a genius child.
Kill him—and let his soul run wild!

"Sister Johnson Marches"
A New Song
1938

Here am I with my head held high!
What's de matter, honey?
I just want to cry:
It's de first of May!

Here I go with my banner in my hand!
What's de matter, chile?
Why we owns de land!
It's de first of May!

Who are all them people
  Marching in a mass?
  Lawd! Don't you know?
That's de working class!

It's de first of May!

ZORA NEALE HURSTON
Mules and Men
1935

Zora Neale Hurston was the Harlem Renaissance writer who produced the most impressive work during the 1930s, publishing the books that eventually elevated her to her current status as one of the most important writers of the period. In the 1920s Hurston had been involved in the Renaissance, participated in the publication of *Fire!!*, and associated with Harlem's bohemian element; she also had written some poetry and several prize-winning short stories. In the 1930s she published two books of folklore, including *Mules and Men* in 1935, and three novels, among them her masterpiece of 1937, *Their Eyes Were Watching God*. Yet she did not receive the critical acclaim in the 1930s that she garners today. By the mid-1930s the Harlem Renaissance had passed her by. Many critics, especially African Americans, dismissed her work, accusing it of either being exploitative of the black experience, or of lacking a social or political perspective.

Mules and Men was Hurston's second book, published a year after her first novel *Jonah's Gourd Vine*. It consists of two sections: a presentation of the folk tales and stories that she had collected during a series of research trips to the South, and a brief section of conjure stories and rituals. Even her harshest critics acknowledged her talent for presenting these stories and her knack for capturing the language of the people she interviewed.

Mules and Men

These stories were collected in a lumber camp at Loughman, Florida, a company town in central Florida south of Kissimmee. To gain the confidence of the local men, most of whom were wanted by the law for some offense or another, Hurston passed herself off as a fugitive bootlegger. The camp offered access material from a confined population that had drifted in from all over the South.

V.

Y'all ever hear dat lie 'bout big talk?" cut in Joe Wiley.

"Yeah we done heard it, Joe, but Ah kin hear it some 'gin. Tell it, Joe," pleaded Gene Oliver.

During slavery time two ole niggers wuz talkin' an' one said tuh de other one, "Ole Massa made me so mad yistiddy till Ah give 'im uh good cussin' out. Man, Ah called 'im everything wid uh handle on it."

De other one says, "You didn't cuss *Ole Massa*, didja? Good God! Whut did he do tuh you?"

"He didn't do *nothin'*, an' man, Ah laid one cussin' on 'im! Ah'm uh man lak dis, Ah won't stan' no hunchin'. Ah betcha he won't bother *me* no mo."

"Well, if you cussed 'im an' he didn't do nothin' tuh you, de nex' time he make me mad Ah'm goin' tuh lay uh hearin' on him."

Nex' day de nigger did somethin'. Ole Massa got in behind 'im and he turnt 'round an' give Ole Massa one good cussin' an Ole Massa had 'im took down and whipped nearly tuh death. Nex' time he saw dat other nigger he says tuh 'im. "Thought you tole me, you cussed Ole Massa out and he never opened his mouf."

"Ah did."

"Well, how come he never did nothin' tuh yuh? Ah did it an' he come nigh uh killin' *me*."

"Man, you didn't go cuss 'im tuh his face, didja?"

"Sho Ah did. Ain't dat whut you tole me you done?"

"Naw, Ah didn't say Ah cussed 'im tuh his face. You sho is crazy. Ah thought you had mo' sense than dat. When Ah cussed Ole Massa he wuz settin' on de front porch an' All wuz down at de big gate."

De other nigger wuz mad but he didn't let on. Way after while he 'proached de nigger dat got 'im de beatin' an' tole 'im, "Know whut All done tuhday?"

"Naw, whut you done? Give Ole Massa 'nother cussin'?"

"Naw, Ah ain't never goin' do dat no mo'. Ah peeped up under Ole Miss's drawers."

"Man, hush yo' mouf! You knows you ain't looked up under ole Miss's clothes!"

"Yes, Ah did too. Ah looked right up her very drawers."

"You better hush dat talk! Somebody goin' hear you and Ole Massa'll have you kilt."

"Well, Ah sho done it an' she never done nothin' neither."

"Well, whut did she say?"

"Not uh mumblin' word, an' Ah stopped and looked jus' as long as Ah wanted tuh an' went on 'bout mah business."

"Well, de nex' time All see her settin' out on de porch Ah'm goin' tuh look too."

"Help yo'self."

Dat very day Ole Miss wuz settin' out on de porch in de cool uh de evenin' all dressed up in her starchy white clothes. She had her legs all crossed up and de nigger walked up tuh de edge uh de porch and peeped up under Ole Miss's clothes. She took and hollered an' Ole Massa come out an' had dat nigger almost kilt alive.

When he wuz able tuh be 'bout agin he said tuh de other nigger; "Thought you tole me you peeped up under Ole Miss's drawers?"

"Ah sho did."

"Well, how come she never done nothin' tuh *you*? She got me nearly kilt."

"Man, when Ah looked under Ole Miss's drawers they wuz hangin' out on de clothes line. You didn't go look up in 'em while she had 'em on, didja? You sho is uh fool! Ah thought you had mo' sense than dat, Ah claire Ah did. It's uh wonder he didn't kill yuh dead. Umph, umph, umph. You sho ain't got no sense atall."

. . . .

Joe Wiley said: "Ah jus' got to tell this one, do Ah can't rest."

In slavery time dere was a colored man what was named John. He went along wid Ole Massa everywhere he went. He used to make out he could tell fortunes. One day him and his Old Massa was goin' along and John said, "Ole Massa, Ah kin tell fortunes." Ole Massa made out he didn't pay him no attention. But when they got to de next man's plantation Old Massa told de landlord, "I have a nigger dat kin tell fortunes." So de other man said, "Dat nigger can't tell no fortunes. I bet my plantation and all my niggers against yours dat he can't tell no fortunes.

Ole Massa says: "I'll take yo' bet. I bet everything in de world I got on John 'cause he don't lie. If he say he can tell fortunes, he can tell 'em. Bet you my plantation and all my niggers against yours and throw in de wood lot extry."

So they called Notary Public and signed up de bet. Ole Massa straddled his horse and John got on his mule and they went on home.

John was in de misery all that night for he knowed he was gointer be de cause of Ole Massa losin' all he had.

Every mornin' John useter be up and have Old Massa's saddle horse curried and saddled at de door when Ole Massa woke up. But this mornin' Old Massa had to git John out of de bed.

John useter always ride side by side with Massa, but on de way over to de plantation where de bet was on, he rode way behind.

So de man on de plantation had went out and caught a coon and had a big old iron wash-pot turned down over it.

There was many person there to hear John tell what was under de wash-pot.

Ole Massa brought John out and tole him, say: "John, if you tell what's under dat wash pot Ah'll make you independent, rich. If you don't, Ah'm goin' to kill you because you'll make me lose my plantation and everything I got."

John walked 'round and 'round dat pot but he couldn't git de least inklin' of what was underneath it. Drops of sweat as big as yo' fist was rollin' off of John. At last he give up and said: "Well, you got de ole coon at last."

When John said that, Ole Massa jumped in de air and cracked his heels twice befo' he hit de ground. De man that was bettin' against Ole Massa fell to his knees wid de cold sweat pourin' off him. Ole Massa said: "John, you done won another plantation fo' me. That's a coon under that pot sho 'nuff."

So he give John a new suit of clothes and a saddle horse. And John quit tellin' fortunes after that.

Going back home Ole Massa said: "Well, John, you done made me vast rich so I goin' to Philly-Me-York and won't be back in three weeks. I leave everything in yo' charge."

So Ole Massa and his wife got on de train and John went to de depot with 'em and seen 'em off on de train bid 'em goodbye. Then he hurried on back to de plantation. Ole Massa and Ole Miss got off at de first station and made it on back to see whut John was doin'.

John went back and told de niggers, "Massa's gone to Philly-Me-York and left everything in my charge. Ah want one of you niggers to git on a mule and ride three miles north, and another one three miles west and another one three miles south and another one three miles east. Tell everybody to come here—there's gointer be a ball here tonight. The rest of you go into the lot and kill hogs until you can walk on 'em."

So they did. John goes in and dressed up in Ole Massa's swaller-tail clothes, put on his collar and tie; got a box of cigars and put under his arm, and one cigar in his mouth.

When the crowd come John said: "Y'all kin dance and Ah'm goin' to call figgers."

So he got Massa's biggest rockin' chair and put it up in Massa's bed and then he got up in the bed in the chair and begin to call figgers:

"Hands up!" "Four circle right." "Half back." "Two ladies change." He was puffing his cigar all de time.

'Bout this time John seen a white couple come in but they looked so trashy he figgered they was piney woods crackers, so he told 'em to g'wan out in de kitchen and git some barbecue and likker and to stay out there where they belong. So he went to callin' figgers agin. De git Fiddles' was raisin' cain over in de corner and John was callin' for de new set:

"Choose yo' partners." "Couples to yo' places like horses to de traces." "Sashay all." "Sixteen hands up." "Swing Miss Sally 'round and 'round and bring her back to me!"

Just as he went to say "Four hands up," he seen Ole Massa comin' out the kitchen wipin' the dirt off his face.

Ole Massa said: "John, just look whut you done done! I'm gointer take you to that persimmon tree and break yo' neck for this—killing up all my hogs and havin' all these niggers in my house."

John ast, "Ole Massa, Ah know you gointer kill me, but can Ah have a word with my friend Jack before you kill me?

"Yes, John, but have it quick."

So John called Jack and told him; says: "Ole Massa is gointer hang me under that persimmon tree. Now you get three matches and get in the top of the tree. Ah'm gointer pray and when you hear me ast God to let it lightning Ah want you to strike matches."

Jack went on out to the tree. Ole Massa brought John on out with the rope around his neck and put it over a limb.

"Now, John," said Massa, "have you got any last words to say?"

"Yes sir, Ah want to pray."

"Pray and pray damn quick. I'm clean out of patience with you, John."

So John knelt down. "O Lord, here Ah am at de foot of de persimmon tree. If you're gointer destroy Old Massa tonight, with his wife and chillun and everything he got, lemme see it lightnin'."

Jack up the tree, struck a match. Ole Massa caught hold of John and said: "John, don't pray no more."

John said: "Oh yes, turn me loose so Ah can pray. O Lord, here Ah am tonight callin' on Thee and Thee alone. If you are gointer destroy Ole Massa tonight, his wife and chillun and all he got, Ah want to see it lightnin' again."

Jack struck another match and Ole Massa started to run. He give John his freedom and a heap of land and stock. He run so fast that it took a express train running at the rate of ninety miles an hour and six months to bring him back, and that's how come niggers got they freedom today.

. . . .

Larkins White burst out:

And dat put me in de mind of a nigger dat useter do a lot of prayin' up under 'simmon tree, durin' slavery time. He'd go up dere and pray to God and beg Him to kill all de white folks. Ole Massa heard about it and so de next day he got hisself a armload of sizeable rocks and went up de 'simmon tree, before de nigger got dere, and when he begin to pray and beg de Lawd to kill all de white folks, Ole Massa let one of dese rocks fall on Ole Nigger's head. It was a heavy rock and knocked de nigger over. So when he got up he looked up and said: "Lawd, I ast you to kill all de white folks, can't you tell a white man from a nigger?"

Joe Wiley says: "Y'all might as well make up yo' mind to bear wid me, 'cause Ah feel Ah got to tell a lie on Ole Massa for my mamma. Ah done lied on him enough for myself. So Ah'm gointer tell it if I bust my gall tryin'.

Ole John was a slave, you know. And there was Ole Massa and Ole Missy and de two li' children—a girl and a boy.

Well, John was workin' in de field and he seen de children out on de lake in a boat, just a hollerin'. They had done lost they oars and was 'bout to turn over. So then he went and tole Ole Massa and Ole Missy.

Well, Ole Missy, she hollered and said: "It's so sad to lose these 'cause Ah ain't never goin' to have no more children." Ole Massa made her hush and they went down to de water and follered de shore on 'round till they found 'em. John pulled off his shoes and hopped in and swum out and got in de boat wid de children and brought 'em to shore.

Well, Massa and John take 'em to de house. So they was all so glad 'cause de children got saved. So Massa told 'im to make a good crop dat year and fill up de barn, and den when he lay by de crops nex' year, he was going to set him free.

So John raised so much crop dat year he filled de barn and had to put some of it in de house.

So Friday come, and Massa said, "Well, de day done come that I said I'd set you free. I hate to do it, but I don't like to make myself out a lie. I hate to git rid of a good nigger lak you."

So he went in de house and give John one of his old suits of clothes to put on. So John put it on and come in to shake hands and tell 'em goodbye. De children they cry, and Ole Missy she cry. Didn't want to see John go. So John took his bundle and put it on his stick and hung it crost his shoulder.

Well, Ole John started on down de road. Well, Ole Massa said, "John, de children love yuh."

"Yassuh."

"John, I love yuh."

"Yassuh. "

"And Missy *like* yuh!"

"Yassuh. "

"But 'member, John, youse a nigger."

"Yassuh."

Fur as John could hear 'im down de road he wuz hollerin', "John, Oh John! De children loves you. And I love you. De Missy *like* you."

John would holler back, "Yassuh. "

"But 'member youse a nigger, tho!"

Ole Massa kept callin' 'im and his voice was pitiful. But John kept right on steppin' to Canada. He answered Old Massa every time he called 'im, but he consumed on wid his bag.

. . . .

IX.

Everybody laughed but nobody told me a thing. But after a while Box-Car began to sing a new song and I liked the swing of it.

"What's dat you singing, Box-Car?" I asked.

" 'Ah'm Gointer Loose dis Right-hand Shackle from 'Round my Leg.' Dat's a chain-gang song. Thought everybody knowed dat."

"Nope, never heard it. Ain't never been to de gang. How did you learn it?"

"Working on de gang."

"Whut you doin' on de gang, Box-Car? You look like a good boy, but a poor boy."

"Oh, dey put me under arrest one day for vacancy in Bartow. When de judge found out Ah had a job of work. He took and searched me and when he found out Ah had a deck of cards on me, he charged me wid totin' concealed cards, and attempt to gamble, and gimme three months. Then dey made out another charge 'ginst me. 'Cused me of highway shufflin', and attempt to gamble. You know dese white folks sho hates tuh turn a nigger loose, if every dey git dey hands on 'im. And dis very quarters boss was Cap'n on de gang where Ah wuz. Me and him ain't never gointer set hawses." So he went on singing:

> All day long, you heard me moan
> Don't you tell my Cap'n which way I gone
> Ah'm gointer lose dis right hand shackle from 'round my leg.
>
> You work me late, you work me soon
> Some time you work me by de light of de moon
> Ah'm gointer lose dis right hand shackle from 'round my leg.

I learned several other songs. Thanks to James Presley and Slim; and Gene Oliver and his sister brought me many additional tales.

But the very next pay-night when I went to a dance at the Pine Mill, Lucy tried to steal me. That is the local term for an attack by stealth. Big Sweet saved me and urged me to stay on, assuring me that she could always defend me, but I shivered at the thought of dying with a knife in my back, or having my face mutilated. At any rate, I had made a very fine and full collection on the Saw-Mill Camp, so I felt no regrets at shoving off.

The last night at Loughman was very merry. We had a party at Mrs. Allen's. James Presley and Slim with their boxes; Joe Willard calling figures in his best mood. Because it was a special occasion and because I was urged, I actually took a sip of low-wine and found out how very low it was. The dancing stopped and I was hilariously toted off to bed and the party moved to my bedroom. We had had a rain flood early in the afternoon and a medium size rattlesnake had come in out of the wet. I had thrown away a pile of worn out stockings and he was asleep upon them there in the corner by the washstand. The boys wanted to kill it, but I begged them not to hurt my lowly brother. He rattled away for a while, but when everybody got around the bed on the far end of the room and got quiet, he moved in the manner of an hour-hand to a crack where the floor and wall had separated, and popped out of sight.

Cliffert told me the last Loughman story around midnight.

"Zora, did yuh ever hear 'bout Jack and de Devil buckin' 'ginst one 'nother to see which one was de strongest?"

"Naw. Ah done heard a lot about de Devil and dat Jack, but not dat tale *you* know. Tell it."

Jack and de Devil wuz settin' down under a tree one day arguin' 'bout who was de strongest. De Devil got tired of talkin' and went and picked up a mule. Jack went and picked up de same mule. De Devil run to a great big old oak tree and pulled it up by de roots. Jack grabbed holt of one jus' as big and pulled it up. De Devil broke a anchor cable. Jack took it and broke it agin.

So de Devil says, "Shucks! Dis ain't no sho nuff trial. Dis is chillun foolishness. Meet me out in dat hund'ed acre clearin' tomorrow mornin' at nine o'clock and we'll see who kin throw mah hammer de furtherest. De one do dat is de strongest."

Jack says, "Dat suits me."

So nex' mawnin' de Devil wuz dere on time wid his hammer. It wuz bigger'n de white folks church house in Winter Park. A whole heap uh folks had done come out tuh see which one would win.

Jack wuz late. He come gallopin' up on hawseback and reined in de hawse so short till he reared up his hind legs.

Jack jumped off and says: "Wese all heah, le's go. Who goin' first?"

De Devil tole 'im, "Me. Everybody stand back and gimme room."

So he throwed de hammer and it went so high till it went clean outa sight. Devil tole 'em, "Iss Tuesday now. Y'all go home and come back Thursday mornin' at nine. It won't fall till then."

Sho 'nuff de hammer fell on Thursday mornin' at nine o'clock and knocked out a hole big as Polk County.

Dey lifted de hammer out de hole and levelled it and it wuz Jack's time to throw.

Jack took his time and walked 'round de hammer to de handle and took holt of it and throwed his head back and looked up at de sky.

"Look out, Rayfield! Move over, Gabriel! You better stand 'way back, Jesus! Ah'm fixin' to throw." He meant Heaven.

Devil run up to 'im, says, "Hold on dere a minute! Don't you throw mah damn hammer up dere! Ah left a whole lot uh mah tools up dere when dey put me out and Ah ain't got 'em back yet. Don't you throw mah hammer up dere!"

Reprinted with permission.

CRITICISM FROM *NEW CHALLENGE:*
Alain Locke and Richard Wright

In the mid-1930s poet Dorothy West launched *Challenge* in an effort to stimulate the fading Harlem Renaissance. Initially her goals were purely aesthetic; she sought out the best work from established black writers. But she had trouble attracting quality submissions, and she attracted sharp criticism from a number of non-Renaissance younger writers. Chicago-based Richard Wright and Margaret

Walker accused *Challenge* and West of being too insufficiently political, and ignoring the relationship of leftist politics to race and art. In 1937 West recast her magazine as the *New Challenge*, and invited Wright to join her as an associate editor. The new journal committed itself to radical arts and politics; unfortunately editorial clashes between Wright and West, and a shortage of funds limited the new venture to one rather spectacular issue. This issue featured work by Margaret Walker, Ralph Ellison, Langston Hughes, Alain Locke, and Richard Wright, and explored radical issues such as the debate between Marxist and non-Marxist approaches to both black literature and the race problem; it also criticized the Harlem Renaissance for lacking a political and critical perspective, and for catering to white publishers and critics.

Two essays from the July 1937 *New Challenge* are presented here. In the first, Alain Locke's used his review of Claude McKay's autobiography to underscore the failings of the Harlem Renaissance as he saw them. In the second, Richard Wright, just emerging as a major African American literary figure, provides from a Marxist perspective his unfavorable assessment of the Renaissance as well as his blueprint for a more vital and appropriate African American literature. The section of the Wright essay here presents his criticism of the Renaissance.

Alain Locke
"Spiritual Truancy"
New Challenge: A Literary Quarterly
Fall 1937

When in 1928, from self-imposed exile, Claude McKay wrote *Home to Harlem,* many of us hoped that a prose and verse writer of stellar talent would himself come home, physically and psychologically, to take a warranted and helpful place in the group of "New Negro" writers. But although now back on the American scene and obviously attached to Harlem by literary adoption, this undoubted talent is still spiritually unmoored, and by the testimony of this latest book, is a longer way from home than ever. A critical reader would know this without his own confession; but Mr. McKay, exposing others, succeeds by chronic habit in exposing himself and paints an apt spiritual portrait in two sentences when he says: "I had wandered far and away until I had grown into a truant by nature and undomesticated in the blood"—and later,— "I am so intensely subjective as a poet, that I was not aware, at the moment of writing, that I was transformed into a medium to express a mass sentiment." All of which amounts to self-characterization as the unabashed "playboy of the Negro Renaissance".

Real spokesmanship and representative character in the "Negro Renaissance",—or for that matter any movement, social or cultural,—may depend, of course, on many factors according to time and circumstance, but basic and essential, at least, are the acceptance of some group loyalty and the intent, as well as the ability, to express mass sentiment. Certainly and peculiarly in this case: otherwise the caption of race is a misnomer and the racial significance so irrelevant as to be silly. We knew before 1925 that Negroes could be poets; what we forecast and expected were Negro writers expressing a folk in expressing themselves. Artists have a right to be individualists, of course, but if their work assumes racial expression and interpretation, they must abide by it. On this issue, then, instead of repudiating racialism and its implied loyalties, Mr. McKay blows hot and cold with the same breath; erratically accepting and rejecting racial representatives, like a bad boy who admits he ought to go to school and then plays truant. It is this spiritual truancy which is the blight of his otherwise splendid talent.

Lest this seem condemnation out of court, let us examine the record. If out of a half dozen movements to which there could have been some deep loyalty of attachment, none has claimed McKay's whole-hearted support, then surely this career is not one of cosmopolitan experiment or even of innocent vagabondage, but, as I have already implied, one of chronic and perverse truancy. It is with the record of these picaresque wanderings that McKay crowds the pages of *A Long Way from Home*. First, there was a possible brilliant spokesmanship of the Jamaican peasant-folk, for it was as their balladist that McKay first attracted attention and help from his West Indian patrons. But that was soon discarded for a style and philosophy of aesthetic individualism in the then current mode of pagan impressionism. As the author of this personalism,—so unrecognizable after the tangy dialect of the Clarendon hill-folk,

> *'Your voice is the colour o f a robin's breast*
> *And there's a sweet sob in it like rain,*
> *Still rain in the night among the leaves of the trumpet tree'*

McKay emigrated to our shores and shortly adopted the social realism and racial Negro notes of *Harlem Shadows* and *The Harlem Dancer*. These were among the first firmly competent accents of New Negro poetry, and though an adopted son, McKay was hailed as the day-star of that bright dawn. However, by his own admission playing off Max Eastman against Frank Harris and James Oppenheimer, he rapidly moved out toward the humanitarian socialism of *The Liberator* with the celebrated radical protest of *I f We Must Die*; and followed that adventuresome flourish, still with his tongue in his cheek, to Moscow and the lavish hospitality and hero-worship of the Third Comintern. Then by a sudden repudiation there was a prolonged flight into expatriate cosmopolitanism and its irresponsible exoticisms. Even McKay admits the need for some apologia at this point. Granting, for the sake of argument, that the "adventure in Russia" and the association with *The Liberator* were not commitments to some variety of socialism (of this, the author says:—"I had no radical party affiliations, and there was no reason why I should consider myself under any special obligations to the Communists . . . I had not committed myself to anything. I had remained a free agent . . .") what, we may reasonably ask, about the other possible loyalty, on the basis of which the Russian ovation had been earned, viz,—the spokesmanship for the proletarian Negro? In the next breath, literally the next paragraph, McKay repudiates that also in the sentence we have already quoted:—"I was not aware, at the moment of writing, that I was transformed into a medium to express a mass sentiment." Yet the whole adventuresome career between 1918 and 1922, alike in Bohemian New York, literary Harlem and revolutionary Moscow, was predicated upon this assumed representativeness, cleverly exploited. One does not know whether to recall Peter before the triple cock-crow or Paul's dubious admonition about being "all things to all men". Finally, in the face of the obvious Bohemianism of the wanderings on the Riviera and in Morocco, we find McKay disowning common cause with the exotic cosmopolitans,—"my white fellow-expatriates", and claiming that "color-consciousness was the fundamental of my restlessness". Yet from this escapist escapade, we find our prodigal racialist returning expecting the fatted calf instead of the birch-rod, with a curtain lecture on "race salvation" from within and the necessity for a "Negro Messiah", whose glory he would like to celebrate "in a monument of verse".

Even a fascinating style and the naivest egotism cannot cloak such inconsistency or condone such lack of common loyalty. One may not dictate a man's loyalties, but must, at all events, expect him to have some. For a genius maturing in a decade of racial self-expression and enjoying the fruits of it all and living into a decade of social issues and conflict and aware of all that, to have repudiated all possible loyalties amounts to self-imposed apostasy. McKay is after all the dark-skinned psychological twin of that same Frank Harris, whom he so cleverly portrays and caricatures; a versatile genius caught in the ego-centric predicament of aesthetic vanity and exhibitionism. And so, he stands to date, the *enfant terrible* of the Negro Renaissance, where with a little loyalty and consistency he might have been at least its Villon and perhaps its Voltaire.

If this were merely an individual fate, it could charitably go unnoticed. But in some vital sense these aberrations of spirit, this lack of purposeful and steady loyalty of which McKay is the supreme example have to a lesser extent vitiated much of the talent of the first generation of "New Negro" writers and artists. They inherited, it is true, a morbid amount of decadent aestheticism, which they too uncritically imitated. They also had to reckon with "shroud of color". To quote Countee Cullen, they can be somewhat forgiven for "sailing the doubtful seas" and for being tardily, and in some cases only half-heartedly led "to live persuaded by their own". But, with all due allowances, there was an unpardonable remainder of spiritual truancy and social irresponsibility. The folk have rarely been treated by these artists with unalloyed reverence and unselfish loyalty. The commitment to racial materials and "race expression" should be neither that of a fashionable and profitable fad nor of a condescending and missionary duty. The one great flaw of the first decade of the Negro Renaissance was its exhibitionist flair. It should have addressed itself more to the people themselves and less to the gallery of faddist Negrophiles. The task confronting the present younger generation of Negro writers and artists is to approach the home scene and the folk with high seriousness, deep loyalty, racial reverence of the unspectacular, unmelodramatic sort, and when necessary, sacrificial social devotion. They must purge this flippant exhibitionism, this posy but not too sincere racialism, this care-free and irresponsible individualism.

The program of the Negro Renaissance was to interpret the folk to itself, to vitalize it from within; it was a wholesome, vigorous, assertive racialism, even if not explicitly proletarian in conception and justification. McKay himself yearns for some such thing, no doubt, when he speaks in his last chapter of the Negro's need to discover his "group soul". A main aim of the New Negro movement will be unrealized so long as that remains undiscovered and dormant; and it is still the task of the Negro writer to be a main agent in evoking it, even if the added formula of proletarian art be necessary to cure this literary anaemia and make our art the nourishing life blood of the people rather than the caviar and cake of the artists themselves. Negro writers must become truer sons of the people, more loyal providers of spiritual bread and less aesthetic wastrels and truants of the streets.

Reprinted with permission.

Richard Wright
"Blueprint for Negro Writing"
New Challenge: A Literary Quarterly
Fall 1937

The Role of Negro Writing: Two Definitions

Generally speaking, Negro writing in the past has been confined to humble novels, poems, and plays, prim and decorous ambassadors who went a-begging to white America. They entered the Court of American Public Opinion dressed in the knee-pants of servility, curtsying to show that the Negro was not inferior, that he was human, and that he had a life comparable to that of other people. For the most part these artistic ambassadors were received as though they were French poodles who do clever tricks.

White America never offered these Negro writers any serious criticism. The mere fact that a Negro could write was astonishing. Nor was there any deep concern on the part of white America with the role Negro writing should play in American culture; and the role it did play grew out of accident rather than intent or design. Either it crept in through the kitchen in the form of jokes; or it was the fruits of that foul soil which was the result of a liason between inferiority-complexed Negro "geniuses" and burnt-out white Bohemians with money.

On the other hand, these often technically brilliant performances by Negro writers were looked upon by the majority of literate Negroes as something to be proud of. At best, Negro writing has been something external to the lives of educated Negroes themselves. That the productions of their writers should have been something of a guide in their daily living is a matter which seems never to have been raised seriously.

Under these conditions Negro writing assumed two general aspects: 1) It became a sort of conspicuous ornamentation, the hallmark of "achievement." 2) It became the voice of the educated Negro pleading with white America for justice.

Rarely was the best of this writing addressed to the Negro himself, his needs, his sufferings, his aspirations. Through misdirection, Negro writers have been far better to others than they have been to themselves. And the mere recognition of this places the whole question of Negro writing in a new light and raises a doubt as to the validity of its present direction.

The Minority Outlook

Somewhere in his writings Lenin makes the observation that oppressed minorities often reflect the techniques of the bourgeoisie more brilliantly than some sections of the bourgeoisie themselves. The psychological importance of this becomes meaningful when it is recalled that oppressed minorities, and especially the petty bourgeois sections of oppressed minorities, strive to assimilate the virtues of the bourgeoisie in the assumption that by doing so they can lift themselves into a higher social sphere. But not only among the oppressed petty bourgeoisie does this occur. The workers of a minority people, chafing under exploitation, forge organizational forms of struggle to better their lot. Lacking the handicaps of false ambition and property, they have access to a wide social vision, and a deep social consciousness. They display a greater freedom and initiative in pushing their claims upon civilization than even do the petty bourgeoisie. Their organizations show greater strength, adaptability, and efficiency than any other group or class in society.

That Negro workers, propelled by the harsh conditions of their lives, have demonstrated this consciousness and mobility for economic and political action there can be no doubt. But has this consciousness been reflected in the work of Negro writers to the same degree as it has in the Negro workers' struggle to free Herndon and the Scottsboro Boys, in the drive toward unionism, in the fight against lynching? Have they as creative writers taken advantage of their unique minority position?

The answer decidedly is *no*. Negro writers have lagged sadly, and as time passes the gap widens between them and their people.

How can this hiatus be bridged? How can the enervating effects of this long standing split be eliminated?

In presenting questions of this sort an attitude of self-consciousness and self-criticism is far more likely to be a fruitful point of departure than a mere recounting of past achievements. An emphasis upon tendency and experiment, a view of society as something becoming rather than as something fixed and admired is the one which points the way for Negro writers to stand shoulder to shoulder with Negro workers in mood and outlook.

A Whole Culture

There is, however, a culture of the Negro which is his and has been addressed to him; a culture which has, for good or ill, helped to clarify his consciousness and create emotional attitudes which are conducive to action. This culture has stemmed mainly from two sources: 1) the Negro church; 2) and the folklore of the Negro people.

It was through the portals of the church that the American Negro first entered the shrine of western culture. Living under slave conditions of life, bereft of his African heritage, the Negroes' struggle for religion on the plantations between 1820-60 assumed the form of a struggle for human rights. It remained a relatively revolutionary struggle until religion began to serve as an antidote for suffering and denial. But even today there are millions of American Negroes whose only sense of a whole universe, whose only relation to society and man, and whose only guide to personal dignity comes through the archaic morphology of Christian salvation.

It was, however, in a folklore moulded out of rigorous and inhuman conditions of life that the Negro achieved his most indigenous and complete expression. Blues, spirituals, and folk tales recounted from mouth to mouth; the whispered words of a black mother to her black daughter on the ways of men; the confidential wisdom of a black father to his black son; the swapping of sex experiences on street corners from boy to boy in the deepest vernacular; work songs sung under blazing suns—all these formed the channels through which the racial wisdom flowed.

One would have thought that Negro writers in the last century of striving at expression would have continued and deepened this folk tradition, would have tried to create a more intimate and yet a more profoundly social system of artistic communication between them and their people. But the illusion that they could escape through individual achievement the harsh lot of their race swung Negro writers away from any such path. Two separate cultures sprang up: one for the Negro masses, unwritten and unrecognized; and the other for the sons and daughters of a rising Negro bourgeoisie, parasitic and mannered.

Today the question is: Shall Negro writing be for the Negro masses, moulding the lives and consciousness of those masses toward new goals, or shall it continue begging the question of the Negroes' humanity?

. . . .

Social Consciousness and Responsibility

The Negro writer who seeks to function within his race as a purposeful agent has a serious responsibility. In order to do justice to his subject matter, in order to depict Negro life in all of its manifold and intricate relationships, a deep, informed, and complex consciousness is necessary; a consciousness which draws for its strength upon the fluid lore of a great people, and moulds this lore with the concepts that move and direct the forces of history today.

With the gradual decline of the moral authority of the Negro church, and with the increasing irresolution which is paralyzing Negro middle class leadership, a new role is devolving upon the Negro writer. He is being called upon to do no less than create values by which his race is to struggle, live and die.

By his ability to fuse and make articulate the experiences of men, because his writing possesses the potential cunning to steal into the inmost recesses of the human heart, because he can create the myths and symbols that inspire a faith in life, he may expect either to be consigned to oblivion, or to be recognized for the valued agent he is.

This raises the question of the personality of the writer. It means that in the lives of Negro writers must be found those materials and experiences which will create a meaningful picture of the world today. Many young writers have grown to believe that a Marxist analysis of society presents such a picture. It creates a picture which, when placed before the eyes of the writer, should unify his personality, organize his emotions, buttress him with a tense and obdurate will to change the world.

And, in turn, this changed world will dialectically change the writer. Hence, it is through a Marxist conception of reality and society that the maximum degree of freedom in thought and feeling can be gained for the Negro writer. Further, this dramatic Marxist vision, when consciously grasped, endows the writer with a sense of dignity which no other vision can give. Ultimately, it restores to the writer his lost heritage, that is, his role as a creator of the world in which he lives, and as a creator of himself.

Yet, for the Negro writer, Marxism is but the starting point. No theory of life can take the place of life. After Marxism has laid bare the skeleton of society, there remains the task of the writer to plant flesh upon those bones out of his will to live. He may, with disgust and revulsion, say no and depict the horrors of capitalism encroaching upon the human being. Or he may, with hope and passion, say yes and depict the faint stirrings of a new and emerging life. But in whatever social voice he chooses to speak, whether positive or negative, there should always be heard or over-heard his faith, his necessity, his judgement.

His vision need not be simple or rendered in primer-like terms; for the life of the Negro people is not simple. The presentation of their lives should be simple, yes; but all the complexity, the strangeness, the magic wonder of life that plays like a bright sheen over the most sordid existence, should be there. To borrow a phrase from the Russians, it should have a complex simplicity. Eliot, Stein, Joyce, Proust, Hemingway, and Anderson; Gorky, Barbusse, Nexo, and Jack London no less than the folklore of the Negro himself should form the heritage of the Negro writer. Every iota of gain in human thought and sensibility should be ready grist for his mill, no matter how far-fetched they may seem in their immediate implications.

. . . .

Autonomy of Craft

For the Negro writer to depict this new reality requires a greater discipline and consciousness than was necessary for the so-called Harlem school of expression. Not only is the subject matter dealt with far more meaningful and complex, but the new role of the writer is qualitatively different. The Negro writers' new position demands a sharper definition of the status of his craft, and a sharper emphasis upon its functional autonomy.

Negro writers should seek through the medium of their craft to play as meaningful a role in the affairs of men as do other professionals. But if their writing is demanded to perform the social office of other professions, then the autonomy of craft is lost and writing detrimentally fused with other interests. The limitations of the craft constitute some of its greatest virtues. If the sensory vehicle of imaginative writing is required to carry too great a load of didactic material, the artistic sense is submerged.

The relationship between reality and the artistic image is not always direct and simple. The imaginative conception of a historical period will not be a carbon copy of reality. Image and emotion possess a logic of their own. A vulgarized simplicity constitutes the greatest danger in tracing the reciprocal interplay between the writer and his environment.

Writing has its professional autonomy; it should complement other professions, but it should not supplant them or be swamped by them.

The Necessity for Collective Work

It goes without saying that these things cannot be gained by Negro writers if their present mode of isolated writing and living continues. This isolation exists among Negro writers as well as between Negro and white writers. The Negro writers' lack of thorough integration with the American scene, their lack of a clear realization among themselves of their possible role, have bred generation after generation of embittered and defeated literati.

Barred for decades from the theater and publishing houses, Negro writers have been made to feel a sense of difference. So deep has this white-hot iron of exclusion been burnt into their hearts that thousands have all but lost the desire to become identified with American civilization. The Negro writers' acceptance of this enforced isolation and their attempt to justify it is but a defensereflex of the whole special way of life which has been rammed down their throats.

This problem, by its very nature, is one which must be approached contemporaneously from two points of view. The ideological unity of Negro writers and the alliance of that unity with all the progressive ideas of our day is the primary prerequisite for collective work. On the shoulders of white writers and Negro writers alike rest the responsibility of ending this mistrust and isolation.

By placing cultural health above narrow sectional prejudices, liberal writers of all races can help to break the stony soil of aggrandizement out of which the stunted plants of Negro nationalism grow. And, simultaneously, Negro writers can help to weed out these choking growths of reactionary nationalism and replace them with hardier and sturdier types.

These tasks are imperative in light of the fact that we live in a time when the majority of the most basic assumptions of life can no longer be taken for granted. Tradition is no longer a guide. The world has grown huge and cold. Surely this is the moment to ask questions, to theorize, to speculate, to wonder out of what materials can a human world be built.

Each step along this unknown path should be taken with thought, care, self-consciousness, and deliberation. When Negro writers think they have arrived at something which smacks of truth, humanity, they should want to test it with others, feel it with a degree of passion and strength that will enable them to communicate it to millions who are groping like themselves.

Writers faced with such tasks can have no possible time for malice or jealousy. The conditions for the growth of each writer depend too much upon the good work of other writers. Every first rate novel, poem, or play lifts the level of consciousness higher.

SELECTED BIBLIOGRAPHY

The works included in this bibliography by no means represent a complete list of the material available on the Harlem Renaissance. They are a starting place for those interested in pursuing this subject. They include biographical material, critical or historical studies of the movement, examination of non-literary fields, and several of the major anthologies or editions of collected works. Special attention has been given to material on art, music, and theater, areas generally slighted in studies of the movement. In addition to the books included in this bibliography, virtually all of the material published during the Harlem Renaissance is available, either in reprints or in collections of poetry. This is, of course, where anyone interested in pursuing this topic should begin.

Anderson, Paul Allen. *Deep River: Music and Memory in Harlem Renaissance Thought.* Durham: Duke University Press, 2001.

Bruce, Dickson D., Jr. *Black American Writing from the Nadir: The Evolution of a Literary Tradition.* Baton Rouge: Louisiana State University Press, 1989.

The Collected Works of Langston Hughes. 18 Vols. Columbia: University of Missouri Press,

Cooper, Wayne F. *Claude McKay: Rebel Sojourner in the Harlem Renaissance.* Baton Rouge: Louisiana State University Press, 1987.

Davis, Thadious M. *Nella Larsen: Novelist of the Harlem Renaissance, A Woman's Life Unveiled.* Baton Rouge: Louisiana State University Press, 1994

Douglas, Ann. *Terrible Honesty: Mongrel Manhattan in the 1920s.* New York: Farrar, Straus and Giroux, 1995.

Du Bois, W.E.B. *Writings.* New York: The Library of America, 1986.

Early, Gerald. *My Soul's High Song: The Collected Writings of Countee Cullen, Voice of the Harlem Renaissance.* New York: Anchor Books, 1991.

Fabi, M. Giulia. *Passing and the Rise of the African American Novel.* Urbana: University of Illinois Press, 2001.

Gates, Henry Louis, Jr., and McKay, Nellie V., eds. *The Norton Anthology of African American Literature.* New York: W.W. Norton & Company, 1997.

Hemenway, Robert E. Zora Neale Hurston: A Literary Biography. Urbana: University of Illinois Press, 1980.

Huggins, Nathan Irvin. *Harlem Renaissance.* New York: Oxford University Press, 1971.

Hull, Gloria T. Color, Sex, and Poetry: Three Women Writers of the Harlem Renaissance. Bloomington: University of Indiana Press, 1987.

Hurston, Zora Neale. *Novels and Stories.* New York: The Library of America, 1986.

———. *Folklore, Memoirs, and Other Writings.* New York: The Library of America, 1995.

Hutchinson, George. *The Harlem Renaissance in Black and White*. (Cambridge: Harvard University Press, 1995).

Kerman, Cynthia Earl and Eldridge, Richard. *The Lives of Jean Toomer: A Hunger for Wholeness*. Baton Rouge: Louisiana State University Press, 1987

Kirschke, Amy Helene, *Aaron Douglas: Art, Race, and the Harlem Renaissance*. Jackson: The University Press of Mississippi, 1995.

Krasner, David. *A Beautiful Place: African American Theatre, Drama, and Perfromance in the Harlem Renaissance, 1910–1927*. New York: Palgrave McMillan, 2002.

Levy, Eugene. James Weldon Johnson: Black Leader Black Voice. Chicago: University of Chicago Press, 1973,

Lewis, David Levering. *When Harlem Was in Vogue*. New York: Vintage Books, 1982.

———. *W.E.B. Du Bois: Biography of a Race, 1868–1919*. New York: Henry Holt and Company, 1994.

———. *W.E.B. Du Bois: The Fight for Equality and the American Century, 1919–1963*. New York: Henry Holt and Company, 2000.

———, ed. *The Portable Harlem Renaissance Reader*. New York: Penguin Books, 1994.

Lowe, John. *Jump at the Sun: Zora Neale Hurston's Cosmic Comedy*. Urbana: University of Illinois Press, 1997.

McWilliams, Dean. *Charles W. Chesnutt and the Fictions of Race*. Athens: The University of Georgia Press, 2002.

Meisenhelder, Susan Edwards. *Hitting a Straight Lick with a Crooked Stick: Race and Gender in the Work of Zora Neale Hurston*. Tuscaloosa: University of Alabama Press, 1999.

Perpener, John O., III. *African-American Concert Dance: The Harlem Renaissance and Beyond*. Urbana: University of Illinois Press, 2001.

Rampersad, Arnold. *The Life of Langston Hughes*. 2 Vols. New York: Oxford University Press, 1986, 1988.

———, ed. *The Collected Poems of Langston Hughes*. New York: Alfred A. Knopf, 1995.

Scott, William B. and Rutkoff, Peter M. *New York Modern: The Arts and the City*. Baltimore: Johns Hopkins University Press, 1999.

Singh, Amritjit. *The Novels of the Harlem Renaissance: Twelve Black Writers, 1923–1933*. University Park: University of Pennsylvania Press, 1976.

Spencer, Jon Michael. *The New Negroes and their Music: The Success of the Harlem Renaissance*. Knoxville: The University of Tennessee Press, 1997.

Tillery, Tyrone. *Claude McKay: A Black Poet's Struggle for Identity*. Amherst: University of Massachusetts Press, 1992.

Wall, Cheryl A. *Women of the Harlem Renaissance*. Bloomington: Indiana University Press, 1995.

Wintz, Cary D. *Black Culture and the Harlem Renaissance*. College Station: Texas A&M University Press, 1996.

———, ed. *The Harlem Renaissance, 1920–1940*. 7 Vols. New York: Garland Publishing, Inc., 1996.